S0-ARX-608

CONFLICT RESOLUTION AND WORLD EDUCATION

WORLD ACADEMY OF ART AND SCIENCE

3

CONFLICT RESOLUTION AND WORLD EDUCATION

edited by

STUART MUDD

INDIANA UNIVERSITY PRESS

BLOOMINGTON & LONDON

Peace among all peoples requires:
Truth as its foundation
Justice as its rule
Love as its driving force
Liberty as its atmosphere.

JOHN XXIII in "Pacem in Terris"

Originally published by Dr. W. Junk in the Netherlands
First published in the United States 1967

Library of Congress catalog card number: 67-63008
Manufactured in the United States of America

Contents

PART II: CONFLICT RESOLUTIONS

A. *The Idea of a World University*

B. *Transnational Projects Practically Contributing to Conflict Resolutions*

APPENDICES

Editor's Preface

Hereux celui qui porte en soi un Dieu, un idéal de Beauté, et qui lui obéit;
Idéal de l'art; Idéal de la science; Idéal de la Patrie; *
Idéal des vertus de l'Evangile.

LOUIS PASTEUR

* La Patrie for modern man is becoming le Monde. Ed.

This book is based upon a Symposium held at the Consiglio Nazionale delle Ricerche, in Rome, September 9–12, 1965, in connection with the third Plenary Session of the World Academy of Art and Science. The Symposium was convened by Dr. HUGO BOYKO, then Secretary-General, now President of the WAAS. The dual themes of the Symposium were causes of conflict and means of conflict resolution and the genesis of a World University.

The range of conflicts discussed was wide: the struggle of the infant to achieve identity; marital conflict and processes of resolution; conflict between nations and legal aspects of their resolution; the historical unreality of the confrontation between East and West in the Cold War; conflict among animals (which often proves to be more "humane" than conflict between humans); and finally an effort to delineate features of a world capable of peace under law.

The contributing authorities were equally diverse: the human physiologist, Professor GAETANO MARTINO; the political scientist, Professor GEORGE E. G. CATLIN; the novelist, MORRIS L. WEST; the student of family life, Professor EMILY H. MUDD; H.E. ABBA EBAN; the international jurist, Dr. MAX HABICHT; the historian, JOHN U. NEF; the zoologist, J. L. CLOUDSLEY-THOMPSON; the present Editor.

Obviously the entire range of conflicts could not even be sampled in a single symposium. The chapters may be considered as probes in depth in their respective areas. A number of contributions have been added, therefore, in areas not covered in the original Symposium: the difficult intrafamilial adjustments of the formative years and the seeking of foci for dedication in youth, by the distinguished psychiatrists, Professors LEON J. SAUL and ERIK H. ERIKSON; capital-labor struggle and adjustment, by the Labor Negotiator, Professor GEORGE M. TAYLOR; the United Nations in its many roles, by H. E. U THANT; the oecumenical concern of the World Council of Churches, by its General Secretary, Dr. W. A. VISSER 'T HOOFT; analyses of various approaches to the formal study of conflict and conflict resolution by Dr. M. J. STROUP, and Drs. R. L. SISSON and R. L. ACKOFF.

The genesis of a World University of a new kind is the principal current preoccupation of the World Academy of Art and Science. The conception of a disseminated University, without a campus of its own but with interacting units in universities in various parts of the world, is developed by President BOYKO, and variations on this theme are presented by several authors. The initial units will be departments in existing universities, whose teaching and research activities are transnational in scope and significance, and whose administrators are profoundly concerned with human welfare. Appropriate means of liaison and coordination have yet to be worked out.

Dr. HAROLD TAYLOR has made a comprehensive survey of the institutions of the world which approximate or might become world universities. A summary of this survey and relevant bibliography are included here with his kind permission. The final section of the volume describes a number of transnational enterprises congruent in attitude with the World University.

The Editor of this Volume III of the World Academy of Art and Science enjoyed also the privilege of editing Volume II, "The Population Crisis and the Use of World Resources". To have worked with the scores of authors, expert in many disciplines, and to have found them so uniformly humanistic in attitude, so deeply concerned with achieving a fine quality of life for *all* of mankind, has truly been a profound inspiration.

The World Academy of Art and Science was established in 1960 as a forum "for distinguished scientists and scholars to discuss the vital problems of mankind, independent of political boundaries or limits – whether spiritual or physical; a forum where these problems will be discussed objectively, scientifically, globally and free from vested interests or regional attachments." [1]

This profound concern for the good of mankind has been expressed in many idioms by the contributors to Volumes I, II and III. Expressed in the idiom of biology it declares our belief that the only practicable unit of survival for modern man is the *human species*. (2, 3)

1. Manifesto of World Academy of Art and Science, in "Science and the Future of Mankind," p. 367. Dr. W. Junk, Publishers, The Hague, Netherlands, 1961. American edition. Indiana University Press, Bloomington, Indiana, 1964.
2. BROCK CHISHOLM, in "The Population Crisis and the Use of World Resources," Dr. W. Junk, Publishers, The Hague. Netherlands 1964, p. 341. American edition, Indiana University Press, Bloomington, Indiana, 1964. "The Population Crisis, Implications and Plans for Action," Revised and abridged paper-back edition, Indiana University Press, Bloomington, 1965, p. 279.
3. HUDSON HOAGLAND, ibid. p. 442.

The social relevance of one of the World Religions is cogently set forth in the chapter in this volume by Dr. VISSER 'T HOOFT. The President of the World Academy, Dr. Hugo BOYKO, and the Editor of the present volume will be extremely grateful for suggestions as to suitable scholars who might set forth authentically the Social Relevance of other World Religions. It is our hope that such contributions may become the focal subject of a future Plenary Meeting of the World Academy.

STUART MUDD

CONFLICT RESOLUTION AND WORLD EDUCATION

Education in Our Changing Times

by

U Thant

Secretary-General of the United Nations

I have chosen to speak on the subject of "Education in Our Changing Times," because I feel that the present generation has a great responsibility to educate itself, not only to ensure its own survival, but the survival of mankind itself.

We are all aware of the ringing pledge of the United Nations Charter "to save succeeding generations from the scourge of war." Today it is not simply a question of saving succeeding generations from the scourge of war – it is more a question of saving mankind itself from total annihilation. With the progress we have made in the development of nuclear weapons and long-range missiles, with the ushering in of the era of push-button warfare, and with all the dangers that the world faces of war by accident even more than by design, I feel that I am not overstating the case when I put the choice before the present generation in these striking terms.

In this second half of the twentieth century, I consider that the primary task of the educationist everywhere is to dispel certain age-old assumptions. It seems to be assumed, for example, that there are no more than two sides to a problem. As a matter of fact, almost every problem has more than two sides. It is also fallacious to paint human beliefs and human societies in terms of pure black and white. There are various shades in between.

Basing himself on these new principles, the educationist should be concerned primarily with the greatest question before us – the question of human survival. War, which has often been in the past an instrument of national policies, should no longer feature in the settlement of disputes. With the advent of the atomic age, the very concept of war has undergone a tremendous change. War no longer means the controlled employment of violence, with defined targets and limited objectives. It means an uncontrolled unleashing of weapons of mass destruction, probably resulting in the annihilation of all that human ingenuity and effort has built over the years.

Reprinted from *United Nations Review*, Volume 10, Number 6, June 1963

The United States and the Soviet Union now control between them almost the whole of the world's nuclear arsenal. Their common interest is to ensure that existing restraints on the use of this devastating power are not weakened, but strengthened. This means that some system must be found to limit and control the nuclear arms race before it gets out of hand through the spread of weapons to more and more powers, or through the development of weapons which are uncontrollable.

In seeking proper remedies for war, one must be clear about the causes of the disease. Disparities in wealth and living standards between nations no doubt affect the stability of the world; and while programs to assist developing countries in their efforts to reduce these disparities are urgently necessary, they will not in themselves diminish the risk of global war; in fact, the devastating wars which "twice in our lifetime" have "brought untold sorrow to mankind" were started by wealthy and advanced countries. Nor does the creation of larger regional blocs or even a federation of nations make wars less likely—except perhaps between the members themselves. The level of armaments and relative military strength between states does not itself make war more or less probable. Nor are ideological differences the fundamental cause of war; there have been fierce wars between ideologically similar states.

All such factors – economic, military, ideological – may contribute to the causes of wars. What turns these factors into wars is the psychological or emotional frame of mind, which replaces rational thinking. This state of mind, fed daily by mass media propagating sensationalism and suspicion, develops into a condition bordering on obsession, which renders peaceful settlement of disputes difficult if not impossible, and leads us nearer to thinking in terms of a solution by force, which means international anarchy.

The only way out of anarchy in any circumstance – whether local, regional or worldwide – is through the creation of some form of government. Between nations, this has been done peacefully by voluntary union or forcibly by conquest. But in the present world situation neither of these procedures offers hope of a solution.

A voluntary union, or even federation, is possible only between states of roughly similar internal character; it cannot be expected – and may not work – between ideologically different groups of states. And conquest is almost equally unimaginable; war has ceased to be practicable, except on a tiny local scale, as any large-scale military action would probably end as a suicidal adventure.

Do Away with Cold War

This leaves us with the necessity of having to try to form a world authority within the limitations of the present world set-up, across the barriers of the cold war. But to be worth having, it need not be complete or flawless. Anything capable of mitigating the present anarchy would represent a valuable advance.

An effective world authority, like any other governmental system, must be based on power. It cannot grow out of a paper constitution or a Charter or the formation of international agencies in specific fields, though all these in themselves may make useful contributions. As nation-states grew out of the unifying power of the stronger feudal lords, so must a society of nations grow out of the needs of its largest and most powerful constituent members.

It is impossible to conceive in our day of a world authority that could physically overawe the giant states of the United States of America and the Soviet Union. All that seems possible is to employ the strength of the two giants to back a system of preventing war between other countries. But how is war to be prevented in disputes between the two giants themselves? It seems to me that one of the first steps to be taken is to attempt to do away with the cold war which has been such a marked feature of international relations since the end of the Second World War.

We in the United Nations are all too familiar with the cold war. The curious thing about the cold war is that it is not a battle for more territory, or even for more political power. As it is waged in the United Nations, it is a battle for the votes of the uncommitted and for the minds of the unconverted. History is full of examples of religious intolerance, but the ideological fanaticism that we see today seems to me sometimes to be even more implacable, and certainly more deadly and dangerous to the human race, than the religious fanaticism which marked the history of past centuries and occasioned such extreme instances of man's inhumanity to man.

One remarkable feature of the cold war is that each side is so completely convinced of its own rightness. The doctrines of capitalism and communism have, in fact, undergone some subtle changes since the major exponents of these theories expounded their dogmas. There is no doubt that some of the theories of communism, for example, were influenced by the conditions of extreme *laissez-faire* of private enterprise, the ruthless exploitation of labor, including the labor of women and children, and the accumulation of wealth and power in the hands of a few, that marked the rise of capitalism in the eighteenth and nineteenth centuries. While communist dogma may still speak of capitalism as though it has remained unchanged over the last century, in fact capitalism has undergone a change. Even in the capitalist countries, society has awakened to the dangers of unrestricted private enterprise, and the societies practising the most advanced theories of private enterprise have found it necessary to adopt, at the same time, stringent laws to avoid the danger of extreme concentration of economic power in the form of monopolies. Far from labor's being exploited, united labor has learned its own strength. Small men and women everywhere have in a way become capitalists, with a stake in the development of their own societies. Social welfare legislation has made sure not only that child labor is outlawed, but that children are given opportunities for education and for choosing their own careers.

On the other hand, while some capitalists may not wish to concede this point, I believe that communism too has undergone many changes. For example, there are many communists in the world today who do not believe in the inevitability of war between the two rival systems of society. In the Soviet Union the leaders talk in terms of competitive coexistence. I can well understand why they should wish to compete with the capitalist societies to provide better standards of living for their own people, since they believe in the inherent superiority of their system, and this would be the surest way of demonstrating it.

While thus the practice of capitalism and of communism has perhaps come a little closer than the extreme antithesis assumed by dogmatists in the past, there is still the ideological fanaticism to which I referred and which complicates our existence. Each side is convinced that it alone represents the true philosophy of peace and that the other side is a warmonger. Both sides mistrust the intentions of the other and are also very much afraid that one side might achieve some technological breakthrough in the field of missilery or nuclear warfare, or even defence systems against nuclear attack, which gives it an advantage over the other. If this atmosphere of mistrust and fear continues and if, meanwhile, the stockpiling of nuclear arms and the development of more deadly engines of destruction should continue unchecked, surely the danger of total annihilation of mankind to which I referred earlier is becoming "nearer, clearer, deadlier than before."

It is in this context that I feel that I should address myself today mainly to the younger generation. Those who are leaving an institution of learning today will in due course be responsible as citizens, as mothers and as enlightened members of the public in shaping not only the policies of their country but – what is even more important – the minds of the young.

Their first task, I think, should be to try to understand each other better and to remove in this process the fear and mistrust that characterize the attitudes of the major protagonists of the cold war.

I believe that the prime need today is this need for better understanding, especially the better understanding of the other man's problems and of his point of view. We live in an age of technological miracles. The other day we saw an astronaut take off at 9 a.m. and return to the earth at 7:30 p.m. the next day, after having completed 22 orbits around the globe. Some months earlier we had the fantastic spectacle of two astronauts, one of whom was in orbit for four days, and the other for three days, practically in tandem. Now there is a race to the moon. Already the aeronautical industry is talking in terms of aircraft which will travel at two to three times the speed of sound. In a world which is thus shrinking, it is essential that the human mind must open out, and that we must realize that we all have a common interest in survival and that this interest binds us together.

Some time ago there was an epoch-making conference in Addis Ababa of the heads of state and other officials of the independent countries of Africa. It was a matter of great personal regret to me that although I had been invited in a personal capacity to attend this historic meeting, I was not able to do so. Most of the countries represented at this conference had achieved their independence only during the last decade or so. The heads of state assembled in Addis Ababa were naturally concerned that the African people still subject to colonial rule should obtain their independence soon. But even more striking was their concern with their interdependence, and their emphasis on the establishment of a machinery for regular consultations and concerted action on common problems. This meeting has an important lesson for us – for individuals as well as nations – the lesson of our mutual interdependence.

Atmosphere of Confidence

One fact of our interdependence is our common interest in survival, which can be realized only by better understanding because such understanding is the key to the solution of our most pressing global problems. As I pointed out earlier, there are very few international issues today which can be settled on the basis of a clear-cut judgement that one side is right and the other is wrong. International problems have become so complicated, and so many different elements enter into them, that a simple clear-cut judgement in terms of black and white is no longer possible. Nor can these issues be settled by the imposition of the will of the stronger on the weaker, for history shows that no issue can be settled on a permanent basis by superior force. This in fact would be a good reason for outlawing war, because wars do not solve any problems; in fact, they leave more problems unsolved in their wake, and give rise to more new problems as the years go by, than the problems that they were supposed to solve.

How then can we solve the issues of the world today? We can do so only by creating an atmosphere of confidence to replace the present atmosphere of mistrust. We can solve great issues only by discussion and debate, by negotiation and give-and-take, by conciliation and compromise. It is only in this way that these problems will remain solved and not raise their ugly heads again, as they surely will if they are suppressed rather than solved.

The solution of these great issues is, of course, one of the primary functions of the United Nations. I would be the first to concede that the United Nations is far from being perfect. But I also feel that people often criticize the United Nations because of a basic misunderstanding of its nature. The United Nations is not a world government, nor is its General Assembly a world legislature. It is, in a sense, of course, the parliament of mankind, as it gives opportunities for the large and the small countries equally to have their say on major issues, and this is the original meaning of a parliament.

But it is not a world legislature with the authority to pass laws binding on all member governments; its resolutions are more in the nature of recommendations than of statutes. But the United Nations does offer a machinery for multilateral diplomacy, which did not exist before. As it makes greater progress toward universality over the years, it enables its member governments to hold a simultaneous conversation with the rest of the world, which would not be possible through the normal channels of bilateral diplomacy. And the means it adopts to solve the issues which it faces, big and small, are the very means of persuasion and negotiation which I advocated a moment ago.

I believe that one of the major tasks of education in our changing times is to create in the young the willingness to tolerate differences of opinion and the desire to try to understand different points of view. There was a time not so long ago when religious fanaticism was so great that the hatred of the Saracen for the Christian was no less than that of the Christian for a heretic in his own faith. It is only during the last century or so that religious tolerance has more and more come into its own. Today what we need to do is to practise the cult of political tolerance so as to reach the goal of ideological coexistence as the first imperative of survival on our planet, because truly the only alternative to coexistence is no-existence.

In the search for better understanding, we also have to minimize differences of race, color and nationality. I am an Asian who has lived for some time in the Western world. I think I can say without fear of contradiction that, while we may have a different sense of values, we do not have a different concept of civilization. A civilized Asian is no different from a civilized European or American. But each of them is very different from his own uncivilized compatriots. If we can minimize these differences of race and color and nationality at the same time that we make an effort for better understanding, we shall find it easier to live together on this planet.

There is only one more thought that I should like to share with you. I said a moment ago that the Asian and his Western counterpart may have a different sense of values. I believe that this is particularly true in the field of education. While one has to take all generalizations with reservation, I think it is safe to say that the main aim of education in the West is the development of the intellect. The massive progress of science and technology has tended to stress the intellectual rather than the moral and spiritual values. In Asia, if I may say so, the traditional aim of education is to impress on the young the importance of the mind rather than the body, and, even more basically, the importance of the spirit rather than the mind. Education thus becomes inward looking, and the aim of education is the discovery of one's self rather than the discovery of things external to us.

Today I feel that both approaches are inadequate, and that it is not enough to stress in education either purely moral and spiritual or purely mental and intellectual values. Education cannot mean merely the development of our intellect or of all our potentialities, for there are potentialities for evil in us as well as for good. Nor can it mean mere preparation for life, but rather to make the world a better place to live in. Our educators should realize as clearly as possible what kind of potentialities they are to develop in their students; what kind of life they are to educate young people for. The ideals and values which constitute the essential elements of culture must first be clearly understood and appreciated.

What we therefore need is a synthesis of these values – spiritual and moral as well as intellectual – with the aim of producing a fully integrated human being who is inward looking as well as outward looking, who searches his own mind in order that his nobler self may prevail at all times, and at the same time recognizes his obligations to his fellow men and the world around him; because while the world is shrinking, humanity is multiplying, and each of us has to recognize his essential kinship to every other member of the human race.

Introduction

by

GAETANO MARTINO
Professor of Human Physiology, University of Rome, Italy

It is both a great honour and a profound satisfaction for me to take the chair at this plenary meeting of our Academy. In these days we shall discuss subjects of great and vivid interest not only in a strictly scientific field but also – as I would like to add – in the human and moral domains. In extending a most cordial welcome and best wishes, also on behalf of all Italian Fellows of the Academy, to the Secretary General and Presidium of the W.A. A.S., to those Fellows who will take part in our work, and to all people who have desired to honour us with their gratifying presence, I beg to express my joyfully moved feelings that Rome has been chosen as the seat of such an important event. Doubtless, many other cities in the world would have been just as worthy to be hosts, but perhaps no one more than Rome could express fully that spirit, those essential values, we invoke to enlighten and guide us in the tasks we have set ourselves.

It is surely by such essential and never ending values, as expressed by this eternal city, that has been inspired the Presidium of our Academy in launching the project of creating a World University, when referring expressly both to the message of fraternity and peace addressed to the world by the late Pope JOHN XXIII in the celebrated Encyclical "Pacem in Terris", and to the resolution by the United Nations' General Assembly to proclaim 1965 "a year of international collaboration."

That message and this resolution have the precise aim of reminding all mankind of those fundamental values I have just mentioned. Without them it would be extremely difficult, not to say impossible, to weave the fabric of a solidarity which, by attracting the greatest number of peoples on earth, helps to constitute a basis of that international society so ardently desired by men.

Politics is not sufficient to attain such a goal. We should not let ourselves be immobilized by politics which, apart from all other considerations, may often compel us to wait. Progress must find other ways, other means. Among these ways and means science and culture hold a leading position.

They can materialize that effective progress which directs the march of mankind towards reciprocal trust and steadily closer, more sincere and fruitful cooperation among the peoples.

I have said "effective progress". But what is the meaning of such words today?

The old "quarrel" concerning the inner nature of human progress between the illuminist and the romanticist conceptions is well known. The former maintained that the historical process marking mankind's long and tormented way did not necessarily imply a continuous improvement of man; it can show, side by side with admirable and stupendous highlights of civilization, discouraging and mortifying decline and deviations. According to the latter, on the contrary, progress consisted of a chain of always ascending events, so that even certain seemingly obscure times were always a step higher than those having preceded them.

That quarrel is to be deemed superseded today, because the problem troubling the conscience of modern men, and with greater reason of modern scientists, is only how to see whether a fact, or a sequence of facts, are apt to produce effective progress.

Such an identification needs a criterion of valuation which can obviously be but of a moral nature. Only by judging them on a moral scale can we ascertain whether such facts, or such a fact, lead to real or fictitious progress.

If, for instance, the project of a World University which will be discussed here, should succeed in materializing to a concrete institution, we shall, in my opinion, stand before an effective progress. If the results of research by learned men all over the world could converge in a single World University centre, many problems hindering or slowing down the march of civilization today could evidently be solved more easily.

Another effective progress will be achieved if the continued efforts by students from various nations permit us to identify with precision the causes of conflicts. Because only by discriminating between the real causes and the fictitious ones shall we be in a position to adopt measures aiming at the consolidation of justice and peace in those tormented regions of the world most likely to kindle and spread sparks of conflagration.

We shall also stand before effective progress if we succeed in solving the grave problems of nutrition in their relation to world population; the problem of education on which the integral formation of man depends so much both from the moral and the spiritual angles; the problems of rendering fertile the immense reaches of our planet now barring human life from penetrating and expanding there.

To my mind, however, the enactment of the plan of a World University should be the aim of our main and immediate endeavours. Above all, this would greatly facilitate the solution of the other problems I have just mentioned.

Amongst these, the problem of the ratio between population increase, standard of living and the development of the natural resources on our globe is of particular importance today. It is well known that various organs exist with the task of establishing common programmes for a most rational and propitious utilization of such resources. In this connection, I refer especially to the F.A.O. Moreover, many international conferences have deepened the study of this interesting subject. But as has been observed with good reason, there is no organization capable of studying this problem in its complexity. Well, such an organization could find its fitting location in the World University or in some body closely connected with it.

Moreover, the birth of a World University recruiting the cooperation of scientists and experts from various countries would be both symbol and reality of a more extensive and intensive human solidarity.

All of you know, of course, that we in Europe have been trying for years to establish a European University. Its creation was foreseen in the 1957 Rome Treaties which gave rise to the two great European Communities, the economic and the atomic, which in line with the earlier Coal and Steel Community were intended to make possible the practically total integration of the economies in the six countries forming the so-called Little Europe.

The promoters and makers of those Treaties – and I had the honour of being one of them – had visualized the European University not only as a study centre particularly connected with the functioning and the problems of the Community, but also as a link of cohesion for the spiritual and cultural unity of Europe.

The European University was supposed to function as an ideal beacon for the new generations of European students, warning them against the dangers connected with the lasting inner divisions and contrasts on the already too blood drenched European soil, and accustoming them to live in a climate deprived of all crude nationalistic ambitions and tempered by the balmy and invigorating breeze of friendliness and fraternity.

This is not the fitting occasion to recall the reasons why that project has not yet been able to become concrete reality. But tracing back the lengthy and complicated events which have marked the development of the European University still so far from its final aim, I cannot help being in complete agreement with those who want the planned World University to bypass the traditional schemes of an international university, conceived simply as a meeting place and study centre for teachers and students from various parts of the world. In other words, we have to form a centre of academic activity to gather and evaluate the results achieved in all countries of the world which are connected with the solution of problems concerning all mankind. I am convinced that the creation of such a university, while giving an example which could not be disregarded in Europe, would clear the way for a steadily widening mobilization of scientists in all the world. This would have a twofold effect. It would reinforce international solidarity in a sector of the greatest importance and it would render all the peoples of the world conscious of the fact that only by uniting their endeavours could be created the premises for the attainment of the supreme aims – peace, liberty, security, and well-being – which all men and women, wherever they live, crave for in the depth of their hearts.

A careful and impartial interpretation of the reality in the world we are living in today induces us to assent, to welcome and to contribute most generously and enthusiastically to the initiative of our Academy. We stand in need of increasingly capable instruments for rousing the interest of the most qualified men and organizations in the supreme task of eliminating the causes of unbalance, disorders, sickness and misery. This is the only way to create that basic, lasting and efficient solidarity among the peoples which should facilitate the development of a specifically political action.

In concluding my address, I want to express the wish, that our work could represent a real contribution to the fight that the human race is now waging for its very salvation.

PART I: CAUSES OF CONFLICT

Pax Mundi

by

George E. G. Catlin

"We must never confuse error with the person who errs" — John XXIII.

This globe has existed for several millions of years. There is no reason to suppose that it – and, subject to certain conditions, the human race with it – will not last for some millions of years more. It is suitable that an eminent and world-wide Conference such as this should assess basic priorities; and make an analysis of those factors which threaten human survival. These can be distinguished from those factors, medical, educational, industrial and political, which may be beneficial for human welfare but which are broadly irrelevant to survival, and which humanity has still millions of years of leisure on its hands to think about.

It may be that future studies of ethology will demonstrate that non-human animals avoid mortal conflict by allowing respect for spheres of influence and by general recognition of the different functional status of certain individuals and groups; and it may occur to us that this same formula may also apply in resolving conflict problems between human beings, who are also animals, although less well instinctually endowed than the rest.

I may add, without vouching for its scientific accuracy, that recent research, with small fishes in the reefs, by Professor Konrad Lorenz, of the Max Planck Institute for Behavioral Studies in Bavaria, is reported as indicating that this world of small fry divides into what are called "communist" or collectivist fish, who swim in shoals, are drab in coloration but tend to red, whereas there are, of a different species, what are termed "capitalist" fish, so highly coloured as to look as if daubed with paint, individualists who swim alone, but who yet bellicosely attack like fish of their own kind. Nevertheless these two types can co-exist without mutual adverse attention in a large enough pond.

If, again, our bourgeois democracy, in the shape of traditional parliamentary government, came to an end tomorrow, the human race would no more perish than it did under those Roman Emperors, in whose age the great historian Gibbon said that he would have chosen to live. But there is little purpose in fighting a war to save the world for democracy, if there is no world left at the end. If an aggressive dictatorship or an enraged and emotional people's democracy started up a nuclear war of massive retaliation in order "to save face," and was unable to arrest the war-game, "seeing no way out," reiterating the sophistry that "we have all got to die sometime," even before we have produced the children of another generation, then, whatever the abacus calculations of some chess-playing Dr. Strangelove, the human race might physically perish. Or, at least, all intellectual and civilized leadership lost, it might plunge into the Dark Age of some violent cultural reverse. Confronted by such catastrophe, to argue about how intransigent we should be about forms of government and of economy may, by contrast, be a matter for discussion by fools.

To use an illustration from the non-human animal world. If, in the interests of the progressive modernization of the whaling industry, and to satisfy the greed for profit of various nations – some capitalist ones such as the Japanese and some, be it noted, orthodox Communist – the blue whale becomes extinct, no skill of man or science ever, at any future time, will put the blue whale back into the waters again; and it is dubious whether the Creator will oblige His human apes by doing so, despite their destructive mania.

One of the main targets of censorship and repression has to be private war as it springs from international anarchy. There must always be a political union of theory and practice; and social scientists should not shy away from a problem because it has inconvenient practical consequences.

In a remarkable New Year message, of 1964, to Nikita S. KHRUSHCHOV, President Lyndon B. JOHNSON wrote:

"All the work of the chemist in the laboratory, the scientist in space, and the agronomist in the field will be in vain unless we can learn to live together in peace. No feat of physical science can compare with the feat of Political Science which brings a just peace to the earth."

I have quoted the passage elsewhere before [1] but, like the Bible and the poets, its truth warrants re-quotation.

In this connection, it is also well to recall the comment of Albert EINSTEIN: "Our world faces a crisis as yet unperceived by those possessing the power to make great decisions for good or evil. The unleashed power of the atom has changed everything save our modes of thinking, and thus we drift towards unparalleled catastrophe."

Since the days of Thomas HOBBES political theorists have wondered and lamented that political science, so magisterially outlined by ARISTOTLE, has not matured or advanced so fast or far as it should. Economics and psychology, much younger social sciences, have conspicuously overtaken it in

1. G. CATLIN: Political and Sociological Theory and its Applications (University of Michigan Press and Cresset, 1964), pp. *103–104*.

empirical accuracy and in power of prediction. HOBBES himself, not unlike MACHIAVELLI, suggested pessimistically that no study could be expected to advance when those rash enough to tell the truth only placed themselves thereby at the mercy of those able to do them harm.

Today, when the whole world stands, in HOBBES' own words, in "fear of violent death" and of an apocalyptic last judgement of fire, and when indeed, in the words of the mediaeval hymn, the *Dies Irae*, all may be dissolved in a very fervent heat, we can perhaps summon up courage to despise opposition. We can set forth how far social science has carried us; and most seriously address ourselves – since all science begins in the practical and ends in the practical – to exploring how far it can carry us in these problems of peace and war which, along with the alarming wastages of the irreplaceable resources of nature, have first priority among the concerns of mankind.

Within the last few years, in Toronto under Dr. N. ALCOCK, in Michigan, in Washington, in Oslo and Stockholm, in London and elsewhere, Peace Research Institutes have sprung up, addressing themselves to this central problem in the malfunctioning of the body politic. I ventured to suggest the issue (beyond what could be done by the London Institute) to your Secretary General – and the praesidium of the World Academy of Art and Science in its wisdom has decided to take up the discussion of what the Academy itself, beginning with this Rome Conference, could do towards the advancement of learning and science in this practical field of conflict, peace and war.

The general consensus has been that the problem should be treated, fundamentally, as one of "the Causes of Conflict." Here it would seem to fall, and it is the intention of this Conference that it should be treated, in three parts:

(1) The psychological, sociological and anthropological (and some would add biological) problem of Conflict itself. It is an issue which has certainly preoccupied psychologists and ethnologists in recent years and, as you will be aware, there is now a quite vast literature on the subject. This will occupy the attention, with a view to initiating further research, of one of our subsections.

(2) There is the sociological and historical issue of Group Conflict, including Race and Class Conflict, where such distinguished students as Professor Gunnar MYRDAL and Her Excellency Dr. Alva MYRDAL – with their Institute supported by the Swedish Government, just as this Academy likewise enjoys the patronage of the King of Sweden – are making a most promising contribution.

(3) Finally, there is the limited but in history pre-eminent, case of that kind of conflict between States which is officially called war or which, in our more discreet or maybe more hypocritical epoch, is not so called (no war has been declared, according to international protocol, in Vietnam) but

actually is such. This is a section where the specific problem has been of peculiar concern to myself over the last thirty years and which has, indeed, been at the core of my own work in political analysis.

Dr. ALCOCK, whose work is known to the Pugwash Group and who continued his missionary initiative at its London Conference, in his pioneer pamphlet made one statement which I am confident you will regard as wisdom of the first order.[1] For scientific advance, as he said, it is necessary to define with precision the problem and to set the right questions. Most of our failures here, in political and sociological science, have been due to indulgence in vague rhetoric, acceptance of uncriticized political superstitions and disregard of this salutary warning. By way of contrast, it will be noted that the Philadelphia group, centred on the University of Pennsylvania but with international ramifications, has directed much of its attention (in accord with the sociological style of approach, of which some of us have seen and encouraged the initiation) to precise quantitative and statistical studies.

In meditating recently on this matter I have found myself asking a question which may seem simple to the point of naiveté. Only a few months ago two Soviet astronauts not only orbited in space but one of them was able to step outside his aircraft and not only to swim with the craft, but slowly to turn somersaults. He was indeed attached to the parent craft by a rope, which we may choose to regard as a symbol of the just limits, in these experiments, of scientific doubt. The American Major James McDivitt from the spacecraft *Gemini* has recently performed a similar feat. Nevertheless, it is clear that the miracle-working was undertaken with great confidence in view of precise mathematical and scientific work, which had been perfected in the preceding time, so that there was what approached to human certainty that these startling and untested experiments would prove successful.

The questions which seized my mind were: "Why cannot we do in the social sphere, with all its urgencies, what the astronauts could do so confidently in the physical sphere: not only turn somersaults but return safe to firm ground?" and "What equivalent can we find in the social and political spheres to these precise calculations which the American and Soviet scientists had made, ahead of time, in these astronaut experiments?" What, if any, were the equally, or approximately equal, firm principles in political science upon which we could base ourselves? And here, and throughout this address, I am accepting provisionally the truth of the statement of the analytical philosopher, Professor A. J. AYER, in his Comte Memorial Lecture (1964), that "the differences between these generalizations [in the social sciences] and those that can be found to govern other natural phenomena is nowhere more than a difference of degree."

1. NORMAN Z. ALCOCK: The Bridge of Reason, published by the Canadian Peace Research Institute.

Are there, then, if we wish to exercise control against disasters in politics, hypotheses as well tested as those principles which enable us to prognosticate that astronauts can fearlessly turn somersaults in space? Are there any equivalents at all of the $E = mc^2$ formula, amazingly simple and amazingly subtle? Is there something even as assured as, in Economics, contemporary Business Cycle analysis? My answer is "Yes." We are on the verge, it is my assertion, of discovering them. Nevertheless objections can be taken before we start.

Plain common-sense, we may be told, can supply us with all the answers we seek. The late and saintly Pope JOHN XXIII, in his *Pacem in Terris*, exhorted all men of goodwill to support the authority of an international organization against an insurgent and erosive nationalism. Over a century and a half ago, the philosopher KANT insisted that such an authority must be set up, although he hedged his remarks with typical Kantian hesitations and reservations. The vision of the poet DANTE, in *De Monarchia*, enabled him to demonstrate the necessity for the same road to peace. It would be open for us to say, for example, that what we want is the restoration of the Roman Empire, whose head, according to the ancient prayer, would "rule all barbarous peoples by his might" (Roman Missal, pre-revision Good Friday office).

The common-sense, however, which tells us that an apple drops to the ground or (quite falsely) that the sun can be seen going around the earth is something quite different from the elegant scientific formula which sets forth why, under given and hypothetical conditions, this must be so – or the reverse – and why it is so; or from the scientific research which reaches out to this formula, using terms with exact precision, terms which are also so far as is useful, quantitative.

Further, these common-sense affirmations are by no means entirely non-controversial or, in this sense, indeed "common". The notion of an international Leviathan was certainly not advocated either explicitly or by intention by Thomas HOBBES – quite the contrary – although we may yet argue that it was indeed implicit in his logic. If, however, I urged this model upon you for your acceptance, many of you, I am confident, would start out of your chairs to repudiate it. And the President of France is, at this moment, pressing, with wide popular consent and support, for just such a revival of nationalism as that to which we have referred with distaste.

A further objection to our procedure is in vogue and needs to be answered. It can be said that these are grave matters, not for the analysis of social scientists, but of popular or philosophical principle, moral issues not patient of this kind of analytical approach. I would certainly not, on my personal record, wish to depreciate Political Philosophy: I have written too much of it. If we reply that, granted that the human race desires and, indeed, for its survival to day must have stable peace, then this is the agreed moral end, and it is for social scientists to see to the fitting means, we can be told that this is not so. We can be told that quite fundamental ideological objections, such as once obtained between Christians and Moslems or between Protestants and Catholics, preclude any attainment of stable peace on this side of decisive victory for the right. We can further be told that, although peace and survival may be good things, they can only be considered in the moral context of freedom and justice.

I am inclined to regard much of this line of objection as cant and nonsense, political vote-hunting superstition and rhetoric. There is indeed a present cleavage in the world not (fortunately) so much between East and West, or even North and South, as between the so-called "capitalist" and the so-called "communist" camp. However, Mr. Averell HARRIMAN has repudiated the word "capitalist" as an adequate polemic description of the United States economy (as has also General EISENHOWER), and President JOHNSON has rightly insisted that his economy today is something totally dissimilar from the "capitalism" attacked by MARX. Likewise, as to "communism," it is a system advocated from Pythagoras to the early Christians of Jerusalem (and the treatment of Ananias and Sapphira was scarcely of a "voluntary" character) and from monasticism to the contemporary kibbutzim of Israel. A question may be raised of its industrial efficiency in the modern world of adventure, private initiative and competition; but I do not observe that the Soviet Ilyushin airplane fails to compete. On the contrary, if we look away from doctrinaire abstractions to practice, we see, on the one hand, a guide-line policy or *économie directive* in conservative and capitalist France (more so than under the Socialist Government of Britain) and a system of Liberman theory and of factory competition, measured by profits, being introduced in today's Soviet Union.

If we are to concentrate on "cold war" ideological objections, allegedly insoluble, then I can only comment that conflicts about the Real Presence of God, between Catholics and Protestants, would logically seem to be even more profound and matters of principle than whether an economy is to be planned, semi-planned or unplanned... We have to address ourselves to the dispassionate consideration of what is effective by the joint consideration of the best technical minds facing complex technical problems, and not to indulge ourselves by protestations about who, in our subjective view, has been right in the past or must be right now. The first alone is the business of the scientist; the second we can leave to the hired attorney.

Atheism, if it is official doctrine, along with the secular Marxist religion, for Russian (and Chinese) communists, is also unashamedly proclaimed in innumerable Western universities. Nor is materialism in practice the prerogative of either East or West. Some day our children, if they survive so long, will regard these disputes as on a par with the allegedly "insoluble" disputes between Christian and Moslem, precluding co-existence.

We do well to bear in mind the admonition of JOHN XXIII, tinged with infallibility, that human beings evolve from doctrinal origins and that the heresies, rightly condemned, which they proclaim in their youth may be very different from the objective practice of their maturity. The communism of LENIN is not that of STALIN; is not that of KRUSHCHOV; and may be not that of KRUSHCHOV's successors.

How, then, shall we proceed? I wish to begin by stating, as a hypothesis for our research, a very simple principle, not dissimilar from that which, from the days of RICARDO, the economists have adopted, to systematize their science, as touching the pursuit of exchangeable wealth and of prosperity. I want, also, here to utter the caution that I am not at all stating the tautology that "what a man desires, as ends, he desires." Many men ardently desire the means to achieve their desired ends: but they lack the knowledge how to master those means. One major end of human aspiration today is to achieve stable civil peace internationally; but, conspicuously, we lack the knowledge of the assured means. Some say that what we require is the rule of law. But what law do we require; who makes it; and how do we establish it? In the words of President Andrew JACKSON about the then Chief Justice: "John Marshall has given his decision: now let him execute it."

My initial principle, as foundation of the relevant political structure and its working models, is this: "Every man, being offered the opportunity of power, without disproportionate cost, wills to have it." One corollary of this could be that the costs of non-consensual power should be raised so high that people, like some animals, become content to confine themselves to their own area of influence, the area for which they can obtain recognition and legitimacy. Without costs the general law of expansion will take its course.

Upon the precise definition of "power," as used here, I have spent some pages in my *Systematic Politics* [1] so that it is not obnoxious to the objections which Bishop BUTLER advanced against the crude and too general statements of HOBBES. Incidentally, "power" does not mean "influence" (as George WASHINGTON noted about governmental power) or, again, the immediate exercise of control; but the sure capacity for the act of control. The dictum or principle applies equally to those who are governed by fear of such as may control them; to those ambitious of control; and to those who, being inspired by the most ideal ends, seek to have the co-operation of their fellows in assuring the means to their realization.

The only superficial exceptions are the lazy or vegetable man; and those who have already achieved the ends of their desires in the enjoyment of an untroubled and contented life – but who, if disturbed, will yet have to fight for the means to preserve it. The problem of the lazy man I leave to the psychologists but suggest that we have here, not a genuine exception, but a matter of slowness of temper. There are also the "other-worldly men" – who yet, in history, have been known to fight very vigorously to persecute

1. Systematic Politics, University of Toronto Press and George Allen and Unwin, 1963

those who did not share their views about the other world and the way to it as the all-important ideal of salvation.

If we accept this fundamental hypothesis, which happens to be one which in some fashion political scientists and political sociologists have debated anew since the "Twenties," and in which debate I have taken some part, certain consequences follow, both of a theoretical and of a practical nature.

The hypothesis is not only patently capable of empiric test but, the mental basis (as Bryce said) of political propositions being usually psychological, psychological experiments should be able greatly to refine it. Further, although the quest of power may be, within the agreed framework of discussion, the efficient cause, the very reference to conditions and costs indicates the existence of other factors, economic, demographic, psychological and the rest. Here also there is a fruitful field for research, in indicating the rôle they play in reducing or increasing the costs of power-action. It is a work to which I hope that our conflict-study groups will address themselves, perhaps with some statistical precision. Specific social factors, of an irritant quality, can be isolated in group and racial conflicts. Some of these factors (such as nationalism and tribalism), despite Marx, will probably not be found to be economic.

Let us, then, now look to the side of the costs. If indeed there is relevant power available, everybody is interested in acquiring it. If every state can have a nuclear bomb without disproportionate costs, we must expect run-away dissemination. If what is going to emerge, to satisfy the demand for peace, is a world authority, the interest of all states in having a share in its power contributes to its construction. There is no lack of would-be claimants. But it is obvious enough that playing the world policeman is, in any sense, a costly operation; and, having counted these costs, many will shy away or not pay their dues – and many were not serious contenders anyhow. Further, any authority is not only a "power" but a "recognized power": and the trouble for a world authority is to obtain precisely this consensus of recognition.

Freedom from control by an alien interest, not an authority recognized as for our benefit, however interpreted, is a quite intelligible advantage. The issue here is likely to turn on the meaning of "benefit" or "vital" or "real" interest. The fusion of the nations of England and Scotland, with the abandonment of local sovereignty, was in the interest of both. (I regret to say that the happy result was achieved, in no small part, by financial corruption, aided by the discreet distribution of honours to appease the vanity of Scottish noblemen). We may disapprove in general, ethically, logically or practically, of our neighbour's dreams, ideologies or blueprints. But what we fear is that he may acquire the power to impose these, when unwanted, upon us. Here is the crux. Here is why we resent being required to regard him as an authority or even part of an authority. And we propose to make him pay heavy costs for exercising power over us.

Two issues here arise which we can, briefly, call the rational and the irrational. Power, it is necessary to insist, is of two kinds. The one, perhaps the more difficult to construct, but often the more lasting and stable, is a rational co-operative power. It rests upon a wide measure of consent. "Let us now reason together." The other, dominative power, also (as has been emphasized since the days of David HUME) requires some measure of assent, but not of the same wide or explicit kind. One of the major tasks of the social scientist today is to study the ways and means of increasing preference for co-operative power. Thus the example set by the lawyers in the law courts and also in our political assemblies is a disastrous one. Here the object, as in war itself, is to score points; to represent one's client as entirely right and white, and the other side as fit to be adjudged by the court totally wrong and black. Unfortunately in the political arena there is no professional judge and, as yet, in the arena of arms no judge at all. Often political science gains more from studying the structure of industry than of civil affairs; and, in industry, the technique of the round table conference, especially of the type where each participant is invited to have the imagination to put himself in the shoes of the other, is a technique most definitely worthy of further research, with a view to its application in political affairs. The inadequacy of political agencies and sovereignties – with their accompanying suppositions, legal and popular, which were developed in the Seventeenth Century as a protection of civil peace against, for example, the greed of the French baronage – to operate effectively in the international and democratic system of today, seeking international peace, may be patent but still requires reiterated and unqualified demonstration. We have basically to reverse our concepts of sovereignty and to cut clear from the Westphalian system of small states claiming unqualified sovereignty to themselves.

Incidental to this theme for science of research and to persistent political co-operation, it is worthy of remark that the NATO set-up in France, preoccupied with defence, has as yet no section interlocking with the patent endeavours towards disarmament which are the preoccupation of the Conference set up in Geneva. No need has, as yet, been seen for such integration of effort.

However, there is not only need for painful patient training in constructive collaboration, in which we have to get away from ancient traditions, since the Seventeenth Century, of absolute state sovereignty. We still have, periodically, to confront the urgent problem of irrational aspirations to dominative power, power to impose by force this or that system of ends. We have, further, to reckon out the costs of these confrontations. In parenthesis let me add that the Chinese, broadly speaking, have been for millennia a peaceful people. President NYERERE described them as "a reasonable people." We have to ask ourselves how far, objectively, they have ceased to be rational now. How far are the mass claims of the "have-not" countries and races irrational claims? And how far will their economic advancement indeed best be advanced, on their part, by war and refusal of co-existence? How far are we cursed by unanalysed and irrational prejudices, idées fixes and mental stereotypes? Does aggression pay? To take an illustration from the argument of a Nobel Prize-winner of before the First World War, Sir Norman ANGELL: How far does war not pay? Or, on the contrary, is it the one route – and the illusion to the contrary ANGELL's own? Is the one war worth fighting that which involves paying the heavy costs, not of democracy *per se* (however consensually desirable), but of setting up an effective and decisively armed World Authority?

It is not my task here to anticipate the results of the very research with which you and this Academy will concern yourselves. It is one of the most presumptuous – but, alack! also one of the most common – errors to do just this.

However, having given some years of attention to this matter (indeed ever since the last days of the First World War), I may perhaps have the temerity to put forward certain suggestions for your consideration and further research.

(1) The techniques of co-operative power require further study. These techniques are probably neither particularly democratic nor particularly public. They seek results by whatever may be indeed the efficient means. They are probably those of the round table of plenipotentiaries, where each is prepared, if not to put himself in the position of the other side in making a bargain, at least to be intelligently aware of the strength of the opponent's case. They are almost certainly not the techniques of the defense attorney and of the prosecuting attorney, although these latter are customary in the party fights of the world's legislatures. It is not remarkable that statesmen trained in these wrong political methods should fail to find the right ones in international discussion. Above all, avoid zeal and avoid rhetoric. The world will live a long time yet and even genuine grievances, as distinct from pretended ones, can await the opportune time for solution. Some things matter vitally: most things don't. It is better to weigh up power and to bargain than to be dead. The formal or ceremonial peaceful fight can replace the actual animal fight.

(2) New physical and technical inventions, if we press forward with their development, can often alleviate conflict by providing a solution to what might otherwise seem to be insoluble difficulties in appeasement. For example, highly technical research can provide means of detection of menacing nuclear experiments which detection, prior to these discoveries, would have required objectionable and spying-on-the-spot inspection.

(3) Hate is psychologically energizing and satisfying to the vulgar and animal side of men, an ape-cousin and full of original sin. This is one of the prostitute attractions of war itself. Nevertheless, no man who expresses it, save as a charade, should ever be suffered in any position of power. In the

last World War and before, we discovered how Hitler's and Mussolini's wilfully militaristic and aggressive language, as menacing, provoked its own nemesis, stirred alarm and led to the downfall of whose who used it. Fundamentally this demagoguery was politically stupid. Today, the Chinese leaders, who cheerfully talk about the death of millions and invite ostracism, should learn this lesson and re-study CONFUCIUS, who was very wise.

(4) One major cause of war would seem to lie in the emotion of the populace, stirred up and exploited whether by the sincere fanaticism or by the ambition for power of demagogues, so that the cession of a single acre of "the sacred soil" of A country, or such nonsense, cannot be a matter of a bargain with B country. The remedy would seem to lie in regarding the whole affair of politics, as of economics, as more a business matter, open to arbitration, such as it was regarded in the Eighteenth Century when the stress lay on good administration. Today the Swiss Constitution seems to be among the most appropriate, which is one of perpetual coalition of experts according to elected party proportions. The demands of the political *consumers* have to be taken into account, even with statistical precision; but it also has to be recognized that this consumer demand is often self-contradictory, e.g. for peace but also intransigently for *la gloire*. The responsibility of the Government is that of the expert and long-range *producer* of political goods.

(5) Allied, as a rider, to this last point is the extreme danger of making an issue of "what is right." In effect this means the claim of each litigant to reject compromise and to insist "on principle" in being judge and jury in his own case, imposing his judgement upon his opponent, in the absence of a recognized tribunal. The remedy lies in a recognized tribunal backed by force and solely competent to declare, for purposes of political actuality, what is just and to punish those who reject due process of law. What orators may think is right or wrong is, as HOBBES said, irrelevant. This is not, however, to deny the rational obligation of positive law to conform to natural law, both logical and empirically based on human nature and its fundamental demands.

(6) In the early Twentieth Century it was held that a major cause of war was "the Merchants of Death," the armaments manufacturers. This commercial cause of war was probably exaggerated, although not negligible. In the Eighteenth Century it was held that a major cause of war was "journalists." This may be worth further study.

(7) It is now possible to revert to the more purely scientific considerations of power. Some countries, owing to their inherent natural resources, their populations and wealth and their technical high development are in the actual position of being super-Powers. At the present time there are two. At least on the level of conventional (not to speak of revolutionary) warfare China may be a third. Assuming sacrifice of national sovereignty and integration in close unions, there may be more. It is yet not in the interest of

any emergent World Authority that their number shall be multiplied. If these super-Powers can reach an *entente*, then the desired objective of establishing a stable World Authority enters the area of the practicable. However, let us be clear, the costs to be paid are going to be heavy. For the first time, the human ideal of enforcing peace comes within sight. Since armed conflict will be suicidal for civilization and for themselves, the fundamental self-interested power impulses of the super-Powers can be gratified by such a *condominium*.

(8) Superficially the power-interests of smaller countries, such as France, will be adversely affected. In some cases – not France, but possibly China – a way of accomodation may be found in the allocation and recognition of an adequate field of influence, roughly corresponding with that of Chinese emigration. This is a case where the maxim, so easy to enunciate and so difficult to implement, of "peaceful change" in the areas of power would seem to apply. What, however, is the power interest of the rest? They cannot, by the decree of Nature, themselves on their own hope to attain to super-Power rank. They are, as it were, but minor dukes and barons, ripe for "mediatization." The ruler of France is a pretty minor duke. If, however, they decide, as alternative, to oppose the effectiveness of the super-Powers, they can only do this by entering into a federation of opposition which will require just such a surrender of sovereignty for a negative and ineffective local purpose as they can constructively achieve for an effective wider purpose.

The answer would seem to be that, surrendering outmoded concepts and practices, which fulfilled their functions in the different conditions of the Seventeenth Century, they should explore what maximum effective power they can exercise under a system of constitutional or at least normal and organic consultation, thereby giving themselves not a smaller but a *greater* share, though this consultation is the shaping of policy, in the effective exercise of world power. To use an analogy from another sphere, like the representatives of the States of the American Union, they would achieve the dignity of Senatorial rank. This could be achieved in a Union of all Europe or, on the principle of *entia non sunt multiplicanda* – an essential principle if we are ultimately to get an effective world organization – of an Atlantic Union. It would carry us beyond our present purpose to discuss here the merits of these. It is sufficient that (a) we have confronted the problem of the demand for shares in power; (b) we have offered to all, but especially to the super-Powers, the determinant prospect of exercising still more power. *L'Union fait la force.*

I put forward these proposals to you provisionally. It is irrelevant that for me personally they seem to be mature enough to warrant their being made the bases for practical policy, to be both commended and pressed. It is for this distinguished body, in its committees, to analyse them and perhaps to reject them as neither scientific deductions in human politics, from what we know whether it be of psychological motivation or of environmental animal conduct, and hence unsound; or as contrary to the recorded trends of history. I do not yet know these answers. Here is the field for investigation.

What I have, however, endeavoured to say is that this problem of war between states is immemorial but, nevertheless, is a form of social disease today so critical that it insists upon urgent solution; and that it is not only of interest but the professional duty of political and social scientists to apply themselves to this end. I have raised the question whether one course (although there are of course, others) of this persistently recurrent trouble of war may not lie in the very traditional sovereign structure of the states themselves, designed in the past for the more limited function of the preservation of the civil and local peace, putting down the dangerous notion that *chaque baron est souverain dans sa baronnie*.

Above all, I have submitted to you that, whatever the solutions of this problem at which you may arrive, they will have to take into account that appetite of men, groups and nations for power, as means to their several ends, which is the fundamental hypothesis or even axiom upon which the whole science of politics turns.[1]

1. Cf. G. E. G. Catlin: Systematic Politics (University of Toronto Press and G. Allen & Unwin, 1963), ch. 3, and Science and Method of Politics (Knopf and Routledge, 1927; Archon, 1964), for development of this theme. Also Political and Sociological Theory and its Applications (University of Michigan Press and Cresset, 1964), ch. 5.

The Struggle for Identity

by

MORRIS L. WEST
Novelist, Canberra, Australia

It is my belief, and I should like to state it clearly at the beginning of this talk, that the causes of all conflict are buried deep in the sub-soil of the individual mind. The root of all dissension is the struggle of the individual to discover, affirm and maintain his personal identity against all that threatens, or appears to threaten it.

This struggle begins at the first moment after birth, when the tiny human animal finds itself adrift in a strange and hostile environment. He is no longer lapped in the warm fluid of the womb. His nourishment is no longer automatic. He is subject to heat and cold, to hunger and pain, to the eccentric attentions of other human beings whom he knows only by touch and smell, and by their association with comfort or discomfort.

Even in a family group which offers him – as many do not – love, nurture and security, he finds that his desires and demands are thwarted, that he is forced, on the one hand, to accomodate himself and, on the other, to assert himself with his feeble resources, against those who are stronger than he. Even before he begins to be aware of himself, the seeds of conflict are planted. He has begun his dialectic with life – the argument that will last until the day he dies.

When his conscious life begins – when he starts to know, and to know that he knows – the argument becomes more and more vivid, and more charged with emotion. Reason enters into it – but how much reason depends on the degree of education, enlightenment, tolerance and love which exists within the family group. If there is much love, much enlightenment, the child accomodates himself more readily and asserts himself less avidly, because his identity is recognised, interpreted and maintained by those around him. In the light of this recognition, the disciplines to which he is subjected take on an acceptable meaning. The paradox of existence is no longer a threat to his identity, but a guardian of it.

Alone he is weak. Inside the unit he is strong. He is independent, but he recognises his dependence. He may claim rights because they arise out of a mutuality of recognised duty. He can accept an order in society because the analogue of order in the family has prepared him for it. He is not hostile to the idea of a spiritual level of existence, because a notion of creative order and moral principle has been part of his formation.

This, of course, is the ideal picture of how an identity – a balanced and secure identity – is created. However, even in this ideal environment, a variety of identities and identity goals is established and these are subject to later challenge. The need is apparent for a fundamentally and universally valid understanding of identity.

But when the family structure is unstable, or when it is broken by internal or external stresses, the child's notion of his own identity becomes clouded. He is forced back to the avid and solitary search. More than this, when he is thrust out, inevitably, into a wider society, he will have no armour against the new challenges which will be made against his insecure self.

The challenges are many and various. "Who are you?" – And the fledgling human knows only that he is here, a cosmic accident out of an act called the act of love.

"What are you?" – And this simple question has a whole category of answers – by colour, race, nationality, creed or social station. To answer in one category is only to provoke a challenge in another.

"Why are you?" "What do you want?" .... the inquisition goes on and on, relentlessly, until the exasperated spirit retreats into itself, or fights back to wrest the inquisitor from his chair and sit there in his place.

At this point of exasperation, language breaks down. It is no longer an instrument of communication, but a collection of symbols, fluid, personal, esoteric and obscurantist; so that the commerce of society sounds like the Tower of Babel.

And here, precisely, is where the social conflict begins. In the community, the city, the nation, man is still separate. Each one makes a different affirmation of identity; each has his own identity goal. The goals are often contradictory and antipathetic. Even when they are similar, they are never identical.

Those with similar goals tend to agglomerate. They make the groups, the sects, the unions, the parties within a given society. They have made a discovery, you see, – the same discovery that they might have made less painfully in an evolved family group – that to maintain an identity, one has to sacrifice a part of it to the group, in the hope that the sacrifice may be fruitful and the return more abundant than the gift. Sometimes it is so, sometimes not. A free society demands a lesser price from the individual than a collectivised one; but a price is still exacted.

Yet, in spite of its compensations, the group is not enough. Its solidarity can never assuage the essential solitude of the individual. It may give him support while he seeks his own identity. It may even reveal to him certain aspects of that identity. It may protect him from exploitation and injustice. It may give him certain defined and attainable goals. But it cannot create an identity for him. If it claims to do so, it is launching him upon a lie, which will ultimately destroy the individual and the group.

So, inside the groups, the tensions of unrealised identity still exist. Tensions develop within the groups themselves, and they tend to agglomerate again under the guidance of a central regulating authority, with all its mechanisms of government.

It is, in one sense, a constructive step. Out of the perennial conflict of interests – individual conflicts, group conflicts – there grows the notion of a community of interest, a pragmatic acceptance of imperfection, and an aspiration to a less imperfect state of affairs. But if too much hope is based upon it, it degenerates into paternalism on the part of the government and infantilism on the part of the governed.

The individual seeks identity in a community – only half aware that he will not find it there in fulness. The community seeks identity in a larger community, and the large community is forced to make a collective affirmation to create a collective identity, whether it be religious, racial, national, lingual or political.

The individual tends to accept this identity as a substitute for a more basic one. He is even prepared to accept, in self defence, the ghetto mentality. Anything is better than the vacuum which he senses at the core of himseif. Now he can say – I am Greek, I am Russian, American. I am Catholic, I am Buddhist, I am Asian, or Semite, or Negro . . . .

To be collective is better at least than not to be at all, or to be an unnamed dustmote, floating restlessly and aimlessly on the winds of change. But it is not enough – not half enough for the man who lives under my skin. He is still threatened and challenged. He is still tormented by the same questions – Who am I? Why am I? Where am I going? He is still the primal battlefield: between the certainty he desires and the doubt he knows: between the love he has to spend and the hate by which he seeks to protect his vulnerable heart. His waking is beset by the fear that hostile others, or a hostile environment, may rob him of his small attainment. Disaster stalks him on the highway, or on the stock exchange. Death stares at him out of a dark alley, or out of a mushroom cloud. His sleeping is now glorious with the visions of what knowledge may reveal to him, now haunted by nightmares that he has conjured out of his own ignorance.

In the solitary hours which make up most of his life, it is no longer enough that he should know himself for Greek, German, Copt or Confucian, Negro or Caucasian. He is still in conflict, and sometimes he is tempted to kill himself because he can see no tangible enemy. Sometimes he creates an enemy, or worse still, lets the community create one for him, like a carnival barker who sets up coconuts, and then sells the balls to throw at them.

And here is the shape of the greatest conflict of all – war between the nations. Those who direct the destinies of great human communities, are themselves under test. They know that if they cannot satisfy the human cravings of the people, for identity, for security, for a minimal dignity and physical comfort, they will be ousted by a vote or by a revolution. They know, too, that they cannot control the vast physical forces of the planet, the economic complexities, the great demographic movements of history. So, all too often, they try to divert the people – no longer with bread and circus games, but by fear: fear of nameless enemies, faceless fates and illusory threats. They raise the beast in man to fight fairy-tale monsters. So, man ends up fighting himself, seeing in the face of his dying adversary what he has sought in vain all his life – the mirror image of his true self.

It is in order to avoid this repetitious tragedy that man has tried, from time to time, to create supra-national organisations to reconcile the conflicts between nations, as the nation tries to reconcile conflicts between individuals and groups.

But just as the reconciliation of the individual with the group is never complete and never wholly satisfactory, so the reconciliation of the nations with a supra-national entity can never be complete or wholly successful. The pressure of self interest is too great. The divergence of identity goals is too wide.

What then? Do we despair? Do we abandon all hope and abrogate all effort? Do we do collectively what some individuals do – set ourselves in fugue, into a state of flight from existence, whose end is total withdrawal and total madness? And for us, remember, total madness means total war and the annihilation of civilisation as we know it. It is a possibility which hangs over us every day, which is increased by every local conflict, in every part of the world.

I want to talk now for a little while about one of the symptoms of this collective insanity, which is also a symptom of insanity in the individual: the breakdown of communication – and specifically, the breakdown of language as a means of communication – between individuals and communities.

It is a fact, I think, that human experience always outstrips the means to communicate it. New concepts are slow of acceptance because we lack words, or even symbols to convey them. On the night before he died, the great Albert EINSTEIN uttered the same thought to his son: "If only I had more mathematics." We have the mathematics now, but we still lack the languages. The languages which we have are tainted by history, not yet adapted to our present, and still incapable of compassing our visions of the future.

For example, one of the great problems in religious unity is that every great religion is expressed in verbalisms which belong to other ages, other climates of experience, earlier stages of knowledge. And man still lives in the echo of atavistic magic, so that he is often afraid to examine the origin and the meaning of the age old formulae.

In politics it is the same. Do you remember the book of Judges – How the men of Galaad asked the man of Ephraim to identify himself "They asked him then – Say "Shibboleth" and he answered "Sibboleth" .... So immediately they took him and killed him at Jordon Ford."

In the affairs of the nations, we still use the Shibboleth – the catchword. What is a democrat, a republican, a monarchist, a socialist, a communist, a Stalinist, a Trotskyite, a liberal, a capitalist exploiter, an imperialist ....? The words mean different things to different people. They are variable symbols – often the symbols of a deep emotional and intellectual confusion. Certainly no man should be killed for them. Yet we stand in danger of a universal holocaust because of them. They are the trigger-words of a Pavlovian reflex. For millions of people all over the world, they can be made an incitement to irrational destruction.

We need in all our schools a new approach to the teaching of language – a care for the sanctity of language, one of the noblest gifts we have, and yet the easiest to be debased by the sophist, or perverted by the tyrant.

There is a sanctity, too, in the symbols which men have created to express their deepest spiritual yearnings and aspirations. We have to cultivate wisdom enough to interpret them to our children, courage to defend them against the iconoclast, and vigilance to preserve them against exploitation by the rabble-rouser. My symbol is not your symbol, but what it expresses is common to us both: the elevation of man out of the jungle that spawned him, into an image of the God Who made him.

I am a theist and a Christian. This is the foundation of my identity. I desire only that you respect it, as I respect yours, whatever it may be. I seek in our relationship not the ground of contradiction, but the area of agreement. Each of us carries the burden of his own history, which is still a determinant of his identity. But we can still assume a common responsibility for the history which remains to be written – the future. We dare not abandon that to the politicians and the professional myth-makers.

There is no fundamental reason why the Star of David should be set in contradiction to the Crescent of Islam, nor the Buddha smile against the grimace of the dying Christ, nor the Hammer and Sickle against the Stars and Stripes. Each symbol began as a symbol of identity and of hope. They have been debased only by the malice of the past, and by a present misuse as symbols of conflict.

Which brings me, by a round turn, to the core of my contribution to this symposium. The roots of conflict are planted in the individual. The flowering of hope – if hope there be – will come from the individual.

Man is a political animal, yes. Man is a gregarious animal, yes. He has need of social regulation if he is to grow to his full stature as a single person. But I affirm, with all possible emphasis, that the group, the society, the nation, the supra-national body, must all be devoted to, and responsible to, the individual.

Historically, my dear colleagues, all the great forward steps of civilisation have been those dictated by a communal concern for individual identity, and for the individual rights which arise out of it.

The Gautama recorded as the symbols of his first steps in the way of enlightenment, an old man, a sick man, a dead man, and a man with a shaven head who had no home. Moses the Lawgiver, brought down from the Fiery Mountain the Decalogue: a code for individual man, by which the most complex society might still regulate itself. The core of the Gospel of Christ was: "So long as you did it to the least of My brethren, you did it to Me." The great popular revolutions which have changed, in a century, the face of our planet, were founded first on a declaration of individual rights; and, no matter how much violence has been done, how much they have been perverted, their progress to betterment, where betterment has come, has been because of this substratum of fundamental truth: that collective man is a myth, and individual man is made in a Divine image.

And we – we, colleagues in this international academy – where do we stand? Our position, I think, is very clear. We know, none better, that the one hope to avert conflict is the idea – the idea that is shaped first in the brain of a man, is tested by free debate in a free forum and is then sent out, not to be rammed down man's neck so that he either swallows it or chokes on it, but to take root and grow quietly like a flower in a garden, to propagate itself in liberty and reseed itself far beyond the place of its original planting.

One flower is the genesis of millions more. Light one candle, and a million other can be lit from it. Help one man to discover, affirm and maintain his true identity, and you preserve the hope of survival of the whole human species.

Preventive Psychiatry and World Problems

by

LEON J. SAUL
Professor of Clinical Psychiatry, University of Pennsylvania, Philadelphia

The basic goal of medicine is prevention. Dramatic and enormously helpful as is cure, for example by the antibiotics, the real triumph of medicine is in the virtual elimination of diseases – such as smallpox and typhoid. Prevention has been achieved by understanding the basic cause and combatting it.

The basic cause of emotional disorders is now known, and it is now known that emotional disorders comprise not only the *private* suffering of neurotic thoughts and feelings and of psychosomatic symptoms, but also the character and behavior disorders, including *anti-social* acting out as criminal and criminoid behavior and even in the fomenting of wars.

The emotional disorders are the roots of the world's hate, violence, evil, and suffering. *The world's brutality and folly are expressions and symptoms of emotional disorders. The basic cause of emotional disorders is faulty childrearing* during the earliest, most tender, most formative years, from birth or even from conception, to age 4, 5, 6, or 7 – for convenience expressed as "0 to 6." The pine seedling grows straight of its own nature if given proper soil and climate. The human being matures into an adult of good will, a good citizen, spouse and parent if given the proper emotional soil and climate. It is resoundingly true that "as the twig is bent the tree is inclined." Our world of brutality, madness and folly is the result of the gnarled and twisted personalities who make it up, and this warping, with exceptions so rare as to be neglible, is the direct result of just one fundamental cause; atrocious child-rearing, expecially from 0 to 6. We are a world of inclined trees because we were bent as twigs.

But let us perceive clearly, sharply, and definitely that *there are people of good-will and people of cruelty and violence.* It is not so simple as group against group, nation against nation, race against race. In every group (except homogeneously selected ones) there are adults who, because they are mature, are men and women of good-will who want to solve conflicts and problems by reason, generosity, and considerateness; and in every group are those who, through faulty childrearing, have failed to mature adequately and who therefore feel inferior and frustrated and hence are filled with fear and hate and frequently with readiness to violence. There are those who love people because they were raised with love and those who hate people because they suffered at their hands in childhood.

Man is unique in the animal kingdom in the extent and intensity with which he organizes the destruction of his species – of his own kind and of himself. This is not because of his nature.

He is, in fact, in his nature as good a citizen and family man and woman as, say the wolves. But his nature is warped by injurious treatment during the critical, earliest months and years, when the imprinting and conditioning take effect for life. This early mishandling generates the child's hostility and resentment against those in power over it, and the child continues these feelings against others for life, just as a puppy who is mistreated grows into a frightened, slinking, dangerous cur. If people cause the child suffering, it hates them and it fails to mature properly because its human relations are disturbed. It feels the inner warping which causes a sense of anxiety and inferiority and frustration because it cannot be defined and combatted; this child fails to mature adequately and as an adult remains in large part the frustrated, frightened, hostile child he once was. We all remain very much the children we once were. If we had a world of happy children, loving because they are loved, understood and well-treated, then we would have a world in which good-will would predominate instead of callousness and brutality as today.

The scientific evidence for the folk saying that as the twig is bent the tree is inclined, is now overwhelming and conclusive. But there is emotional resistance to its acceptance, stemming from several sources including (1) psychological inertia against new knowledge and new ways of thinking; (2) the guilt and shame of parents and a refusal to accept the responsibility which comes from a realization that "the hand that rocks the cradle rules the world," that, as HOOVER said, "If we had one generation of properly reared children, we would have Utopia itself." People much prefer the old thinking and are enmeshed in the prejudice that it is all heredity, even though there is not a scrap of evidence (except possibly for extremes of psychoses) to support it. Even if there were, it could not gainsay the thoroughly established body of evidence for the permanent after-effects of early treatment of the young.

This evidence is drawn from folk wisdom, as in the quotations above and in others, such as "the child is father to the man." It was expressed by the Jesuit educators as: Give me the child until he is six and you can have him for the rest of his life.

The modern scientific evidence can be classified as follows:

(1) Clinical evidence comes from general psychiatry exemplified by ADOLPH MEYER (1936) whose "Life Chart" showed the effects throughout life of the early influences.

It also comes, and more powerfully, from psychoanalysis. All the different disagreeing psychoanalytic schools are founded upon FREUD's demonstration of the fact that the child lives on in every adult and if this is a good, affectionate child because it has been raised with good relations to its family members, the adult matures properly, while if it is a disturbed child because it has not been properly treated, there is a failure of the development of the capacity to love in the home which spreads toward other human beings in society.

(2) Sociological evidence also supports these findings. For example:

(*a*) Anthropology – MARGARET MEAD, (1949), RUTH BENEDICT (1934), and many others have shown that the personality traits in common of adults in a given culture are determined by how they are reared in childhood.

(*b*) Criminology – the various studies, only now bearing fruit, which show gross disorders in childhood to be at the root of criminal behavior will probably not stand up because, although the field is definitely far enough advanced to show the *cause* of criminal behavior, it is not so far advanced, in all probability, that it can *predict* with certainty that crime and no other disorder of personality will be the outcome. Crime and the hostility of people to each other emerge very clearly, however, as simply one form of behavior disorder.

Direct sociological studies such as "The Authoritarian Personality"(1) and the studies of what made people Nazis or Anti-Nazis also show the determining effect of the home environment, emotionally speaking, during the earliest years.

Since we live in an age of laboratory sciences, clinical observations are not accorded full scientific weight. It is therefore gratifying to turn to:

(3) Animal ethology, the direct observation of animals in natural or semi-natural state (K. LORENZ (1952), WM. THORPE (1961), N. TINBERGEN (1963), for example) and also to

(4) Laboratory experiments with animals which bear upon this subject:

(*a*) There is now a series of fascinating experiments by psychoanalysts with animals to establish some of the basic principles (e.g. MASSERMAN (1943), SEITZ (1959)).

(*b*) The modern work of conditioned reflex scientists such as HOWARD LIDDELL (1956) has cast a new light upon the phenomena of conditioning and it is interesting that people like LIDDELL have gotten a good deal of understanding from dynamic psychiatrists and analysts of the nature of the reactions of their animals. The animals subjected to traumatic influences, especially in the early years, develop severe neurotic reactions, also antisocial reactions, and often are not curable or are curable only through a long process of deconditioning.

(*c*) The other field of work is "imprinting", exemplified by the experiments of HARLOW (1959) and by HESS (1958, 1959).

In all this laboratory work one can see the power of the newborns' intense need for attachment, normally and naturally to the mother but, in her absence, to substitutes. It also shows, particularly the work of HARLOW with monkeys and of LIDDELL with twin kids, how this relationship and therefore all other relationships can be deranged in the early years with permanent after-effects.

To summarize, using a sentence of HESS: "Students of behavior generally agree that the early experiences of animals (including man) have a profound effect on their adult behavior."

The kind of world we have is made by the kind of people who constitute it. The great discovery of our century is not the nature of the atom, but is the fact that properly reared children mature by their own inner nature into constructive adults of good-will, good spouses, good parents, and good citizens – while conversely, the improperly reared child is warped in his development and reacts blindly with rage and hate which cause inner psychological suffering, psychosomatic disorders, marital discord, (with about one marriage in three ending in divorce or separation), alcoholism, crime and the criminoids who support it and, in the ultimate, behavior that leads to tyrannies and to wars. The child simply continues into adult life the loves and the hates and violences of childhood. If he loves his family, he loves others for life; if he hates them, he hates others for life; and a pattern of violence leads to violence. *There is no problem of the world that could not readily be solved by good will all around.* It is a matter of rearing sufficient numbers of children properly so that the mature adults of good will(1) form a sizeable percentage of the population and(2) can gain the organization and power to run a reasonable, peaceful world.

There is not one scrap of conclusive evidence that heredity plays any critical, important role in all these emotional and character disorders, despite the extremely deep-seated prejudice in favor of it. In contrast, the evidence for the conditioning effects of influences during the earliest years, drawn from all fields, is overwhelming and conclusive.

Thus we can pin-point the single, general, central cause of the diverse emotional disorders with their devastating destructive effects: Faulty influences of omission or commission during the earliest years, "0 to 6" which fill the child with hostility to those close to it. These children are "conditioned" to hate and, like old dogs, they do not learn new tricks.

This finding leads to many conclusions and corollaries. One is that forms of organization alone, important though they are, will never solve the world's basic problems. But all fields dealing with people can have and should have the great goal of solving our problems at their one great source – rearing our young properly. This involves adequate living conditions, physical and emotional. It has to do with economics, housing, social conditions, education. It should be the central long range concern of science, education, church and state if we are ever to start moving toward a world in which the mature adults of good will do not suffer crime, tyrannies, and wars through the behavior of those who, through no fault of their own, have been warped in their emotional development by faulty influences especially during their 0–6, and therefore grow up hating.

Of course there are many related fundamental points, but the essential has been stated. It cannot be passed off as "Parent-Teachers Associations stuff". The connection is vital between the child and the man. As the twig is bent the tree *is* inclined. The child *is* father to the man. The emotional development must no longer be neglected for over-emphasis on the physical and intellectual.

The prevention of emotional disorders with their consequences in the *private* suffering of neuroses, psychoses, and addictions, and in *acting out* as crime, tyranny and war, can only be achieved at their *source* in the imprinting and conditioning which occurs during earliest childhood. This is a staggering task – but the survival of humanity is now at stake. LINCOLN said, "Determine that a thing can and shall be done and then we shall find a way."

REFERENCES

ADORNO, T. W., FRENKEL-BRUNSWICK, ELSE, et al., The Authoritarian Personality. N.Y., Harper and Bros., 1950.

BENEDICT, RUTH, Patterns of Culture. Boston, Houghton Mifflin, 1934.

HARLOW, H. F., Love in Infant Monkeys. *Sci. Amer.*, 200, 1959, *68–74*.

HESS, E. H., "Imprinting" in Animals. *Sci. Amer.*, 198, 1958, *81–90*.

— Imprinting, An Effect of Early Experience. *Science*, 130, 1959, *133–141*.

LIDDELL, H., Emotional Hazards in Animals and Man. Springfield, Ill., Chas. C. Thomas, 1956.

LORENZ, KONRAD, King Solomon's Ring. N.Y., Thom. Y. Crowell Co., 1952.

MASSERMAN, JULES, Behavior and Neurosis. Chicago, Univ. of Chicago Press, 1943.

MEAD, MARGARET, Male and Female, N.Y., Morrow, 1949.

MEYER, ADOLPH, The Meaning of Maturity. *Our Children*, N.Y., 1936 (no publisher given).

SAUL, L. J., The Hostile Mind. N.Y., Random House, 1956.

— Emotional Maturity. Philadelphia, J. B. Lippincott Co., 2nd ed., 1960.

— Early Influences on Development and Disorders of Personality. *Psychoanalyt. Quart.*, 34, 1965, *327–390*.

SEITZ, P.F.D., Infantile Experience and Adult Behavior in Animal Subjects: II Age of Separation from the Mother and Adult Behavior in the Cat. *Psychosom. Med.*, 21, 1959, *353–378*.

THORPE, W. H. & LADE, B. I., The Songs of Some Families of the Order Passeriformes. *Ibis*, 103, 1961, *231–259*.

TINBERGEN, NIKOLAAS, Social Behavior in Animals. N.Y., Wiley, 1963.

Youth: Fidelity and Diversity

by

ERIK H. ERIKSON
Professor of Human Development, Harvard University, Cambridge

The subject of this paper is a certain strength inherent in the age of youth. I call it the sense of and the capacity for Fidelity. Such a strength, to me, is not a moral trait to be acquired by individual effort. Rather, I believe it to be part of the human equipment evolved with socio-genetic evolution. This assertion I could not undertake to defend here; nor could I make plausible the fact that, in the schedule of individual growth, Fidelity could not mature earlier in life and must not, in the crises of youth, fail its time of ascendance if human adaptation is to remain intact. Nor (to complete the list of limitations) could I review the other stages of life and the specific strengths and weaknesses contributed by each to man's precarious adaptation. We can take only a brief look at the stage of life which immediately precedes youth, the school age, and then turn to youth itself. I regret this; for even as one can understand oneself only by looking at *and* away from oneself, one can recognize the meaning of a stage only by studying it in the context of all the others.

The school age, which intervenes between childhood and youth, finds the child, previously dominated by play, ready, willing, and able to apply himself to those rudimentary skills which form the necessary preparation for his culture's tools and weapons, symbols and concepts. Also, it finds him eager to realize actual roles (previously play-acted) which promise him eventual recognition within the specializations of his culture's technology. I would say, then, that Skillfulness is the specific strength emerging in man's school age. However, the stage-by-stage acquisition during individual childhood of each of man's evolutionary gains leaves the mark of infantile experience on his proudest achievements. As the play age bequeaths to all methodical pursuits a quality of grandiose delusion, the school age leaves man with a naive acceptance of "what works".

As the school child makes methods his own, he also permits accepted

Reprinted from "Youth: Change and Challenge", Basic Books Publishing Co., Inc., New York 1963 methods to make him their own. To consider as good only what works, and to feel accepted only if things work, to manage and to be managed, can become his dominant delight and value. And since technological specialization is an intrinsic part of the human horde's or tribe's or culture's system and world image, man's pride in the tools that work with materials and animals extends to the weapons which work against other humans as well as against other species. That this can awaken a cold cunning as well as an unmeasured ferocity rare in the animal world is, of course, due to a combination of developments. Among these we will be most concerned (because it comes to the fore during youth) with man's need to combine technological pride with a sense of identity: a double sense of personal self-sameness slowly accrued from infantile experiences and of shared sameness experienced in encounters with a widening part of the community.

This need too is an evolutionary necessity as yet to be understood and influenced by planning: for men – not being a natural species any more, and not a mankind as yet – need to feel that they are of some special kind (tribe or nation, class or caste, family, occupation, or type), whose insignia they will wear with vanity and conviction, and defend (along with the economic claims they have staked out for their kind) against the foreign, the inimical, the not-so-human kinds. Thus it comes about that they can use all their proud skills and methods most systematically against other men, even in the most advanced state of rationality and civilization, with the conviction that they could not morally afford not to do so.

It is not our purpose, however, to dwell on the easy perversion and corruptibility of man's morality, but to determine what those core virtues are which – at this stage of psychosocial evolution – need our concerted attention and ethical support; for antimoralists as well as moralists easily overlook the bases in human nature for a strong ethics. As indicated, Fidelity is that virtue and quality of adolescent ego strength which belongs to man's evolutionary heritage, but which – like all the basic virtues – can arise only in the interplay of a life stage with the individuals and the social forces of a true community.

At this point, it may be necessary to defend the use of the word "virtue" in this context. It once had the connotation of an inherent strength and of an active quality in something to be described: a medicine or a drink, for example, was said to be "without virtue" when it had lost its spirit. In this sense, I think, one may use the term "basic virtues" to connote certain qualities which begin to animate man pervasively during successive stages of his life, Hope being the first and the most basic.(1) The use of such a term, however, for the conceptualization of a quality emerging from the interplay of individual growth and social structure calls to mind dreaded "naturalist" fallacies. All I can say here is that newer concepts of environment (such as the *Umwelt* of the ethologists) imply an optimum relation of inborn potentialities and the structure of the environment. This is not to deny the special problems adhering to the fact that man creates his environment and both lives in it and judges his own modes of living.

The evidence in young lives of the search for something and somebody to be true to is seen in a variety of pursuits more or less sanctioned by society. It is often hidden in a bewildering combination of shifting devotion and sudden perversity, sometimes more devotedly perverse, sometimes more perversely devoted. Yet, in all youth's seeming shiftiness, a seeking after some durability in change can be detected, whether in the accuracy of scientific and technical method or in the sincerity of conviction; in the veracity of historical and fictional accounts or the fairness of the rules of the game; in the authenticity of artistic production (and the high fidelity of reproduction) or in the genuineness of personalities and the reliability of commitments. This search is easily misunderstood, and often it is only dimly perceived by the individual himself, because youth, always set to grasp both diversity in principle and principle in diversity, must often test extremes before settling on a considered course. These extremes, particularly in times of ideological confusion and widespread marginality of identity, may include not only rebellious but also deviant, delinquent, and self-destructive tendencies. However, all this can be in the nature of a moratorium, a period of delay, in which to test the rock-bottom of some truth before committing the powers of body and mind to a segment of the existing (or a coming) order. "Loyal" and "legal" have the same root, linguistically and psychologically; for legal commitment is an unsafe burden unless shouldered with a sense of sovereign choice and experienced as loyalty. To develop that sense is a joint task of the consistency of individual life history and the ethical potency of the historical process. . . . . .

Let a great tragic play tell us something of the elemental nature of the crisis man encounters here. If it is a prince's crisis, let us not forget that the "leading families" of heaven and history at one time personified man's pride and tragic failure. Prince Hamlet is in his twenties, some say early, some late. We will say he is in the middle of his third decade, a youth no longer young and about to forfeit his moratorium. We find him in a tragic conflict in which he cannot make the one step demanded simultaneously by his age and his sex, his education, and his historical responsibility.

If we want to make Shakespeare's insight into one of "the ages of man" explicit, we know that such an endeavor seems reprehensible to the students of drama, if undertaken by a trained psychologist. Everybody else (how could he do otherwise?) interprets Shakespeare in the light of some prevailing if naive psychology. I will not try to solve the riddle of Hamlet's inscrutable nature, because his inscrutability is his nature. I feel sufficiently warned by Shakespeare himself, who lets Polonius speak like the caricature of a psychiatrist:

And I do think – or else this brain of mine
Hunts not the trail of policy so sure
as it hath used to do – that I have found
The very cause of Hamlet's lunacy.

Hamlet's decision to play insane is a secret which the audience shares with him from the start, without their ever getting rid of the feeling that he is on the verge of slipping into the state he pretends. "His madness," says T. S. ELIOT, "is less than madness, and more than feigned."

If Hamlet's madness is more than feigned, it appears to be aggravated at least fivefold: by habitual melancholy, an introverted personality, Danishness, an acute state of mourning, and love. All this makes a regression to the Oedipus complex, postulated by ERNEST JONES as the main theme of this as of other great tragedies, entirely plausible(2). This would mean that Hamlet cannot forgive his mother's recent illegitimate betrayal, because he had not been able as a child to forgive her for having betrayed him quite legitimately with his father; but, at the same time, he is unable to avenge his father's recent murder, because as a child he had himself betrayed him in phantasy and wished him out of the way. Thus he forever postpones – until he ruins the innocent with the guilty – his uncle's execution, which alone would free the ghost of his beloved father from the fate of being,

doom'd for a certain term to walk the night
and for the day confined to fast in fires.

No audience, however, can escape the feeling that he is a man of superior conscience, advanced beyond the legal concepts of his time, consumed by his own past and by that of his society.

One further suggestion is inescapable, that Hamlet displays some of the playwright's and the actor's personality: for where others lead men and change the course of history, he reflectively moves characters about on the stage (the play within the play); in brief, where others act, he play–acts. And indeed, Hamlet may well stand, historically speaking, for an abortive leader, a still-born rebel.

We shall return to this in another context. In the meantime, all that has been stated can only support a biographic view which concentrates on Hamlet's age and status as a young intellectual of his time: for did he not recently return from studies at Wittenberg, the hotbed of humanist corruption, his time's counterpart to Sophist Athens (and today's existentialist centers of learning)?

There are five young men in the play, all Hamlet's age mates, and all sure (or even overdefined) in their identities as dutiful sons, courtiers, and future leaders. But they are all drawn into the moral swamp of infidelity, which seeps into the fiber of all those who owe allegiance to "rotten" Denmark, drawn by the multiple intrigue which Hamlet hopes to defeat with his own intrigue: the play within the play.

Hamlet's world, then, is one of diffuse realities and fidelities. Only through the play within the play and through the madness within the insanity, does Hamlet, the actor within the play-actor, reveal the identity within the pretended identities – and the superior fidelity in the fatal pretense.

The core of his estrangement is identity confusion. His estrangement from existence itself is expressed in the famous soliloquy. He is estranged from being human and from being a man: "Man delights me not; no, nor woman either"; and estanged from love and procreation: "I say we will have no more marriage." He is estranged from the ways of his country, "though I am native here and to the manner born"; and much like our "alienated" youth, he is estranged from and describes as "alienated" the overstandardized man of his day, who "only got the tune of time and outward habit of encounter."

Yet Hamlet's single-minded and tragically doomed search for Fidelity breaks through all this. Here is the essence of the historical Hamlet, that ancient model who was a hero on the folk stage for centuries before Shakespeare modernized and eternalized him(3):

> *He was loth to be thought prone to lying about any matter, and wished to be held a stranger to any falsehood; and accordingly he mingled craft and candor in such a wise that, though his words did not lack truth, yet there was nothing to betoken the truth and to betray how far his keenness went.*

It accords with the general diffusion of truth in Hamlet that this central theme is announced in the old fool's message to his son:

Polonius: This above all: to thine own self be true
And it must follow, as the night the day,
Thou canst not then be false to any man.

Yet it is also the central theme of Hamlet's most passionate pronouncements, which make his madness but an adjunct to his greatness. He abhors conventional sham, and advocates genuineness of feeling:

Seems, madam! Nay, it is; I know not "seems."
'Tis not alone my inky cloak, good mother,
Nor customary suits of solemn black,
Nor windy suspiration of forced breath,
No, nor the fruitful river in the eye,
Nor the dejected'haviour of the visage,
Together with all forms, moods, shows of grief
That can denote me truly: these indeed seem,
For they are actions that a man might play;
But I have that within which passeth show;
These but the trappings and the suits of woe.

He searches for what only an elite will really understand – "honest method":

I heard thee speak me a speech once, – but it was never acted; or, if it was, not above once; for the play, I remember, pleased not the million. . . ! it was (as I received it, and others, whose judgments, in such matters, cried in the top of mine) an excellent play, well digested in the scenes, set down with as much modesty as cunning. I remember, one said there were no sallets in the lines to make the matter savoury, nor no matter in the phrase that might indict the author of affection; but called it an honest method.

He fanatically insists on purity of form and fidelity of reproduction:

. . . let your own discretion be your tutor; suit the action to the word, the word to the action, with this special observance, that you o'erstep not the modesty of nature; for anything so overdone is from the purpose of playing, whose end, both at the first and now, was, and is, to hold, as 'twere, the mirror up to nature; to show virtue her own feature, scorn her own image, and the very age and body of the time his form and pressure.

And finally, the eager (and overeager) acknowledgment of genuine character in his friend:

Since my dear soul was mistress of her choice
And could of men distinguish, her election
Hath seal'd thee for herself; for thou hast been
As one, in suffering all, that suffers nothing,
A man that fortune's buffets and rewards
Hast ta'en with equal thanks; and bless'd are those
Whose blood and judgment are so well co-mingled
That they are not a pipe for fortune's finger
To sound what stop she please. Give me that man
That is not passion's slave, and I will wear him
in my heart's core, ay, in my heart of heart,
As I do thee. Something too much of this.

This, then, is the Hamlet within Hamlet. It fits the combined playactor, the intellectual, the youth, and the neurotic that his words are his better deeds, that he can say clearly what he cannot live, and that his fidelity must bring doom to those he loves: for what he accomplishes at the end is what he tried to avoid, even as he realizes what we would call his negative identity in becoming exactly what his own ethical sense could not tolerate: a mad revenger. Thus do inner reality and historical actuality conspire to deny tragic man the positive identity for which he seems exquisitely chosen. Of course, the audience all along has sensed in Hamlet's very sincerity an element of deadliness. At the end he gives his "dying voice" to his counterplayer on the historical stage, victorious young Fortinbras, who in turn insists on having him born

... like a soldier to the stage
For he was likely, had he been put on,
To have proved most royally.

The ceremonial fanfares, blaring and hollow, announce the end of this singular youth. He is confirmed by his chosen peers, with the royal insignia of his birth. A special person, intensely human, is buried – a member of his special kind.

To be a special kind, we have said, is an important element in the human need for personal and collective identities – all, in a sense, pseudospecies. They have found a transitory fulfillment in man's greatest moments of cultural identity and civilized perfection, and each such tradition of identity and perfection has highlighted what man could be, could he be all these at one time. The utopia of our own era predicts that man will be one species in one world, with a universal identity to replace the illusory superidentities which have divided him, and with an international ethics replacing all moral systems of superstition, repression, and suppression. Whatever the political arrangement that will further this utopia, we can only point to the schedule of human strengths which potentially emerge with the stages of life and indicate their interdependence on the structure of communal life. In youth, ego strength emerges from the mutual confirmation of individual and community, in the sense that society recognizes the young individual as a bearer of fresh energy and that the individual so confirmed recognizes society as a living process which inspires loyalty as it receives it, maintains allegiance as it attracts it, honors confidence as it demands it.

Let us go back, then, to the origins of that combination of drivenness and disciplined energy, of irrationality and courageous capability which belong to the best discussed and the most puzzling phenomena of the life cycle. The puzzle, we must grant throughout, is in the essence of the phenomenon. For the unity of the personality must be unique to be united, and the functioning of each new generation unpredictable to fulfill its function.

Of the three sources of new energy, physical growth is the most easily measured and systematically exercised, although its contribution to the aggressive drives is little understood. The youthful powers of comprehension and cognition can be experimentally studied and with planning applied to apprenticeship and study, but their relation to ideological imagination is less well known. Finally, the long delayed genital maturation is a source of untold energy, but also of a drivenness accompanied by intrinsic frustration.

When maturing in his physical capacity for procreation, the human youth is as yet unable to love in that binding manner which only two identities can offer each other; nor to care consistently enough to sustain parenthood. The two sexes, of course, differ greatly in these respects, and so do individuals, while societies provide different opportunities and sanctions within which individuals must fend for their potentials – and for their potency. But what I have called a psychosocial moratorium, of some form and duration between the advent of genital maturity and the onset of responsible adulthood, seems to be built into the schedule of human development. Like all the moratoria in man's developmental schedules, the delay of adulthood can be prolonged and intensified to a forceful and a fateful degree; thus it accounts for very special human achievements and also for the very special weaknesses in such achievements. For, whatever the partial satisfactions and partial abstinences that characterize premarital sex life in various cultures – whether the pleasure and pride of forceful genital activity without commitment, or of erotic states without genital consummation, or of disciplined and devoted delay – ego development uses the psychosexual powers of adolescence for enhancing a sense of style and identity. Here, too, man is never an animal: even where a society furthers the genital closeness of the sexes, it does so in a stylized manner. On the other hand, the sex act, biologically speaking, is the procreative act, and there is an element of psychobiological dissatisfaction in any sexual situation not favorable in the long run to procreative consummation and care – a dissatisfaction which can be tolerated by otherwise healthy people, as all partial abstinences can be borne: for a certain period, under conditions otherwise favorable to the aims of identity formation. In the woman, no doubt, this dissatisfaction plays a much greater role, owing to her deeper engagement, physiologically and emotionally, in the sex act as the first step in a procreative commitment of which her monthly cycle is a regular bodily and emotive reminder.

The various hindrances to a full consummation of adolescent genital maturation have many deep consequences for man which pose an important problem for future planning. Best known is the regressive revival of that earlier stage of psychosexuality which preceded even the emotionally quiet first school years, that is, the infantile genital and locomotor stage, with its tendency toward autoerotic manipulation, grandiose phantasy, and vigorous play.(4) But in youth, auto-erotism, grandiosity, and playfulness are all immensely amplified by genital potency and locomotor maturation, and are vastly complicated by what we will presently describe as the youthful mind's new historical perspective.

The most widespread expression of the discontented search of youth is the craving for locomotion, whether expressed in a general "being on the go," "tearing after something," or "running around"; or in locomotion proper, as in vigorous work, in absorbing sports, in rapt dancing, in shiftless Wanderschaft, and in the employment and misuse of speedy animals and machines. But it also finds expression through participation in the movements of the day (whether the riots of a local commotion or the parades and campaigns of major ideological forces), if they only appeal to the need for feeling "moved" and for feeling essential in moving something along toward an open future. It is clear that societies offer any number of ritual combinations of ideological perspective and vigorous movement (dance, sports, parades, demonstrations, riots) to harness youth in the service of their historical aims; and that where societies fail to do so, these patterns will seek their own combinations, in small groups occupied with serious games, good-natured foolishness, cruel prankishness, and delinquent warfare. In no other stage of the life cycle, then, are the promise of finding oneself and the threat of losing oneself so closely allied.

In connection with locomotion, we must mention two great industrial developments; the motor engine and the motion picture. The motor engine, of course, is the very heart and symbol of our technology and its mastery, the aim and aspiration of much of modern youth. In connection with immature youth, however, it must be understood that both motor car and motion pictures offer to those so inclined passive locomotion with an intoxicating delusion of being intensely active. The prevalence of car thefts and motor accidents among juveniles is much decried, although it is taking the public a long time to understand that a theft is an appropriation for the sake of gainful possession, while automobiles more often than not are stolen by the young in search of a kind of automotive intoxication, which may literally run away with car and youngster. Yet, while vastly inflating a sense of motor omnipotence, the need for active locomotion often remains unfulfilled. Motion pictures especially offer the onlooker, who sits, as it were, with the engine of his emotions racing, fast and furious motion in an artificially widened visual field, interspersed with close-ups of violence and sexual possession – and all this without making the slightest demand on intelligence, imagination, or effort. I am pointing here to a widespread imbalance in adolescent experience, because I think it explains new kinds of adolescent outbursts and points to new necessities of mastery. The danger involved is greatly balanced in that part of youth which can take active charge of technical development, manages to learn and to identify with the ingeniousness of invention, the improvement of production and the care of machinery, and is thus offered a new and unlimited application of youthful capacities. Where youth is underprivileged in such technical experience, it must explode in riotous motion; where it is ungifted, it will feel estranged from the modern world, until technology and nontechnical intelligence have come to a certain convergence.

The cognitive gifts developing during the first half of the second decade add a powerful tool to the tasks of youth. J. Piaget calls the gains in cognition made toward the middle teens, the achievement of "formal operations."(5) This means that the youth can now operate on hypothetical propositions, can think of possible variables and potential relations, and think of them in thought alone, independent of certain concrete checks previously necessary. As Jerome S. Bruner puts it, the child now can "conjure up systematically the full range of alternative possibilities that could exist at any given time."(6) Such cognitive orientation forms not a contrast but a complement to the need of the young person to develop a sense of identity, for, from among all possible and imaginable relations, he must make a series of ever narrowing selections of personal, occupational, sexual, and ideological commitments.

Here again diversity and fidelity are polarized: they make each other significant and keep each other alive. Fidelity without a sense of diversity can become an obsession and a bore; diversity without a sense of fidelity, an empty relativism.

The sense of ego identity, then, becomes more necessary (and more problematical) wherever a wide range of possible identities is envisaged. Identity is a term used in our day with faddish ease; at this point, I can only indicate how very complicated the real article is.(7) For ego identity is partially conscious and largely unconscious. It is a psychological process reflecting social processes; but with sociological means it can be seen as a social process reflecting psychological processes; it meets its crisis in adolescence, but has grown throughout childhood and continues to re-emerge in the crises of later years. The overriding meaning of it all, then, is the creation of a sense of sameness, a unity of personality now felt by the individual and recognized by others as having consistency in time – of being, as it were, an irreversible historical fact.

The prime danger of this age, therefore, is identity confusion, which can express itself in excessively prolonged moratoria (Hamlet offers an exalted example); in repeated impulsive attempts to end the moratorium with sudden choices, that is, to play with historical possibilities, and then to deny that some irreversible commitment has already taken place; and sometimes also in severe regressive pathology, which we will illustrate presently. The dominant issue of this, as of any other stage, therefore, is that of the active, the selective, ego being in charge and being enabled to be in charge by a social structure which grants a given age group the place it needs – and in which it is needed.

In a letter to Oliver Wendell Holmes, William James speaks of wanting to "rebaptize himself" in their friendship – and this one word says much of what is involved in the radical direction of the social awareness and the social needs of youth. From the middle of the second decade, the capacity to think and the power to imagine reach beyond the persons and personalities in which youth can immerse itself so deeply. Youth loves and hates in people what they "stand for" and chooses them for a significant encounter involving issues that often, indeed, are bigger than you and I. We have heard Hamlet's declaration of love to his friend Horatio, a declaration quickly broken off – "something too much here." It is a new reality then, for which the individual wishes to be reborn, with and by those whom he chooses as his new ancestors and his genuine contemporaries.

This mutual selection, while frequently associated with, and therefore interpreted as a rebellion against or withdrawal from, the childhood environment, is an expression of a truly new perspective which I have already called "historical" – in one of those loose uses of an ancient and overspecialized word which sometimes become necessary in making new meanings specific. I mean by "historical perspective" something which every human being newly develops during adolescence. It is a sense of the irreversibility of significant events and an often urgent need to understand fully and quickly what kind of happenings in reality and in thought determine others, and why. As we have seen, psychologists such as PIAGET recognize in youth the capacity to appreciate that any process can be understood when it is retraced in its steps and thus reversed in thought. Yet it is no contradiction to say that he who comes to understand such a reversal also realizes that in reality, among all the events that can be thought of, a few will determine and narrow one another with historical fatality, whether (in the individual instance) deservedly or undeservedly, intentionally or unintentionally.

Youth, therefore, is sensitive to any suggestion that it may be hopelessly determined by what went before in life histories or in history. Psychosocially speaking, this would mean that irreversible childhood identifications would deprive an individual of an identity of his own; historically, that invested powers should prevent a group from realizing its composite historical identity. For these reasons, youth often rejects parents and authorities and wishes to belittle them as inconsequential; it is in search of individuals and movements who claim, or seem to claim, that they can predict what is irreversible, thus getting ahead of the future – which means, reversing it. This in turn accounts for the acceptance by youth of mythologies and ideologies predicting the course of the universe or the historical trend; for even intelligent and practical youth can be glad to have the larger framework settled, so that it can devote itself to the details which it can manage, once it knows (or is convincingly told) what they stand for and where it stands. Thus, "true" ideologies are verified by history – for a time; for, if they can inspire youth, youth will make the predicted history come more than true.

By pointing to what, in the mind of youth, people "stand for," I did not mean to overemphasize the ideological explicitness in the meaning of individuals to youth. The selection of meaningful individuals can take place in the framework of pointed practicalities such as schooling or job selection, as well as in religious and ideological fellowship; while the methods of selection can range from banal amenity and enmity to dangerous play with the borderlines of sanity and legality. But the occasions have in common a mutual sizing up and a mutual plea for being recognized as individuals who can be more than they seem to be, and whose potentials are needed by the order that is or will be. The representatives of the adult world thus involved may be advocates and practitioners of technical accuracy, of a method of scientific inquiry, of a convincing rendition of truth, of a code of fairness, of a standard of artistic veracity, or of a way of personal genuineness. They become representatives of an elite in the eyes of the young, quite independently of whether or not they are also viewed thus in the eyes of the family, the public, or the police. The choice can be dangerous, but to some youths the danger is a necessary ingredient of the experiment. Elemental things are dangerous; and if youth could not overcommit itself to danger, it could not commit itself to the survival of genuine values – one of the primary steering mechanisms of psychosocial evolution. The elemental fact is that only when fidelity has found its field of manifestation is the human as good as, say, the nestling in nature, which is ready to rely on its own wings and to take its adult place in the ecological order.

If in human adolescence this field of manifestation is alternately one of devoted conformism and of extreme deviancy, of rededication and of rebellion, we must remember the necessity for man to react (and to react most intensively in his youth) to the diversity of conditions. In the setting of psychosocial evolution, we can ascribe a long-range meaning to the idiosyncratic individualist and to the rebel as well as to the conformist, albeit under different historical conditions. For healthy individualism and devoted deviancy contain an indignation in the service of a wholeness that is to be restored, without which psychosocial evolution would be doomed. Thus, human adaptation has its loyal deviants, its rebels, who refuse to adjust to what so often is called, with an apologetic and fatalistic misuse of a once good phrase, "the human condition."

Loyal deviancy and identity formation in extraordinary individuals are often associated with neurotic and psychotic symptoms, or at least with prolonged moratorium of relative isolation, in which all the estrangements of adolescence are suffered. In Young Man Luther I have attempted to put the suffering of a great young man into the context of his greatness and his historic position.(8)

It is not our purpose, however, to discuss what to many youths is the most urgent question, and yet to us the most difficult to answer, namely, the relation of special giftedness and neurosis; rather, we must characterize the specific nature of adolescent psychopathology, or, even more narrowly, indicate the relevance of the issue of fidelity to the psychopathology of youth.

In the classical case of this age group, FREUD's first published encounter with an eighteen-year-old girl suffering from "petite hystérie with the commonest of all ... symptoms," it is interesting to recall that at the end of treatment FREUD was puzzled as to "what kind of help" the girl wanted from him. He had communicated to her his interpretation of the structure of her neurotic disorder, an interpretation which became the central theme of his classical publication on the psychosexual factors in the development of hysteria.(9) FREUD's clinical reports, however, remain astonishingly fresh over the decades, and today his case history clearly reveals the psychosocial centering of the girl's story in matters of fidelity. In fact, one might say, without seriously overdoing it, that three words characterize her social history: sexual infidelity on the part of some of the most important adults in her life; the perfidy of her father's denial of his friends' sexual acts, which were in fact the precipitating cause of the girl's illness; and a strange tendency on the part of all the adults around the girl to make her a confidante in any number of matters, without having enough confidence in her to acknowledge the truths relevant to her illness.

FREUD, of course, focused on other matters, opening up, with the concentration of a psychosurgeon, the symbolic meaning of her symptoms and their history; but, as always, he reported relevant data on the periphery of his interests. Thus, among the matters which somewhat puzzled him, he reports that the patient was "almost beside herself at the idea of its being supposed that she had merely fancied" the conditions which had made her sick; and that she was kept "anxiously trying to make sure whether I was being quite straightforward with her" – or perfidious like her father. When at the end she left analyst and analysis "in order to confront the adults around her with the secrets she knew," FREUD considered this an act of revenge on them, and on him; and within the outlines of his interpretation, this partial interpretation stands. Nevertheless, as we can now see, there was more to this insistence on the historical truth than the denial of an inner truth – and this especially in an adolescent. For, the question as to what confirms them irreversibly as a truthful or a cheating, a sick or a rebellious type is paramount in the minds of adolescents; and the further question, whether or not they were right in not accepting the conditions which made them sick, is as important to them as the insight into the structure of their sickness can ever be. In other words, they insist that the meaning of their sickness find recognition within a reformulation of the historical truth as revealed in their own insights and distortions, and not according to the terms of the environment which wishes them to be "brought to reason" (as Dora's father had put it, when he brought her to FREUD).

No doubt, Dora by then was a hysteric, and the meaning of her symptoms was psychosexual; but the sexual nature of her disturbance and of the precipitating events should not blind us to the fact that other perfidies, familial and communal, cause adolescents to regress in a variety of ways to a variety of earlier stages.

Only when adolescence is reached does the capacity for such clear regression and symptom formation occur: only when the historical function of the mind is consolidated can significant repressions become marked enough to cause consistent symptom formation and deformation of character. The depth of regression determines the nature of the pathology and points to the therapy to be employed. However, there is a pathognomic picture which all sick youth have in common and which is clearly discernible in FREUD's description of Dora's total state. This picture is characterized first of all by a denial of the historical flux of time, and by an attempt to challenge retrospectively, while retesting in the present all parental premises before new trust is invested in the (emancipated) future.

The sick adolescent thus gradually stops extending experimental feelers toward the future; his moratorium of illness becomes an end in itself and thus ceases to be a moratorium (Dora suffered from a "taedium vitae which was probably not entirely genuine," FREUD wrote). It is for this reason that death and suicide can be at this time such a spurious preoccupation – one leading unpredictably to suicide (and to murder) – for death would conclude the life history before it joins others in inexorable commitment (Dora's parents found "a letter in which she took leave of them because she could no longer endure life. Her father ... guessed that the girl had no serious suicidal intentions.") There is also a social isolation which excludes all sense of solidarity and can lead to a snobbish isolation which finds companions but no friends (Dora "tried to avoid social intercourse," was "distant" and "unfriendly"). The energy of repudiation which accompanies the first steps of an identity formation (and in some youngsters can lead to the sudden impulse to annihilate) is in neurotics turned against the self ("Dora was satisfied neither with herself nor with her family").

A repudiated self in turn cannot offer loyalty, and, of course, fears the fusion of love or of sexual encounters. The work inhibition often connected with this picture (Dora suffered from "fatigue and lack of concentration") is really a career inhibition, in the sense that every exertion of skill or method is suspected of binding the individual to the role and the status suggested by the activity; thus, again, any moratorium is spoiled. Where fragmentary identities are formed, they are highly self-conscious and are immediately put to a test (thus Dora obviously defeated her wish to be a woman intellectual). This identity consciousness is a strange mixture of superiority, almost a megalomania ("I am a majority of one", one of my patients said), with which the patient tries to convince himself that he is really too good for his community or his period of history, while he is equally convinced of being nobody.

We have sketched the most obvious social symptoms of adolescent psychopathology, in part to indicate that, besides the complicated structure of specific symptoms, there is in the picture presented of each stage an expression of the dominant psychosocial issue, so open that one sometimes wonders whether the patient lies by telling the simple truth or tells the truth when he seems most obviously to lie.

The sketch presented, however, also serves as a comparison of the isolated adolescent sufferer with those youths who try to solve their doubt in their elders by joining deviant cliques and gangs. FREUD found that "psychoneuroses are, so to speak, the negative of perversions,"(10) which means that neurotics suffer under the repression of tendencies which perverts try to "live out." This has a counterpart in the fact that isolated sufferers try to solve by withdrawal what the joiners of deviant cliques and gangs attempt to solve by conspiracy.

If we now turn to this form of adolescent pathology, the denial of the irreversibility of historical time appears to be expressed in a clique's or a gang's delusion of being an organization with a tradition and an ethics all of its own. The pseudo-historical character of such societies is expressed in such names as "The Navahos," "The Saints," or "The Edwardians;" while their provocation is countered by society (remember the Pachucos of the war years) with a mixture of impotent rage wherever murderous excess does actually occur, and with a phobic overconcern followed by vicious suppression wherever these "secret societies" are really no more than fads lacking any organized purpose. Their pseudo-societal character reveals itself in their social parasitism, and their pseudo-rebellion in the conformism actually governing their habits. Yet the seemingly unassailable inner sense of callous rightness is no doubt due to an inner realignment of motivations, which can best be understood by briefly comparing the torment of the isolated youngster with the temporary gains derived by the joiner from the mere fact that he has been taken into a pseudo-society. The time diffusion attending the isolate's inability to envisage a career is "cured" by his attention to "jobs" – theft, destruction, fights, murder, or acts of perversion or addiction conceived on the spur of the moment and executed forthwith. This "job" orientation also takes care of the work inhibition, because the clique and the gang are always "busy," even if they just "hang around." Their lack of any readiness to wince under shaming or accusation is often considered the mark of a total personal perdition, while in fact it is a trademark, an insignia of the "species" to which the youngster (mostly marginal in economic and ethnic respects) would rather belong than to a society which is eager to confirm him as a criminal and then promises to rehabilitate him as an ex-criminal.

As to the isolate's tortured feelings of bisexuality or of an immature need for love, the young joiner in social pathology, by joining, has made a clear decision: he is male with a vengeance, she, a female without sentimentality; or they are both perverts. In either case, they can eliminate the procreative function of genitality altogether and can make a pseudo-culture of what is left. By the same token, they will acknowledge authority only in the form chosen in the act of joining, repudiating the rest of the social world, where the isolate repudiates existence as such and, with it, himself.

The importance of these comparative considerations, which have been stated in greater detail elsewhere, lies in the impotent craving of the isolated sufferer to be true to himself, and in that of the joiner, to be true to a group and to its insignia and codes. By this I do not mean to deny that the one is sick (as his physical and mental symptoms attest), nor that the other can be on the way to becoming a criminal, as his more and more irreversible acts and choices attest. Both theory and therapy, however, lack the proper leverage, if the need for (receiving and giving) fidelity is not understood, and especially if instead the young deviant is confirmed by every act of the correctional or therapeutic authorities as a future criminal or a lifelong patient.

In Dora's case, I have tried to indicate the phenomenology of this need. As to young delinquents, I can only quote again one of those rare newspaper reports which convey enough of a story to show the elements involved. Kai T. ERIKSON and I have used this example as an introduction to our article "The Confirmation of the Delinquent."(11)

JUDGE IMPOSES ROAD GANG TERM FOR BACK TALK

Wilmington, N. D. (UP) – A "smart alecky" youth who wore pegged trousers and a flattop haircut began six months on a road gang today for talking back to the wrong judge.

Michael A. Jones, 20, of Wilmington, was fined $ 25 and costs in Judge Edwin Jay Roberts Jr's superior court for reckless operation of an automobile. But he just didn't leave well enough alone.

"I understand how it was, with your pegged trousers and flattop haircut," Roberts said in assessing the fine. "You go on like this and I predict in five years you'll be in prison."

When Jones walked over to pay his fine, he overheard Probation Officer Gideon Smith tell the judge how much trouble the "smart alecky" young offender had been.

"I just want you to know I'm not a thief," interrupted Jones to the judge.

The judge's voice boomed to the court clerk: "Change that judgement to six months on the roads."

I quote the story here to add the interpretation that the judge in this case (neither judge nor case differs from a host of others) took it as an affront to the dignity of authority what may have also been a desperate "historical" denial, an attempt to claim that a truly antisocial identity had not yet been formed, and that there was enough discrimination and potential fidelity left to be made something of by somebody who cared to do so. But instead, what the young man and the judge made of it was likely, of course, to seal the irreversibility and confirm the doom. I say "was likely to," because I do not know what happened in this case; we do know, however, the high recidivity of criminality in the young who, during the years of identity formation, are forced by society into intimate contact with criminals.

Finally, it cannot be overlooked that at times political undergrounds of all kinds can and do make use of the need for fidelity as well as the store of wrath in those deprived in their need by their families or their societies. Here social rejuvenation can make use of and redeem social pathology, even as in individuals special giftedness can be related to and redeem neurosis. These are matters too weighty to be discussed briefly and, at any rate, our concern has been with the fact that the psychopathology of youth suggests a consideration of the same issues which we found operative in the evolutionary and developmental aspects of this stage of life.

To summarize: Fidelity, when fully matured, is the strength of disciplined devotion. It is gained in the involvement of youth in such experiences as reveal the essence of the era they are to join – as the beneficiaries of its tradition, as the practitioners and innovators of its technology, as renewers of its ethical strength, as rebels bent on the destruction of the outlived, and as deviants with deviant commitments. This, at least, is the potential of youth in psychosocial evolution; and while this may sound like a rationalization endorsing any high-sounding self-delusion in youth, any self-indulgence masquerading as devotion, or any righteous excuse for blind destruction, it makes intelligible the tremendous waste attending this as any other mechanism of human adaptation, especially if its excesses meet with more moral condemnation than ethical guidance. On the other hand, our understanding of these processes is not furthered by the "clinical" reduction of adolescent phenomena to their infantile antecedents and to an underlying dichotomy of drive and conscience. Adolescent development comprises a new set of identification processes, both with significant persons and with ideological forces, which give importance to individual life by relating it to a living community and to ongoing history, and by counterpointing the newly won individual identity with some communal solidarity.

In youth, then, the life history intersects with history: here individuals are confirmed in their identities, societies regenerated in their life style. This process also implies a fateful survival of adolescent modes of thinking in man's historical and ideological perspectives.

Historical processes, of course, have already entered the individual's core in childhood. Both ideal and evil images and the moral prototypes guiding parental administrations originate in the past struggles of contending cultural and national "species," which also color fairytale and family lore, superstition and gossip, and the simple lessons of early verbal training. Historians on the whole make little of this; they describe the visible emergence and the contest of autonomous historical ideas, unconcerned with the fact that these ideas reach down into the lives of generations and re-emerge through the daily awakening and training of historical consciousness in young individuals.

It is youth, then, which begins to develop that sense of historical irreversibility which can lead to what we may call acute historical estrangement. This lies behind the fervent quest for a sure meaning in individual life history and in collective history, and behind the questioning of the laws of relevancy which bind datum and principle, event and movement. But it is also, alas, behind the bland carelessness of that youth which denies its own vital need to develop and cultivate a historical consciousness – and conscience.

To enter history, each generation of youth must find an identity consonant with its own childhood and consonant with an ideological promise in the perceptible historical process. But in youth the tables of childhood dependence begin slowly to turn: no longer is it merely for the old to teach the young the meaning of life, whether individual or collective. It is the young who, by their responses and actions, tell the old whether life as represented by the old and as presented to the young has meaning; and it is the young who carry in them the power to confirm those who confirm them and, joining the issues, to renew and to regenerate, or to reform and to rebel.

I will not at this point review the institutions which participate in creating the retrospective and the prospective mythology offering historical orientation to youth: obviously, the mythmakers of religion and politics, the arts and the sciences, the stage and fiction – all contribute to the historical logic preached to youth more or less consciously, more or less responsibly. And today we must add, at least in the United States, psychiatry; and all over the world, the press, which forces the leaders to make history in the open and to accept reportorial distortion as a major historical factor.

I have spoken of Hamlet as an abortive ideological leader. His drama combines all the elements of which successful ideological leaders are made: they are the postadolescents who make out of the very contradictions of adolescence the polarities of their charisma. Individuals with an uncommon depth of conflict, they also have uncanny gifts, and often uncanny luck with which they offer to the crisis of a generation the solution of their own crisis – always, as Woodrow Wilson put it, being "in love with activity on a large scale," always feeling that their one life must be made to count in the lives of all, always convinced that what they felt as adolescents was a curse, a fall, an earthquake, a thunderbolt, in short, a revelation to be shared with their generation and with many to come. Their humble claim to being chosen does not preclude a wish to universal power. "Fifty years from now," wrote Kierkegaard in the journal of his spiritual soliloquy, "the whole world will read my diary." He sensed, no doubt, that the impending dominance of mass ideologies would bring to the fore his cure for the individual soul, existentialism. We must study the question (I have approached it in my study of young Luther) of what ideological leaders do to history – whether they first aspire to power and then face spiritual qualms, or first face spiritual perdition and then seek universal influence. Their answers often manage to subsume under the heading of a more embracing identity all that ails man, especially young man, at critical times: danger from new weapons and from natural forces aggravated by man's misuse of nature; anxiety from sources within the life-history typical for the time; and existential dread of the ego's limitations, magnified in times of disintegrating superidentities and intensified in adolescence.

But does it not take a special and, come to think of it, a strange sense of calling, to dare and to care to give such inclusive answers? Is it not probable and in fact demonstrable that among the most passionate ideologists there are unreconstructed adolescents, transmitting to their ideas the proud moment of their transient ego recovery, of their temporary victory over the forces of existence and history, but also the pathology of their deepest isolation, the defensiveness of their forever adolescing egos – and their fear of the calm of adulthood? "To live beyond forty", says Dostoevsky's underground diarist, "is bad taste." It warrants study, both historical and psychological, to see how some of the most influential leaders have turned away from parenthood, only to despair in middle age of the issue of their leadership as well.

It is clear that today the ideological needs of all but intellectual youth of the humanist tradition are beginning to be taken care of by a subordination of ideology to technology: what works, on the grandest scale, is good. It is to be hoped that the worst implications of this trend have outlived themselves already in fascism. Yet, in the technological superidentity, the American dream and the Marxist revolution also meet. If their competition can be halted before mutual annihilation, it is just possible that a new mankind, seeing that it can now build and destroy anything it wishes, will focus its intelligence (feminine as well as masculine) on the ethical question concerning the workings of human generations – beyond products, powers, and ideas. Ideologies in the past have contained an ethical corrective, but ethics must eventually transcend ideology as well as technology: the great question will be and already is, what man, on ethical grounds and without moralistic self-destruction, must decide *not* to do, even though he could make it work – for a while.

Moralities sooner or later outlive themselves, ethics never: this is what the need for identity and for fidelity, reborn with each generation, seems to point to. Morality in the moralistic sense can be shown by modern means of inquiry to be predicated on superstitions and irrational inner mechanisms which ever again undermine the ethical fiber of generations; but morality is expendable only where ethics prevail. This is the wisdom that the words of many languages have tried to tell man. He has tenaciously clung to the words, even though he has understood them only vaguely, and in his actions has disregarded or perverted them completely. But there is much in ancient wisdom which can now become knowledge.

As in the near future peoples of different tribal and national pasts join what must become the identity of one mankind, they can find an initial common language only in the workings of science and technology. This in turn may well help them to make transparent the superstitions of their traditional moralities and may even permit them to advance rapidly through a historical period during which they must put a vain superidentity of neonationalism in the place of their much exploited historical identity weakness. But they must also look beyond the major ideologies of the now "established" world, offered them as ceremonial masks to frighten and to attract them. The overriding issue is the creation not of a new ideology but of a universal ethics growing out of a universal technological civilization. This can be advanced only by men and women who are neither ideological youths nor moralistic old men, but who know that from generation to generation the test of what you produce is in the *care* it inspires. If there is any chance at all, it is in a world more challenging, more workable, and more venerable than all myths, retrospective or prospective: it is in historical reality, at last ethically cared for.

REFERENCES

1. For an evolutionary and genetic rationale of this concept of the life cycle, see the writer's "The Roots of Virtue," in *The Humanist Frame*, Sir Julian Huxley, ed. London: Allen and Unwin, 1961; New York: Harper and Brothers. 1961. Also Chapter IV of the author's "Insight and Responsibility", New York: W. W. Norton, 1964; London: Faber and Faber, 1966.
2. ERNEST JONES, *Hamlet and Oedipus*. New York: Doubleday, Anchor, 1949.
3. SAXO GRAMMATICUS, *Danish History*, translated by ELTON, 1894 (quoted in JONES, *op. cit.*, pp. 193–164.
4. The classical psychoanalytic works concerned with psychosexuality and the ego defenses of youth are: SIGMUND FREUD, *Three Essays on the Theory of Sexuality*, standard edition, (London, The Hogarth Press, 1953), vol. 7; and ANNA FREUD, *The Ego and the Mechanisms of Defence*, New York, International Universities Press, 1946. For the writer's views, see his Childhood and Society. New York: W. W. Norton, 1950, sec. ed. 1963; also in Dutch, Finnish, French, German, Hebrew, Italian, Japanese and Spanish.
5. B. INHELDER & J. PIAGET, The Growth of Logical Thinking from Childhood to Adolescence. New York: Basic Books, 1958.
6. JEROME S. BRUNER, The Process of Education. Cambridge: Harvard University Press, 1960.
7. See the writer's "The Problem of Ego-Identity" in Identity and the Life Cycle: Psychological Issues (New York: International Universities Press, 1959), vol. I, no. 1.
8. Young Man Luther. New York: W. W. Norton, 1958; London: Faber and Faber, 1959.
9. SIGMUND FREUD, Fragment of an Analysis of a Case of Hysteria, standard edition (London: The Hogarth Press, 1953), vol. 7.
10. Ibid., p. 50.
11. ERIK H. ERIKSON & KAI T. ERIKSON, "The Confirmation of the Deliquent," *The Chicago Review*, Winter 1957, *10: 15–23*.

Conflict and Conflict Resolution in Families

by

Emily Hartshorne Mudd

Professor in Family Study in Psychiatry, School of Medicine, University of Pennsylvania, Philadelphia

The conduct of human affairs, in contrast to progress in science and technology, has suffered from reliance upon generalities, superstitions, fallacies, and prejudices. There is all too little pertinent research concerning man's relation to his fellows and few guides to aid in the attainment of creative, co-operative and mutually constructive interaction. In this connection certain students of human behavior have become increasingly interested in the family unit as one of the smallest social systems in which the dynamics of interpersonal conflict resolution can be observed. A family historian, Professor Goode, who recently completed a major study of current family patterns in many countries of the world observed, "So many 'facts' need to be corrected. Ideal patterns of family behavior have been thought to be real ones, and a hypothetical harmony in past family relations has been assumed, rather than treated as a hypothesis to be tested." (1)

The experience reflected in the present paper might be considered as a laboratory experiment on a limited scale within a small unit. It reports the causes and diagnosis of conflict, the development of methods for its resolution and the fact that a systematic follow up study after five years indicates successful resolution of the conflict areas in 66% of cases.(2)

Our Division of Family Study at the School of Medicine, University of Pennsylvania, with its marriage and family counseling facilities has been concerned for over 25 years with the analysis of family conflict, its causes and with methods for its alleviation. On the basis of the experience gained, the possibility suggests itself that efforts at conflict resolution in other and larger units might benefit from the conceptual framework and the phi-

By permission from the publishers this article is abridged and reorganized from Chapter II, Family Conflict, its personal and community impact. The Dimensions of Human Conflict. Ed. by Ross Stagner. Wayne State University Press, Detroit, Michigan. 1966. The author wishes to express appreciation to Dr. S. Harvey Mudd for his help in the reorganization of this paper and to Marian Mudd for her suggestions.

losophy of the counseling session. For this reason I accepted the invitation to participate in this symposium on conflict. I propose to discuss the following areas: the generic aspects of family problems, the individual reaction to conflict and stress, what constitutes a crisis, if outside intervention at crucial points in conflict is feasible, and whether methods, if any, have been devised for helping families to become healthy, cooperative and health producing units.

We realize that all families no matter what their cultural affiliation have problems. Actually reports by Professor Kirkendall of papers presented at the World Family Congress, held July 1965 in Rome, indicated a much greater similarity between family problems in the United States with those of Europe and all newly developing countries than a decade ago.(3) Apparently what we are dealing with is not an American problem or a German, a Scandinavian, an Israeli, an Italian, an Australian or a Nigerian one. We are rather dealing with problems growing out of industrialization, urbanization, overpopulation and poverty in our transnational world. What constitutes a problem to an individual family or any one of its members under these or other conditions may vary with each family. Conditions causing conflict to one family may not produce difficulty to their neighbors. What seems important in this small study is to understand at the level of the individual family unit what factors constitute problems and through what processes the conflictual situation can best be handled.

STRESSES AFFECTING INDIVIDUALS AND FAMILIES

At this point some exploration of the various factors which appear to produce conflict and stress in individuals and family units might be helpful. These might stem from environmental and economic conditions; from unfulfilled personal needs, and from less tangible adjustments in roles and value systems necessitated by changes in society.

In the U.S. among recent studies, one by Dr. Srole and his associates is concerned with the relationship between mental disorder and socio-cultural environment in an urban setting.(4) This seems of particular interest to countries undergoing rapid industrialization. These investigators isolated fourteen stress factors which they believed were associated with the mental health risk of these adults. These factors included poor mental health of parents, aggravated by poor physical health, unemployment, financial problems, and the often repeated break-up of the household. The authors concluded that the growing child who perceives his parents negatively rejects them as models for identification, and that adolescence in such families is marked by increasing antagonism toward parents. The individual with such unhappy early conditioning not uncommonly has problems as an adult in finding meaningful work, has financial and social worries, has few close and satisfying relationships, and repeats the negative cycle of his parents' relationship in his own marriage and family. The results indicated that some individuals seemed able to handle more stress than others, and that a situation which, if continued, might produce intolerable stress to one individual or family, with resulting breakdown, could be handled by another family without undue concern.

Moving from consideration of the relation of stress and conflict to mental health in underprivileged families, we will discuss the problem areas highlighted by the middle-class, educated, financially solvent couples who have sought help in their conflicted marriages over a period of years from Marriage Council of Philadelphia, the clinic of the Division of Family Study, in which much of our experience has been gained. We compared the disagreements reported by two hundred of these American husbands and wives with the disagreements checked by one hundred middle class couples who considered themselves to be successfully functioning families and whose communities concurred in this estimate.(5) Both groups ranked their problems in the same order, leading off with disagreement over financial difficulties, followed by personality differences, sexual adjustment, household management, sharing of household tasks, and children. Out of a possible 22 areas of disagreement, infidelity ranks 16th, just above health, while matters of religion and education as the cause of marital difficulty are at the foot of the list. It is of considerable interest that husbands and wives in each group were in substantial agreement although they reported quite independently.

The third general area to which we alluded we called intangible stresses. As many families indicated in our clinical work, these result from the need for fairly constant innovation and improvisation – a condition clearly reflected in recently industrialized nations. Practical demands of economics, child-rearing, adjustment to the disparity of values of a spouse require the ability to assume new role behavior without undue disturbance. However, traditional patriarchal attitudes of male dominance, family power distribution, the rights and duties of spouses are still very much a part of most cultures. The feelings and attitudes, biases and prejudices produced by ambiguities and new requirements in the shifting reality situation undoubtedly are more difficult to reorient than are vocational skills. Without question they receive far less attention and considered effort.

Our general impression, on the basis of our experience, is that role complementarity of husbands and wives has ceased to function effectively in many families. In other words what responsibilities are husbands expected to take and what are wives expected to do. In instances when wives had been drawn into remunerative jobs or other community activities a new role balance based on cultural change had not yet resulted. This same imbalance has been reported from other industrialized countries. The symbolic value of money as family power and status rather than its basic purchasing potential seemed to be the issue causing finances to be listed as problem number one, – a finding not dissimilar to the behavior of nations. In the area of household management, the conflict pattern we have perceived centers about who should do the routine housework chores when both husband and wife are employed – an unlikely issue one generation ago. Conflicts around personality and sex often represent expressions of intense disappointment of inflated expectations, unreal goals and misconceptions of psychological theory in its semi-popularized form. Each partner expects to find for himself or herself some sort of mystical fulfillment in marriage, to find it quickly and without limit. Moreover, a slight knowledge of personality dynamics with its promise of possible change and improvement, may be taken as an open invitation to remodel a reluctant spouse into a preconceived ideal mate. And just what is considered "ideal" behavior of husbands and wives in the multicultural society of the U.S., or in the many nations of the world, varies greatly for many men and women so that often one spouse does not know what the other expects of him or her. In fact, seldom have they thought it important to find out. One generalization about the American family today seems pertinent. That is that each family is trying to work out a set of complementary role behaviors to suit its particular need.

We have discussed stress factors which affect families and have suggested some of the causes of conflict within families. It is obvious that the outcome of continued conflict and stress may lead eventually to a crisis situation. A crisis may also be precipitated by an emergency, by cumulative frustration or uncontrollable rage, or by those transitions in life, to which we are all subjected, where new and perhaps unwanted challenges or responsibilities are thrust upon us. We shall now consider preventive intervention at crisis points in the life of a family, when potential sources of conflict might be anticipated and forestalled.

FAMILY CRISIS, TURNING POINT AND OPPORTUNITY

Professor CAPLAN views the onset of crisis to result from a sudden loss of basic "supplies" that are needed by an individual for his continued functioning.(6) The deprivation of food, shelter, sensory stimuli, or health are physical bases for crisis. Crisis can result from cultural pressures which keep a person at odds with the customs, values and expectations of his community. Our concern will focus on crises which result from frustration of interpersonal needs which are usually satisfied within the family; that is, from situations when a husband or wife, mother, father, or child fails to perceive, respect, or attempt to satisfy the legitimate needs of another family member. Every family at a heightened point of conflict or at the end of endurance of continued frustration is a family in crisis. Crises vary. I heard of a new one from an engineer recently. During counseling he reported that he had just discovered that his wife didn't know that 75% was equal to $\frac{3}{4}$. This raised, he said, serious questions about continuing his marriage.

The characteristics of a crisis are analyzed as follows by Dr. Caplan. The first phase starts with the impact of a stimulus which calls forth the usual problem-solving responses of the individual. As no solution is reached, and the irritation continues, the *second phase* sees a rise in tension along with feelings of helplessness, anxiety, guilt, shame, or other uncomfortable emotions. During the *third phase*, the individual mobilizes all his reserves and problem-solving techniques for a major attack on the source of trouble. Depending on his intelligence, and his current levels of emotional and physical health, he will re-examine the situation, redefine the problem, search for alternatives, and generally use such effective courses of action that he will either work through to an adequate solution or resign himself to an acceptance of the situation. If, however, neither a solution nor the possibility of living with the situation is acceptable, the *fourth* and final phase of a crisis is reached. Basic needs which remain unsatisfied make for continuously increased tension. Such conditions eventually often lead to destructive behavior and major disorganization of an individual or of a family.

All of us have experienced family crises and, in most cases, have weathered both minor irritations and prolonged periods of illness or estrangement. Indeed, we know from experience that individuals and families can emerge from such periods better integrated and more adequate than at the onset of trouble. Stress may be viewed as a potential for challenge and mastery, and crisis as "a transitional period presenting an individual both with an opportunity for personal growth and with the danger of increased vulnerability to mental disorder, the outcome of which in any particular instance to some extent depends on his way of handling the situation." It becomes of obvious interest to examine methods by which families handle crises before they get out of control and require professional or community intervention.

CONFLICT RESOLUTION AS SEEN BY STUDENTS OF THE FAMILY

Methods used by partners in attempting to re-establish equilibrium after conflict fall into three general categories according to Spiegel.(7) First, steps are taken by the husband and wife unilaterally and are generally manipulative attempts to force the other to give in. Thus, one or the other may try coercive force, coaxing with the promise of rewards, verbal, often derogatory, evaluations of the other's conduct, masking the situation by deceits, hypocrisy, mutual agreement to avoid the danger area, and postponing or outwaiting the other. The second phase consists of *modifications of behavior of both marriage partners*. Initially there is a degree of role reversal when each begins to appreciate the point of view of the other by empathetic efforts to understand the other's situation. Joking replaces tension, and as awareness of the extent of the problem grows there is increased willingness to seek professional help. Next come the familiar solving devices of exploring the alternatives and arriving at a compromise. During this second half of conflict resolution, identification with the partner, consideration, and a willingness to meet his needs replace coercion and manipulation. Each partner perceives that changes are necessary in his actions, his role, and makes them. The final phase consists of *consolidating the new behavior patterns,* which hopefully are more satisfying. These changes are rewarded by each perceptive and grateful spouse.

CONFLICT RESOLUTION IN SUCCESSFUL FAMILIES

The group of families who consider themselves to be succesfully functioning, mentioned earlier, were used also to study the dynamics of conflict resolution.(8) These families seem able for the most part to balance the needs of their various members. We know that they are not immune to major sources of stress since, in our years of contact, they have had accidents, fatal illnesses, financial reverses and shown evidence of emotional problems. On the other hand, they seem to bear out the premise made many years ago by Drs. LEVY and MUNROE (9) that a happy family is not without problems, but is rather a family which has learned to handle its problems.

We asked these husbands and wives what they actually *do* when they are having an argument – successful functioning by no means precludes arguing and arguing heatedly, at times with recriminations! Here is what these husbands and wives reported independently. There is a marked absence of violence or physical expression of anger, the characteristic activity during an argument being discussion of the point of disagreement. However, they exhibit a remarkably healthy sense of reality by keeping the blame within the family. A few husbands and wives give in to avoid an argument, but no one threatens to leave home.

Activity during the period immediately following the intensity of conflict may be crucial to the development of increasingly effective methods of reducing future tensions and of handling future disagreements with improved techniques. Husbands and wives in these successful families report activity in the aftermath of conflict that is practical and constructive. Over half of the husbands and even more wives try to figure out what is wrong with *themselves* or the situation. They also talk over the differences calmly and do something nice for the partner. Only a few of the men and women brood, avoid speaking to each other, or try not to think about the problem. Many report working at something while they gain perspective.

The responses of these husbands and wives bolster the impression that these middle class families who perceive themselves as functioning successfully live within an atmosphere of reasonable self control, of continuing communication, of an awareness of the needs of the other, and of considerable self scrutiny. They have a capacity for humor and enjoyment reaching out to life with exuberance. One husband described to us a plan he had devised for helping to keep his household running smoothly. When he notices that his wife is tense or seems to have something on her mind, he arranges for a baby sitter and surprises her with an invitation to dinner out, accepting no excuses. He added that he runs over in his mind recent family events that might be in need of talking over. Away from the children and the demands of the household, this couple talk over grievances, make plans, and enjoy the occasion of being together. Or as another husband put it; "People don't realize that when marriage really works as a partnership, they never had it so good."

These families also reported that while the intensity of their crises were such that they were usually handled within the family, mainly through the co-operative efforts of all members, they did seek help from appropriate professionals when the scope of the problem exceeded their own ingenuity.

CRISIS INTERVENTION

From our own observations of family conflicts, we believe that during a crisis, an intensified desire for help is experienced by the individual or family, which evokes a helping response from those around and that a person is more susceptible to influence by others during a period of disequilibrium. A relatively minor intervention may sway him to a positive course of action at such a time which will then result in comparative stability. These factors underline the opportunity and the responsibility for all professional persons and family members who have contact with troubled individuals and family units. People who perceive their problems as stemming from an unsatisfactory marriage or who find themselves approaching marriage with doubt and undue anxiety may seek help from a number of sources; their friends, a family member, their religious leader, their doctor, their teacher, a psychologist, a social worker or an agency especially equipped to help with marriage and family problems. If such persons, when approached, can make time available to listen, to express interest and concern, and to help the troubled individual explore the solution best for him, her and the family group, much can often be accomplished toward constructive solution. If the problem persists and is serious, the non-professional friend or family member may be able to suggest reliable professional sources of help.

COUNSELING PHILOSOPHY AND GOALS

At this point, an examination in more detail of the techniques of counseling seems indicated. For this we draw on the sources most familiar to us in our clinical experience. The theoretical framework for our approach rests heavily on the findings of ego psychology and dynamic psychiatry.(10) We stress the importance of considering the client in the context of his interpersonal, cultural, economic and social environment. Some basic assumptions are implicit in our work, structuring our goals, our focus, and the role of the counselor.(11) They are:

(1) That each individual has within himself the capacity for self-awareness of those aspects of his behavior which cause pain and difficulty in his human relationships.
(2) That there is a common human motivation for growth and self-realization to increasingly complex and rewarding levels of development.
(3) That apparently small changes within an individual can result in significant improvement in his interpersonal functioning.
(4) That the strengths of a person can be mobilized within an anxiety reducing, accepting, and reality-oriented counselor-client relationship.
(5) That the choices which are an inevitable part of the therapeutic process are those of the client – that he remains responsible for himself and for his family relationships.

The goal of marriage counseling as we see it is to help each partner reach an awareness of his feelings, attitudes, demands, expectations, and responses as these relate to the marriage and to the marriage partner; to understand where they are appropriate or inappropriate, functional or maladaptive; and to change – or possibly become resigned to – the identifiable sources of conflict. We stress that our goals are modest, aiming toward a family situation which affords some degree of comfort and satisfaction to its members rather than attempting fundamental personality reorganization in individuals or the realization of an "ideal marriage." We have found a useful conceptual model for *marriage counseling* to be reciprocal satisfaction of needs which can realistically be met by a husband or wife. When the marriage relationship fails to supply need satisfaction, or fails to meet these needs in ways to which an individual has been accustomed, marital conflict develops.

Some needs cannot be met by the spouse directly. A wife cannot protect her husband from the stresses he faces on a job; but she can be supportive at home and help him find the strength to cope more effectively with his work situation or to change it. A husband cannot bestow a satisfying work career upon a restless and frustrated wife; but he can support and encourage her efforts in self-actualizing projects. The counselor cannot change the stressful social and cultural environment which contributes to and aggravates family conflict. But he or she can use skills in a therapeutic and professional way to encourage the man and woman to develop new ways of resolving these conflicts.

PROCESSES IN MARRIAGE COUNSELING

The counselor's role varies in the U.S. as elsewhere.(12) In our judgment the counselor is most helpful if he possesses certain capacities.(13)

(1) The ability to sustain a compassionate, unbiased, impartial, and understanding relationship with both partners in the marriage.

(2) The ability to see each client realistically without undue judgment or rejection to gain understanding of the patterns of marital interaction.

(3) The ability to maintain confidentiality, and thus to merit the trust of two people. Information is not passed from one partner to the other without their permission.

(4) The ability in a joint interview to maintain a balanced objectivity, when two clients may try to manipulate the counselor, misquote, or otherwise misuse the three-sided counseling relationship.

(5) The willingness to move with the clients at their own pace as they work to choose suitable solutions to their problems.

The counselor functions in several ways; with the individual husband and wife, with groups of husbands and wives, or with family units. In all of his work he tries to promote certain processes.

Persons involved in other areas of conflict resolution may wish to consider the applicability of these processes to their own interests. In marriage counseling these processes are:

(1) To establish and promote communication.

(2) To create a situation in which the partners experience and recognize samples of their interaction as illustrative of behavior destructive or constructive to their relationship.

(3) To help each partner hear the other express positive and negative feelings and needs. To accept these and make constructive efforts to deal with them.

(4) To test reality through the presence of the counselor.

(5) To establish the joint responsibility for the problem and for its solution.

(6) To devise and practice constructive methods for living together with some degree of satisfaction and for meeting future problems with improved ways of coping before they become crises.

Implicit in these processes is the cathartic effect which results from the sharing of feelings and from identifying the problem areas. When counseling is effective we can usually anticipate that the solution of the immediate problem will lead to the utilization of the same processes of resolution when other problems develop. The family will continue to operate at an improved level of integration with more open channels of communication, will not be overwhelmed by disagreements, differences or difficulties, will have more similar perceptions of reality, will recognize and adjust inconsistencies in thinking, and can reconcile to a reasonable degree diverse needs.

A FRAMEWORK FOR PREVENTION OF FAMILY CONFLICT

In concluding this article may we raise the issue of whether successful family living can be promoted and if so how? Could members of the so-called helping professions, along with the behavioral scientists, profitably concentrate upon those modifications of human behavior which might enable individuals to make a more productive use of their opportunities? Such efforts involve the development of personal, interpersonal and social competence, and, for family problems might be undertaken within a broad framework of public health, – for national conflicts within transnational media. In relation to the prevention of family conflict two general approaches seem pertinent; one is education, another cooperative services.

For example, can steps necessary for a more rational and suitable choice of a marriage partner be discovered so that young people can learn of the responsibilities in the married relationship and how to avoid some of the blunders of their parents? If this is possible such approaches could be encouraged through schools, churches and family living. To carry this idea further we suggest that even more direct prevention might aim for increasingly adequate premarital preparation including longer waiting periods between obtaining a marriage license and the wedding, medical examinations to assess mental as well as physical fitness, and conferences with kindly, interested and well trained counselors to explore anxieties and give factual information. Uniform marriage and family laws throughout each country also might discourage a number of ill-considered and undesirable unions with later disintegration. People contemplating marriage, for all their radiant happiness, are people in crisis, if for no other reason than that they will shortly experience a major change in social and personal role. A potentially good marriage can benefit from the concern and the scrutiny of the community. Marriage and its consequences are in reality by no means private affairs.

A few additional thoughts occur concerning possible cooperative services on a broader public health spectrum. For instance, could not family harmony be promoted by welcoming facilities through churches, clubs, organizations, and business auxiliaries, for each new bride and groom or family who move to a strange community? Apartments for families with children whose mothers are employed, which offer suitably staffed day nurseries and recreational activities for teenagers after school and before mother returns from work, have served in Sweden successfully to relieve continuing anxiety for working mothers and their children. Such facilities can do wonders in preventing resentment and deprivation in young children, and unsavory gang influences in teenagers. Why not make them more generally available in urban centers? Furthermore other imaginative approaches might link the vital need of parents of young children for an evening out with the urgency of isolated older men and women to be useful, wanted and in contact with young vitality. This could constitute a Health Resource Service for each group.

CONCLUSION

We have discussed some of the stresses affecting families in the United States and other industrialized nations, the shifting of male-female roles, and the clash of traditional and modern values. Conflict resolution in marriage and family life, based on theoretical premises and illustrated in functioning families, has been indicated. The conceptual framework, goals and processes of counseling have been described noting that a person has first to perceive a problem and then initiate asking for help. The importance of the counselor's role was emphasized. It was mentioned that many couples and other groups in conflict may be more susceptible to help during a period of crisis. We suggest that conflict resolution in various groups might benefit from the use of the conceptual framework and the processes of the counseling session; the unpressured, unaccusing atmosphere, the give and take, the catharsis, the perspective and the support of efforts at new and mutually acceptable behavior and interaction.

Conflict is a part of life itself. However, in nature accomodation is essential to survival. The search for methods of conflict resolution and creative cooperation is not new. The inspiration to resolve conflict was expressed poetically almost two thousand years ago when Jesus said, "Blessed are the peace makers for they shall be called the children of God." The challenge is immediate, – to move beyond the inspiration of ideals to a livable reality.

NOTES

1. GOODE, WILLIAM J. World Revolution and Family Patterns. New York: The Free Press of Glencoe, 1963, p. 267.
2. PRESTON, M. G., MUDD, E. H., FROSCHER, H. B. & PELTZ, W. L., *Social Casework*, 34, *103–111*, 1953. Effects on Casework of Obtaining Research Material.
3. KIRKENDALL, LESTER A. Report on The World Family Congress of 1965 at Rome, *J. Marriage and the Family*, 28, *109–111* (Feb.) 1966.
   MUDD, S., Ed. The Population Crisis and The Use of World Resources. Dr. W. Junk, Publishers, The Hague, and Indiana University Press, Bloomington, Indiana, 1964.
   Humphrey, Hubert, War on Poverty, McGraw-Hill Book Company, Inc. New York, 1964.
4. SROLE, LEO, LANGNER, THOMAS S., MICHAEL, STANLEY T., OPLER, MARVIN O. & RENNIE, THOMAS A. G. Mental Health in the Metropolis: The Midtown Manhattan Study. New York: McGraw-Hill Book Company, Inc., 1962.
   LANGNER, THOMAS A., & MICHAEL, STANLEY T. Life Stress and Mental Health. New York: The Free Press of Glencoe, The MacMillan Company, 1956.
   GURIN, GERALD, VEROFF, JOSEPH, & FELD, SHEILA. Americans View Their Mental Health. Joint Commission on Mental Illness and Health, Monograph Series No. 4, New York: Basic Books. Inc., 1964.
5. MITCHELL, HOWARD E., BULLARD, JAMES W. & MUDD, EMILY H. "Areas of Marital Conflict in Successfully and Unsuccessfully Functioning Families," *J. Health Human Behavior*, III, *88–93*, 1962.
   MUDD, EMILY H. & GOODWIN, HILDA M. "Marital Problems and Marital Adjustment." The Encyclopedia of Mental Health. New York: Franklin Watts, Inc., 1963, pp. 965–978.

6. CAPLAN, GERALD. Principles of Preventative Psychiatry. New York: Basic Books, 1964.
ERIKSON, ERIK H. Childhood and Society (Second Edition). New York: W. W. Norton and Company. 1963.
7. SPIEGEL, JOHN P. "The Resolution of Role Conflict Within the Family," in The Family. NORMAN W. BELL & EZRA F. VOGEL (Eds.), Illinois: The Free Press of Glencoe, 1960, pp. 361–382.
8. MUDD, EMILY H., MITCHELL, HOWARD E. & TAUBIN, SARA B. Success in Family Living. New York: Association Press, 1965.
9. LEVY, JOHN & MUNROE, RUTH. The Happy Family, New York: Alfred A. Knopf, Inc. 1938; rev. 1959.
10. HARTMANN, HEINZ. Ego Psychology and the Problem of Adaptation. (Journal of the American Psychoanalytic Association Monograph Series, No. 1), New York: International Universities Press, 1958.
ERIKSON, ERIK H. Identity and the Life Cycle (Psychological Issues, Vol. 1, No. 1. Monograph 1) New York: International Universities Press, 1959.
ALLEN, FREDERICK H. Psychotherapy with Children. New York: Norton and Company, 1942.
11. MUDD, EMILY H. & GOODWIN, HILDA M. "Counseling with Couples in Conflicted Marriages," The Psychotherapies of Marital Disharmony, Ed. by BERNARD L. GREENE, M. D. The Free Press, New York, 1965, Chapter 3.
12. MUDD, EMILY H. & GOODWIN, HILDA M. "Marriage Counseling," Cyclopedia of Medicine, Surgery, and Specialities, Philadelphia: F. A. Davis Company, XI, 1960, pp. 601–611.
13. APPEL, KENNETH E., "Psychotherapy." *J.A.M.A.*, 172, 1343–1346, March 26, 1960.

Ideas for Social Change

by

GEORGE W. TAYLOR
Harnwell Professor of Industry, University of Pennsylvania, Philadelphia

The thrust of my remarks has been fashioned by two convictions. First: vast changes in the ways of men living and working together – and in their fighting – are coming about with the acceleration of technical knowledge and its application. It consequence, our already interdependent nation is becoming increasingly interdependent. Second: the resulting social problems can be satisfactorily dealt with only by bringing the basic principles of our kind of a democracy to greater fruition. We believe that by reasoning together, under man-made systems of persuasion, people are willing and able to accomodate as between the duties which alone held a society together and the freedom to act personally. Ours is an agreement-making society.

More than ever before, I believe, the affirmation of democracy lies not in the frantic assertion of absolute private authority (i.e., whatever is good for me is good for society) but rather in the willingness to concede that private sovereignty which, if exercised, will victimize the entire community. Despite some notable lapses the viability of the accomodation idea has been demonstrated in the United States. A continually growing interdependence among us over long years has required the assumption of more and more duties in order to achieve stability despite change and economic progress because of it. There has ever been, however, a lag in the adjustment of ideas and institutions to changed circumstances. The dialogue takes time. This could be a serious liability in a world where time now runs against us.

In the formative years of our nation, most of the people earned a living by working on the land. We still carry many of their qualities in our manners and opinions. Fearful of control by others, they created a new kind of government with built-in checks and balances and held high the tenet: "He governs best who governs least." To be sure, there was a recognition of the common need for some limitation upon individual and provincial latitudes. The assignment of even essential functions to the government, however, was in the nature of a reluctant concession made with apprehension. The government was cast in the role of supplicant. These ideas were understandably a product of the environment. There had been oppression by a strong government; it was overthrown to gain freedom. In terms of the agricultural economy, one could reason logically that through his own untrammeled devices a man would have the best chance to create a good life for himself. The imprint of these ideas remains strong upon us.

The desire to be let strictly alone soon came into sharp conflict with the intense economic drive of these same people. They were a striving people and, in their striving, could not leave each other alone. Anyone who has ever watched television, for even a very brief look, has seen how the cattleman's efforts to get ahead by his own devices came into violent conflict with the ways of the sheepherders. The private battles between them became intolerable in their effects upon everybody else in the neighborhood. More fundamentally, the institutionalization of the private war would have defined one's own freedom in terms of the private power to deprive others of their freedom. The idea emerged of limitation of freedom only under law and the Wyatt Earps became the symbol of "the public interest."

Such private struggles, and the creation of new social ideas to manage them, have made our sagas. Building a democratic society involves far more than the resolution of clashes between good and evil; it is the conflict between good and good which poses the greater challenge to the use of reason. Orderly means had to be invented for limiting somebody's or everybody's freedoms in order to preserve the basic freedoms for all.

The limitations were not so extensive to begin with. Since the interdependence of one upon the other was not so great, there was not too much shoving one another around. Even then, a few souls were unwilling, or unable, to accept the personal restraints upon which an orderly life for the community was dependent. Some heroic attempts were made to escape coming to terms with a changing environment. Withdrawal to a Walden and restless moves ever westward ahead of the settlers provide standard themes for the nostalgic epics – the dissenter fights the inexorable course of destiny and, as in the Greek tragedies, goes down with honor.

To most of the people, freedom was the opportunity to settle down and to live and work with others. Solving the problems of that way of life was seen as the key to the desired goals of stability and security. It is fortunate that this was so. Even in the early days, there weren't enough ponds or frontiers to go around. The settle-downers have always seemed to me to be the really daring pioneers. They faced up to the searing and never-ending challenges of adjustment to "togetherness." Only by their efforts could the vision of a democratic society be realized. In many ways, it is far easier to pioneer a land, uninhibited by man-made rules, than to settle down and learn to live and work with others for common purposes. Social inventiveness was called for in the creation of institutions to resolve private conflicts without overturning the ideas of personal freedom.

A big break-through in ideas thus came about when it was acknowledged that one man's freedom is as good as another's. This is far from a self-effectuating principle and it has perplexing aspects. Not the least is assumption of the risk that private rights and power will be irresponsibly exercised. There is also the danger that institutional forms will be inadequate in developing a willingness to accept personal restraints, i.e., will fail to bring about a consent to lose. In such risks, democracy doubtless carries the seeds of its own destruction. It is a "heady" doctrine.

The matters of which we speak come into sharp focus nowadays in the labor-management relationship. We are no longer a nation of farmers. Most people now earn a living by hiring themselves out for a wage or for a salary. They now become subject to the rules of private governments which limit personal latitudes. The employment contract is crucial for most of us.

Seeking increased bargaining power in the making of the employment contract, wage earners successfully fought for unions to represent their interests. Collective bargaining and the strike became standard institutional forms. One may recall how, in the so-called Wagner Act, government support to union formation was rationalized as necessary to insure a counter-balance to the management power which had previously been enhanced through enactment of Corporation laws. Whether or not an appropriate balance of economic power has been, or can be, effected between these private sovereignties is a debate which will never end. Less debatable is the proposition that many a union and many a corporation has amassed a private power beyond anticipation at the time these organizational forms were created. As a result, the burden of all-out conflicts between them often lies heavier upon non-participants than upon those directly involved.

Institutional forms which operate in that way are, sooner or later, likely to be deemed politically unacceptable. They will be reappraised through the political processes of a democracy to which we subscribe. Nevertheless, unions and managements, by and large, insist that they have an inviolate right to be let alone in the conduct of their joint relationship. Our highest national, state and municipal officials are often rebuffed, and sometimes abused, when they express the common interest by pleading, sometimes abjectly, for restraint in the use of private power.

The utter incongruity of this situation would seem to be apparent upon any reasonable or logical analysis. In this age of unprecedented interdependence, many institutional forms of both public and private government need to be changed if the urgent problems of a revolutionary age of science are to be satisfactorily dealt with. The ceding by nations of some of their sovereignty for the common good, as in the Common Market, is hailed as great statesmanship. The states in our own country are called upon to integrate schools as a matter of essential national policy even though some of them insist upon a retention of local sovereignty in the matter. It would seem no more than prudent for those private interests responsible for our labor-management relations to recognize an involvement in the total picture.

That they do so, I suggest, is of central importance to the future of western democracy. The ideological conflict between the east and the west is most sharply drawn at the point of establishment of the wage-earners' conditions of employment. This is particularly evident in the undeveloped countries where exploitation by private interests has been the lot of workers throughout the ages. Our conviction is that the differences between employees and employers can most equitably be reconciled by private agreement between them; the totalitarian nations assert that such differences are irreconcilable and that the exploitation of workers is inevitable under private enterprise.

Our use of the private contract for wage determination has proven, of course, to be the antithesis of employee exploitation. With scant exception, the wage earners of the United States agree. However, the picture gets blurred in transmission abroad. Perhaps some of the trouble lies in our own lack of realization of the function assigned to collective bargaining and in a growing doubt about our ability to make this process work.

In simple terms, access of employees to collective bargaining is counted upon to guarantee them against exploitation in a private enterprise system. Ironic it is that this institution is challenged by enemies abroad as a capitalist device to snare the workers and to divert them from a manifest destiny but is here appraised by many as a means by which a minority of organized workers can exploit the rest of us – non-organized workers, the employers and the consumers.

Current dissatisfactions stem essentially from the strike, i.e., the idea that private differences about employment terms are arbitrable by the relative economic power of unions and of companies. In this sense, the strike is a curious institution. As a means of inducing private settlements, the strike has an obvious value in keeping wage-determination as a private matter. i.e., of keeping the government out. The work-stoppage, or the threat of it, provides a self-interest basis for such modifications of extreme positions as is necessary to bring about the essential meeting-of-minds, i.e., the contract. The strike can thus be viewed as a mechanism for resolving conflict, i.e., the underlying one about employment terms. But as a motive power for inducing private agreement the strike becomes less acceptable. This is a fact of modern-day living. New inducers of private agreements need to be invented – ones which will not export so heavily the costs of agreement-making to the public. More broadly speaking, it is also timely to reappraise the idea that, in establishing the terms of employment, economic might makes economic right.

Precedents encourage an emphasis upon the reasoned approach. They indicate that it is possible to discover substitutes for sheer economic power in labor-management relations. My first experiences in this field were in the settlement of organizational strikes during the late 1920's. These trials by private combat were then standard practice, and had been for almost a century, for deciding the burning issue of whether or not a union would be recognized by the employer for collective bargaining. Organizational strikes got so far out of hand as to become intolerable in a civilized nation. The representation election was invented as a substitute. By their majority vote in an appropriate unit, the employees were accorded a legal right to determine whether or not collective bargaining was to be instituted. Employers, by and large, opposed this solution. They had usually won the organizational strikes but generally lost the elections. Yet, no better solution could be devised. I haven't lately come across anyone, even among the employers, who would go back to the old way as a national policy.

The next dissatisfaction about strikes related to their use in settling day-by-day grievances in the plant. These involved discharges, promotions, job assignments, wage rate adjustments and the like. The rights and the status of the individual employee are intimately involved in grievances. Deciding them by strikes entailed such immense losses of production as to threaten the well-being of all. And, the settlements tended to be inequitable. For example, a discharge for a minor offense would "stick" if jobs were scarce, but discipline for a major employee dereliction would have to be rescinded if business was booming. There are serious limitations to the use of relative economic power as a means for arriving at fair and equitable solutions to some problems.

In particular, a willingness to lose could not be induced because the strike did not meet the criteria of due process. A greater resort to reason and a lesser dependence upon economic brawn was an evident need in grievance settlement. In their own labor agreements, unions and managements gradually evolved provisions for the arbitration of grievances. This made possible the now virtually standard no-strike clause through which the union agrees that there will be no work stoppages during the term of the agreement. An institutional substitute for the strike was successfully devised.

When the idea of voluntary grievance arbitration was first advanced, union and management representatives stood shoulder to shoulder in opposing the intrusion of outsiders into their private domains. Some hardy pioneers, mainly in the needle trades, were willing to experiment with the new-fangled procedure. A major breakthrough in acceptance of the idea of grievance arbitration came in 1941 when the United Automobile Workers and General Motors Corporation agreed upon the first grievance arbitration to be established in a large mass production industry. A very few companies and several unions still prefer the old way but well over 90 percent of all current labor agreements include provisions for the arbitration of grievances and the no-strike clause. There is a general "pointing with pride" to this development as a notable example of social inventivenes in the private sector of the economy.

Although the short-comings of the strike in resolving differences over labor agreement terms are apparent in today's environment, it doesn't follow that compulsory arbitration is the only way out. Indeed, it is no alternative at all if we would hold to the basic principles of a private enterprise society. They include the conviction that wages are to be fixed by private agreements. Those who espouse compulsory arbitration should be called upon, and in no uncertain terms, to get specific about what objective criteria they would use in a bureaucratic determination of "fair and equitable" wages. The reality of the matter is that no such criteria are available for administrative application. Wage determination under compulsory arbitration can only be arbitrary. Therefore, the sanctions by which the state would compel adherence to employment terms objectionable to employees and to employers should be explicitly stated. To urge compulsory arbitration without these specifics is to write a fairy story in which the difficulties of a life to come are brushed lightly aside by the happy phrase – "and they lived happily ever after." At times, I have wondered about the kind of a domestic life that was actually the fate of Snow White and Prince Charming.

The nature of the present crisis in collective bargaining, as it is often termed, depends upon the way the problem is phrased. In terms of democratic principles, the problem relates to the possibility of developing new institutional forms, as alternatives to the strike, that will assist the private agreement-making process. Notable experiments to this end are being undertaken within the private bargaining of those unions and those companies which are willing to essay the difficult pioneering road.

Time does not permit an extended discussion of the various innovations that are being undertaken. They are encouragingly numerous and have some common characteristics. One may note a growing disposition to work out the problems of automation through analytical reasoning rather than by the imposition of terms through superior economic power. Even more general is an awareness of the inadequacy of crisis bargaining in which a host of complex problems are amassed for "hurry up" treatment in a short period before the strike deadline. This can be too much like "Russian roulette." The role of the mediator is being re-assayed and the pros and cons of "outside" recommendations for settlement are being debated.

One of the experiments, inaugurated by agreement between the Kaiser Steel Company and the United Steelworkers of America, involves the participation of outside consultants in the negotiating process. They are designated as "public representatives." In the eyes of most unions and of most companies, this constitutes a direful intrusion of outsiders, who have no responsibility for the success of a union or a company, into private sovereignties. To forestall any such idea from spreading, some of them are concentrating upon the improvement of their own bipartite arrangements. This is all to the good. Success in these endeavors would be most effective in restoring a waning public confidence in collective bargaining.

The so-called Kaiser agreement, nevertheless, is a significant experiment, even if it only serves to spur improvements in bi-partite collective bargaining. The possibilities, however, are far greater than that. As already noted, under the Kaiser agreement, outside consultants have been invited to participate in private negotiations. The "third" parties are given the authority to make recommendations for the resolution of important differences which persist despite assiduous two-party negotiation. Thus, a kind of private mediation by persons acceptable to the parties and informed about their problems, has been invoked. This is a relatively new idea. Perhaps the result will be more reasoning together to resolve differences. At least, that is the objective.

The tri-partite group was also assigned a responsibility, which has been already carried out, for recommending to the parties a rule of reason to govern the sharing by all interested parties, including displaced workers, in productivity gains derived from technological advances. On the face of it, the idea that arbitrament by economic power is not adequate for arriving at equitable solutions, and hence acceptable solutions, of automation problems, seems to have some merit. Yet it has created opposition, and even hostility, among those who would continue collective bargaining "as usual." These reactions bring to mind the initial stages in the development of grievance arbitration. In sharp contrast is the widespread public interest in the Kaiser Plan doubtless because it promises a reasoned approach. Such contrasting reactions have doubtless typified every new institutional development called for over the years whenever the desire of a striving people to be let alone clashes with the common goals of an interdependent people.

From the beginning, the philosophical model of the agreement-making society has been dismissed by skeptics as no more than a "necessary myth" designed to rationalize a disorderly way of life. The rebuttal, I believe, is in the record. The idea of accommodation, nevertheless, does run a continuous competition, sometimes grim, with the "hard stand."

There are always the organizational counterparts of the cattlemen and the sheepherders who want to be let alone in waging private battle to determine whose freedom should be superseded. The yearning for a simple life in Walden currently finds expression in the glorification by some, often in erudite mathematical models, of those days of long ago when business establishments were very small, when there were no unions and when the invisible hand of the market place worked everything out so nicely without any conscious effort. They would not even try to come to terms with a changed environment. There are modern frontiersmen, many with far more power than the Daniel Boones, who are determined to live their own lives among us but without any involvement in the problems of interdependence.

These are the views which contest with the social inventiveness of a democratic society in devising institutional forms and procedures that, by due process, will induce men to accommodate their conflicting interests and join with enthusiasm in the common effort. In this contest, the dialogue is of crucial importance. Less talk about outer space and more thought about the inner spirit might serve to make the dialogue more resultful.

The United Nations in a Changing World

by

U Thant
Secretary-General of the United Nations

There are times, and this is one of them, when the world, in the absence of some tremendous and immediate threat, seems to wallow helplessly in a morass of dispute and discord. In such times it is easy to lose our sense of the urgent necessity of strengthening and developing further an international order capable of withstanding and containing the crises and conflicts of the future. And it is in times like these that spiritual leadership and inspiration are more necessary than ever.

In the great encyclical letter *Pacem in Terris*, Pope John XXIII appealed to men to "spare no labour in order to ensure that world events follow a reasonable and human course." The encyclical, as I pointed out when it was first published in 1963, is very much in harmony with the spirit and objectives of the United Nations Charter. It emphasizes the dignity and worth of the human person, the rights of man and his corresponding duties, "the principle that all states by nature are equal in dignity," the imperative need for disarmament, the importance of economic development of the underdeveloped countries; these are only illustrative of many principles which are to be found also in the Charter and to which the encyclical gives such eloquent expression. In its specific reference to the United Nations it appeals to all peoples to interest themselves in the development of the Organization, to make it "ever more equal to the magnitude and nobility of its task."

Pacem in Terris

An International Convocation to examine the requirements of Peace assembled in New York City from February 17–20, 1965. It was sponsored by the Centre for the Study of Democratic Institutions in observance of International Co-operation Year. Among those who addressed the Convocation was the Secretary-General of the United Nations, U Thant. The text of his address is given here, reprinted from UN Monthly Chronicle, March 1965, Vol. II, No. 3.

Brotherhood between Nations

This recognition by His Holiness Pope JOHN XXIII of the importance of the role of the United Nations in the modern world was reiterated by His Holiness Pope Paul VI when I had the honour of being received in audience by him on July 11, 1963. His Holiness then observed that the Holy See considers the United Nations to be "an instrument of brotherhood between nations, which the Holy See has always desired and promoted, and hence a brotherhood intended to favour progress and peace among men." His Holiness went on to say: "We therefore derive consolation from your visit, and we avail ourselves of the occasion to renew the expression of our esteem and of our hopes for the fundamental programme of the United Nations, especially in regard to the elimination of war, the assistance of developing peoples, and of those in need of defence and promotion, the lawful liberties of individuals and social groups, and the safeguarding of the rights and dignity of the human person. To these sentiments, then, we add our good wishes for the true prosperity of the great Organization of the United Nations, and for the happy success of its activities."

In the two years which have elapsed since the publication of the encyclical *Pacem in Terris*, the need for human solidarity and understanding has, if anything, increased. Our situation is a paradoxical one. We have, at last, both the means and the general desire to secure peace and justice for all. We know all too well the price we shall surely pay for failing to secure that peace and justice. We are not basically disagreed, whatever our ideological differences, about the kind of world we wish to have. The United Nations Charter, already accepted by 115 nations, describes it; the encyclical describes it; and it is also described in many great works of literature, scholarship and prophecy which are the common heritage of all mankind.

What element, then, is lacking, so that, with all our skill and all our knowledge, we still find ourselves in the dark valley of discord and enmity? What is it that inhibits us from going forward together to enjoy the fruits of human endeavour and to reap the harvest of human experience? Why is it that, for all our professed ideals, our hopes and our skill, peace on earth is still a distant objective, seen only dimly through the storms and turmoils of our present difficulties?

Creative Change Required

All great moves forward in the history of mankind have required changes of existing attitudes and states of mind, so that real life can catch up with the creative ideas that underlie our evolution. We are now trying to make the step forward from a world of antagonism, domination and discord to a world of co-operation, equity and harmony. This is a large step and an important break with the past. It is not to be expected, therefore, that men will easily and immediately accept it – and adapt themselves to it. In the preamble to the UNESCO Constitution it is said that, "Since wars begin in the minds of men, it is in the minds of men that the defences of peace must be constructed." The sentence may well provide one key to our present difficulties. It is an aspect of our problems to which the encyclical *Pacem in Terris* is especially relevant.

Thus, although we have abjured war as an instrument of policy, all nations have not yet abjured the state of mind that has so often led to war – the nationalistic urge to dominate and extend, by various means, their spheres of influence, and the conviction of the unquestionable superiority of their own particular traditions, forms and ways of life. Nor has it been possible effectively to eliminate the use of force, whether openly or covertly, as a means of furthering political or other ends. Such attitudes inevitably breed in other nations the fears, resentments and suspicions which historically have also created the atmosphere of tension in which wars break out. Again, although we speak loudly for equal rights and against discrimination, there are still many nations and groups throughout the world who are not prepared to accept the practical consequences of these ideals, while an even greater number still suffer from discrimination or lack of equal opportunity. It is this failure of everyday, practical behaviour to keep pace with professed ideals and aims which makes the promise of our infinitely promising world a mockery for so many of its inhabitants.

We have accepted the idea of the United Nations as a representative instrument for promoting and maintaining international order. This is an important step away from the old and narrowly nationalistic attitudes. We are, however, still a long way from showing that confidence in each other and in the great instrument itself, which alone can make it work for us and give practical reality to the ideals to which all nations have subscribed in the Charter. The fact is that, though our desire for peace is undeniable, our approach to peace is often old-fashioned and more attuned to former times than to our present state. Even the United Nations Charter itself provides a good example of this. Chapter VII, for instance, on action with respect to threats to the peace, breaches of the peace and acts of aggression, plainly stems from the experience of the aggressions of the Axis powers in the thirties, a kind of situation which is unlikely to recur in our world of superpowers armed with hydrogen bombs amid a vastly increased number of smaller independent states. To be candid, some provisions of the Charter, like Chapter VII, were framed with an eye on the potential re-emergence of the Axis powers as a threat to international peace and security. Memories of the war and the ruthlessness of its perpetrators were still very fresh in the minds of the founding fathers of the United Nations when they met in San Francisco. This state of mind explains the concept behind big power unanimity in taking preventive or enforcement measures against aggression, potential and real. This mood was responsible for the formation of the Military Staff Committee and for the ideas behind its composition and functions.

However, the course of history took a new turn. Alignments changed; old enemies became new friends; old comrades-in-arms found themselves in opposite camps, and the United Nations could not function in the way it was intended to function. The provisions of the Charter relating to action with respect to threats to peace and acts of aggression were subjected to various interpretations. I must say in all frankness that in these círcumstances the Charter provisions are somewhat out of date. It is this anachronism in the Charter – the kind of anachronism which is inevitable in our rapidly changing world – that is partly responsible for the present constitutional and political crisis in the United Nations.

Process of Accomodation

We have to work towards a world order in which aggressive nationalism or expansionism are banished as a means of promoting or protecting national interests, where fanaticism is no longer necessary to support a different point of view and where diversity can be preserved without resort to prejudice and hatred. We have seen how the great religions of the world, after lamentable periods of bigotry and violence, have become accommodated to each other, without losing their influence or spiritual independence, by a mutual respect for, and understanding of, the spiritual and moral aims which are common to them all. We must try, both earnestly and urgently, to extend that process of accommodation to the political, ideological, economic and racial alignments of the world. All of our high aims, our vaunted technology, our skill and our real desire to co-operate and to help one another will be of no avail if this adaptation to new circumstances, this general accommodation, this real change of heart, does not come about.

The realignment of political power in the world is a process whose changing outlines frame the political enigma of our times. The forces likely to be released by this process, benign and otherwise, can, however, be foreseen and cannot be ignored. They can, and must, be channelled and directed by a positive effort of all nations working together in the United Nations, if we are to grasp our destiny and mould our future rather than be swept away into a new and appalling age of strife and hatred. It is not enough to be active only when a dire international emergency breaks about our heads. We need to make a constant effort, year in and year out, to strengthen by practice the theory of a peaceful and co-operative world.

Beneath the present political realignments, the world is in fact divided in a number of ways. It is divided economically; it is divided racially; and it is divided ideologically, although this latter division may prove to be less basic than the first two. These divisions must be faced and discussed with reason and determination. We ignore them at our peril, for if they are allowed to persist and grow larger they will unleash, as they already show signs of doing, darker forces of bigotry, fear, resentment and racial hatred than the world has ever seen. We cannot agree to live in such a nightmare, still less to bequeath it to our children.

Forum for Discussion

Though its current problems are great and its present authority uncertain, the United Nations does provide a forum in which these divisions can be discussed and gradually reduced within the framework of the common interest in peace and justice, and with the safeguards that only an organization representative of all peoples, all interests and all motivations can provide. The United Nations has also, on numerous occasions, furnished a machinery through which countries can co-operate to deal with threatening situations and to keep the peace.

As the respect for it grows, the Organization should also serve as a centre for the harmonizing of national policies within the wider interest. We must eventually arrive, in the affairs of the world, at a state of political maturity in which it will be considered statesmanlike, rather than weak, for even a great country to alter its course of action or to change its national policy in the common interest or in deference to the will of the majority. I hasten to add that we are certainly nowhere near to such an idyllic situation today.

These, to my mind, are the compelling reasons why the United Nations must be preserved and strengthened and why the disagreements of the greatest powers, however justified they may be, must not be allowed to disrupt and stultify the Organization. We have seen, in the crisis over arrears in payments to the United Nations budget, an episode that is both depressing and heartening – depressing for the damage done to the effectiveness and dignity of the United Nations – heartening for the loyal and unceasing efforts of the member nations to preserve their Organization by finding a solution. There is no doubt that the relationship between, and the role of, the Security Council and the General Assembly are issues of great importance. These issues will surely continue to occupy the minds of most of us, since they are basic to the great debate now going on. As I have said earlier, the writers of the Charter envisioned complete agreement among the five permanent members of the Security Council, who would be collectively responsible for keeping the peace by supplying arms and men, in certain contemplated situations. These situations, however, did not come about. History took a new turn; the Security Council could not act in the manner it was intended to act, and the General Assembly assumed, or had to assume, certain functions not originally contemplated in the Charter.

Beginning of Great Debate

We are now witnessing the beginning of the great debate – whether the big powers in unison, through the agency of the Security Council, should take exclusive responsibility for maintaining international peace and security while the General Assembly functions as a glorified debating society in political matters, or whether an attempt should be made to secure a fair, equitable, and clearly defined distribution of functions of the two principal organs, in the light of the changing circumstances, and, particularly, bearing in mind the increase in the membership of the Organization, from 50 in 1945 to 114 in 1965. Account will have to be taken of the fact that in the General Assembly are represented, in addition to the big powers, all the other states, the smaller powers, whose understanding, assistance and co-operation are nevertheless essential in regard to decisions involving issues of international peace and security. These issues are serious, and the manner in which they are resolved will affect profoundly the organic growth of the Organization in the years to come. They can only be resolved by a will to compromise and accommodate, in the overriding interest of maintaining peace. The smaller powers are playing, and must play, an essential role as the spokesmen of moderation and common interest in this process and, if a solution is found, much credit will be due to their steadfastness and determination.

Governments, however well and sincerely they may co-operate in the United Nations, cannot by themselves face the great and shifting problems of our age in isolation. The peoples they represent must also give life and reality to the aims and ideals of the Charter, towards which we strive. Here again, we now have the means to achieve a great objective, an enlightened world public opinion. One of the revolutions of our age, the revolution in communications of all kinds, has made a well-informed world public opinion technically possible for the first time in history. Our problem is to ensure a beneficial use of these means of communication. This is a challenge to leaders both temporal and spiritual, to intelligent and creative men and women everywhere. Without real knowledge and understanding and without a determination to learn from the past, to rid ourselves of outmoded prejudices and attitudes, and to face the future together with both hope and wisdom, we shall not succeed in making our aims and ideals a working reality. The encyclical *Pacem in Terris* gives us an inspiring lead towards that change of heart which our great aims so urgently require.

Conflict between Nations

by

ABBA EBAN
Minister of Foreign Affairs, State of Israel, Jerusalem

We live in an age of progressive science and conservative diplomacy. The instruments and techniques of international relations have not been adapted to the shape and mood of our changing world. Diplomacy is provincial in scope. It awakens only to specific local dangers and rarely addresses itself to the total human condition. And it is remedial and not preventive in its method. It is more concerned with putting out fires than with ensuring that they do not erupt. Twenty years after Hiroshima mankind lacks institutions which show any signs of controlling human destiny at its two most crucial points – security and development.

For over a century it has been customary to believe that a peaceful international order would be ensured by the weight of historic forces without specific technical guidance. It was hoped that as men grew more wise and more free the world would spontaneously be redeemed by science and liberty. Today we have attained technical powers beyond previous dreams; and over ninety percent of humanity live in sovereign states. Yet with all this bulk of knowledge and the eruption of freedom the human situation is in profound disarray. Man has never abstained from any folly of which he is capable.

What HUXLEY once called Man's Estate can best be described by comparing it to the more familiar concepts of a national society. Imagine a nation of which one third is abundantly fed and two thirds are undernourished; of which one third is illiterate, one third illeducated and a small minority intensely culturated in science and letters; of which one part has a life expectancy of 70 and another of 39; of which one third has a standard of living thirty times higher than the other two thirds; a nation plunged in general misery and turbulence with a few privileged suburbs living in peace and prosperity. There is only one nation in which such vast disparities exist: it is the Human Nation which inhabits the planet Earth. This is no mere figure of speech. With modern communications and information media the envy which rich nations excite in the poor, the strong amongst the weak, is equivalent to the kind of rancours which would develop in a national society if such disparities of fortune and opportunity prevailed. Everyone now knows what happens on the other side of the fence. I should add that this human nation has no effective police force and that its several provinces or suburbs can be plunged in bloodshed for months and years with none to call a halt.

There is grotesque disparity between the effectiveness of the social and legal restraints with which we prevent disorder and inequality within our states – and the nebulous, ineffective and sporadic techniques which we apply to the society of nations. This is why those who practice statecraft should be intensely modest in their estimate of themselves. They have failed to apply on the universal plane the successes which they have registered in the exercise of their national responsibilities. In our nations we know to suppress violence, to enthrone law, to share resources and to avoid flagrant inequalities. The methodology of transferring these habits and techniques to an international order still eludes us. The result is a series of vulcanic eruptions developing within the past five years in Congo, Cyprus, Cuba, Vietnam, Kashmir and elsewhere. The machinery of international debate and security is only now emerging from paralysis. The billion undernourished, the 700 million illiterate adults, the 500 million suffering from entirely preventable diseases, and the victims of localised wars all testify to the extraordinary weakness which affects man's social intelligence as soon as it peers beyond the national frontier.

One reason why the method of organising an international harmony eludes us is that we seldom address ourselves to the task, whereas science had the creative imagination to conceive entirely new domains of existence – new countries of thought – diplomacy has never taken globalism seriously. Summit meetings still take a microscopic view of few problems – instead of a panoramic view of the total human scene. United Nations Specialized Agencies and conferences bring universal vision to bear on the human torment. But they have never discussed them at a level of authority capable of launching cooperative and decisive action. At the recent convocation in New York on the Papal Encyclical "Pacem in Terris" I suggested that the heads of the governments spend one week together to discuss not the fate of their own nations, but the destiny of the Human Nation. It is precisely in a concern for supra-national interests that governments and blocs have a chance of transcending their rivalries and developing cooperative habits which could, in time, transform their approach to provincial squabbles – the Vietnams, Congos and Kashmirs of our troubled world. Why should not the Presidents and Prime Ministers discuss the world famine, the population explosion, the nuclear power in its hopeful and fearful aspects, the spread of knowledge and the establishment of effective international machinery for conciliation and peace keeping? Not all the matters which engage their time are of greater urgency and dignity.

The United Nations with all its imperfections is still the salient expression of a universal human order, transcending national barriers. It is therefore more important to preserve it in working order than to vindicate its financial and procedural orthodoxies. The United States has acted wisely in acceeding to world opinion on this point. The tenacious pursuit of arms control agreements and a solution of the Chinese representation problem are now the most urgent tasks of the United Nations. All modern statesmen – including those of small nations – must act in a double role: as spokesmen of their particular national interests and at the same time, as representatives of the wider human cause. Universalism far from being the adversary of nationhood may turn out to be its greatest friend – and possibly its last one.

You will understand that I see no hope of progress unless there is a search for innovation in diplomatic thinking similar to the conceptional changes which made this generation so creative in science. I do not say that discussion of global issues is the same as their solution, but discussion is a prior condition of solution. No answer can be better than the question which invites it.

The decision of Pope PAUL to join the deliberations of the United Nations in October, is an imposing expression of the universal conspectus which is needed for twentieth century's diplomacy in the words of TEILHARD DE CHARDIN: "Everything that formerly made for war now makes for peace. Pressed against one another by the increase in their numbers and relationships, forced together by the growth of a common travail, the men of the future will in some sort form a single consciousness."

The Historical Unreality of the Cold War

by

JOHN NEF
Chairman, Center for Human Understanding, University of Chicago

The mechanization, the automation, the astounding speed of travel and transport and communication, the gigantic cities, the growing density of population which is occurring almost everywhere in our time – are all novel. This Academy and the Center for Human Understanding of the University of Chicago have been established to help cope with these unique conditions of existence, which arrest us as scientists, as historians and other students of man, as writers and other artists, as business men and workers of every kind.

I speak as an historian concerned to recognize and understand the processes that have brought the present world into being. Over a period of some four hundred years, going back at least to the late sixteenth century – to the age of CERVANTES, SHAKESPEARE and GALILEI – individuals have played important parts in making this world. Their thought and art, as well as their political, economic and social decisions, have acted upon and interacted with the natural resources of the earth, and with man-made institutions, to produce the astounding conditions which face humanity today. Clearer views of the interplay of historical factors that have produced these conditions may help in our efforts to prepare the public and especially the younger generation to deal with them.

The influence of strongly-held beliefs upon history is undeniable. During the twentieth century powerful beliefs have been derived from historical philosophies which are even now barely a hundred years old. In a recent letter to the *New York Times*, the Spanish Ambassador to France writes: "I submit that Spain and the United States, and their governments, are now on the same side of the ideological conflict that splits the world." If, as these words take for granted, all countries and governments are enrolled on one side or the other of what has come often to be called the "Cold War", it is in no small measure because of beliefs generated by recently formulated interpretations of history.

What are these interpretations?

One is the cycle theory. According to that all great societies – for example the Greco-Roman lasting from Homeric times to the fall of the ancient Roman Empire – have a span as inexorably fixed within time limits as are those slices of existence accorded individual men and women, who seldom last beyond a hundred years, and, if they do, are no longer active agents in the human comedy. The cycle theory, in its modern influential form, was originally sketched by GOBINEAU in his *Essai sur l'inégalité des races humaines*. That appeared in two volumes in 1853 and 1855. The notion of a rigourously fixed term for great societies was given more precision by SPENGLER's *Untergang des Abendlandes*, published at the end of the First World War.

The cycle theory has led people everywhere to believe all societies are doomed by nature to decadence and death. Following SPENGLER's timetable (which TOYNBEE did not effectively alter) the unique modern industrialized society, which now penetrates the entire planet and extends even into outer space, is not the beginning but the end of a cycle. If such an end is inevitable, there seems no use in setting out to build a world society for which there is no precedent. So people assume nothing effective can be done to transcend the ideological conflict of which the Spanish Ambassador wrote.

Powerful in bringing about that ideological conflict are beliefs generated by the marxist, and what, for want of a more descriptive phrase, may perhaps be called the anti-marxist, interpretations of history. These interpretations do not despair of the salvation of present society in the same way as the cycle interpretations do. But they seek salvation in a victory of their side in the ideological conflict. Each summons all peoples to a showdown which can hardly be resolved except by force, instead of to constructive efforts to transcend the conflict and to build a civilization more durable and more united than any that before has flowered.

So, while beliefs based on marxianism or anti-marxianism are not identical in their implications with beliefs derived from the cycle interpretation, they threaten to provide by total war all the evidence that is needed to support it!

Let us now look more closely at these two ideological interpretations of history – the marxist and the anti-marxist. Chapter 26 of *Das Kapital* opens with these words: "We have seen how money is changed into capital; how, through capital, surplus value is made, and from surplus value more capital. But the accumulation of capital presupposes surplus value, surplus value presupposes capitalistic production; capitalistic production presupposes the pre-existence of considerable masses of capital and of labour power in the hands of producers of commodities. The whole movement, therefore, seems to turn in a vicious circle, out of which we can only get by supposing a primitive accumulation (the "previous accumulation" of Adam SMITH) preceding capitalistic accumulation; an accumulation not the result of the capitalistic mode of production but its starting point."

MARX's words bring out the predominant place which he and those all over the world who faithfully follow his thought give to capital as the vital element in the coming of industrialism. MARX goes on to suggest that the *private* accumulation of all property – including of course capital which becomes with marxists practically a synonym for property – was effected mainly by conquest, enslavement, robbery and murder. In political economy, MARX wrote, primitive accumulation played a role which can be appropriately compared to the role of original sin in theology. Virtue with the marxists becomes almost a monopoly of men employed for wages who are summoned to break their chains. Redemption is therefore to be found in a class struggle to oust the private possessors of capital and to substitute the state as the alleged representative of virtuous workers. That struggle would provide the catharsis needed to settle the future of mankind.

Marxian doctrines concerning the origins of the industrialized world have had an astonishing influence on those opponents of MARX who have generated the beliefs that have served as fodder for the other side in the "ideological conflict." It is surprising that since the publication of *Das Kapital*, economists who are anti-communists deal with economic history much as the marxists do. For them too industrialism originated in capital accumulation, only they attribute a virtuous role in the main to capitalists and to competition. In so doing they are partly right, yet their correct refusal to treat business men and capitalists generally as peculiarly corrupted by various forms of villainy or sin, *has not led them to recognize the constructive parts played by disinterested and novel searches for truth, beauty and virtue in the evolution of industrialism, in man's triumph over matter.* The anti-marxists mostly assume, like the marxists, that the basic explanations of the present industrialized world are, for all important purposes, to be found strictly in economic factors derived from material interests.

The present-day state of beliefs, derived from marxist and anti-marxist interpretations of history, reminds one of an apocryphal story. It circulated in the United States during the McCARTHY era. A policeman arrests a man speaking to a crowd in a public square. As the man is being hoisted into a police car several of his audience protest to the policeman that he is making a mistake. "That man is not a communist," they say, "he is an anti-communist." The policeman dismisses the information as irrelevant. "I don't care what kind of a communist he is," he tells them, "I'm against all communists."

How much truth – how much reality – is there in the two interpretations of history – the marxist and the anti-marxist – which are providing so much combustible matter to inflame the violent propensities of men and to influence the political policies and the actions of those who govern?

The beliefs which split human kind today rest on extremely shaky views of history. Like the cycle theories, they provide false impressions of the processes which brought into being the unique materially interdependent world in which we live.

What have all three historical interpretations, which masquerade today as reality, overlooked?

The foundations of the unique world, to which humanity today is committed, were laid before any of these historical interpretations were set forth. A passage written by CHATEAUBRIAND 125 years ago, shows that society had already advanced at the time further towards the conquest of the material world than is generally supposed today. His words show that the recent triumphs of man over matter had been rendered virtually inevitable before GOBINEAU and MARX and SPENGLER, long before BÖHM-BAWERK, VON MISES and others who are treated as champions by the anti-marxists. Neither the anti-marxists not the marxists nor the cycle theorists have done much, if anything, to bring about the present material triumph of man. Their principal contributions have been to the ideologies which are so prevalent today, and these are almost altogether destructive in their implications.

Here are CHATEAUBRIAND's words, written in 1841 in his diary, published posthumously as part of his *Mémoires d'outre tombe:*

When I compare "two globes of our earth, one at the beginning and the other at the end of my life, I no longer recognize what I see," he wrote. He goes on to make clear that he expects this fantastic rate of change to continue, and that he regards as certain, in view of advancing civilization, the triumph over space and time which we have lived to witness.

But he goes farther in his hopes than our world has gone. He takes a "universal society" almost for granted as the impending consequence of the material advances that we have lived to see. What will a "universal society" be like? he asks. Will it be a society in "which there are no particular nations, which will not be French, nor English, nor German, nor Spanish, nor Portugese, nor Italian, nor Russian, nor Tartar, nor Turkish, nor Persian, nor Indian, nor Chinese, nor American – which will be rather all those societies in one? What will be the result for its manners, its sciences, its arts, its poetry? How will the passions felt together according to different peoples in different climates, be expressed?

"What destiny will the stars, new for us, light up? Will their revelation be linked to some new phase of humanity?"

CHATEAUBRIAND's words serve not only to indicate how far by 1841 society had advanced already towards the material conquest of our globe, but how in his time this conquest was linked in the minds of some Europeans with a fusion of *all* peoples, with the coming of a great society transcending national, racial and religious ties.

Is it not sobering to realize how far we now are from such a fusion of peoples and nations? Is it not sobering to realize how far we are from the new phase of humanity of which CHATEAUBRIAND dreamed?

Was this inevitable? The historical evidence is against inevitability. It suggests that men themselves have been responsible. Not least responsible have been the interpreters of history who, often in the name of the human sciences, have provided the emotional beliefs that are said to divide the world.

It is true that nationalism existed before the time of GOBINEAU and MARX, and jealous ,unimaginative nationalism is of course a major obstacle to "universal society." But that kind of uncreative nationalism was given a fresh intensity and bitterness by despair over man as an instrument for good, bred partly by these interpretations of the past. They have infused themselves into the emotions of millions throughout the world who do not know their origins and have no direct acquaintance with the works of their authors. Whatever the national or religious or social persuasions of those who adopted them, the beliefs have often become fanatical, and have worked to set nation against nation, man against man, and man against himself.

The philosophies which were most influential when CHATEAUBRIAND was born – the philosophies of the Enlightenment – had been much less destructively nationalistic. The advent of NAPOLEON – a man whom CHATEAUBRIAND always opposed – did much to disappoint the hopes of the Enlightenment, but after NAPOLEON had gone, CHATEAUBRIAND (like his younger contemporary TOCQUEVILLE) did not regard those hopes as obsolete.

The notion of universal government reaching to the ends of the earth, and including non-Christian states on equal terms with Christian, had been put forward two centuries before CHATEAUBRIAND's time, in a book called *Le nouveau cynée* printed in 1623. That notion has been periodically revived ever since, and if, as CHATEAUBRIAND thought, a universal society is possible, universal government – a world rule of law replacing force – would be a natural consequence.

Perhaps we could justify men's despair of achieving such a society, if the interpretations of history that have come to dominate belief since CHATEAUBRIAND's time were embedded in historical truth. But the actual historical processes that created the conditions of material progress which dazzled CHATEAUBRIAND, were very different from those portrayed by the theorists from whom millions since his time indirectly derive the beliefs behind the cold war. The material conditions CHATEAUBRIAND witnessed were fruits not *only* of capital formation but of human genius and human compassion which transcend economics and economic interests. The best in human nature has been more influential than the worst in bringing them about.

Let us look briefly at the actual – the real – historical processes which have led to the unique civilization which surrounds us today.

The remarkable progress of coal mining and other modern industries began in Great Britain during the reign of the first Queen Elizabeth. An early industrial revolution changed the course of economic endeavor during the late sixteenth and early seventeenth centuries, above all in Great Britain, in the direction of quantity for its own sake. This change in the direction of economic endeavor, which tended for the first time in history to make the cutting of labor costs the major goal of all work, was accomplished not mainly because more private capital was available. It was accomplished by innovations in the realm of the spirit which influenced the uses to which capital, especially private capital, was put. In their minds, some men began to attach an importance to numbers and to quantity for its own sake, both as ends to happiness and as means to thought, for which there were no precedents in any great societies prior to the times of GALILEI and KEPLER, GILBERT and HARVEY, all of whom were born between 1540 and 1590.

In the seventeenth century there arose a novel concern with precise measurements, combined with a novel insistence on tangible evidence as the arbiter in matters of scientific knowledge and with an application of innovations in the realm of mathematical theory, to guide astronomy, physics and biology into channels of reasoning unknown to earlier scientists. The scientific revolution then got in full swing. "Since a babe was born in a manger," WHITEHEAD has written, "it may be doubted whether so great a thing has happened with so little stir." That early scientific revolution led steadily and directly to the recent even more revolutionary discoveries concerning matter and space and those concerning genetics. The application, especially during the last hundred years, of accumulating scientific knowledge, as derived from the scientific revolution, to practical technology was essential to the material conquest of the earth. So the new directions taken by individual minds in the seventeenth century provided one essential foundation for the globe as we find it today.

These innovations in the minds of men lend themselves neither to marxist nor to anti-marxist interpretations of history. Nor to cyclical interpretations.

What have also played an important – and an hitherto almost entirely ignored part – in the material conquest of the earth, are other innovations in the realm of the individual mind and heart. These must also be traced back to the two centuries that followed the Reformation and the rise of Protestantism after 1540. The recent dominant interpretations of history neglect both.

One was the evolution during the seventeenth and eighteenth centuries, alongside and intermingled with the novel quantitative economy, of an economy of delight and commodity. This linked, in ways that were new, the values of beauty (as expressed by art) with the furniture and decorations surrounding families in their homes, and even with the style and the embellishment of warships, forts and firearms. Thus beauty blunted the violent propensities of man during the times of COUPERIN, RAMEAU, BACH, HAYDN and MOZART, which is to say from about 1650 to about 1800.

The other constructive movement was the cultivation, that began a bit earlier, by religious innovators – Catholic as well as Protestant – in times when religion was not touched by marxist or anti-marxist theories, of the virtues Christ exemplified, in connection with simple everyday existence as led beyond the cloister by individuals and families of every social class – the virtues of tenderness, charity and love. Actually the basis of the modern civilized world was not laid, as MARX argued, by a spread in economic relations of greed and avarice. The basis for the modern industrialized world was laid by a spread in all walks of life of better manners and a diminution of violence. A substitution for piracy of bargaining and exchange – out of which both sides derived satisfaction - marked the evolution of commerce in early modern times. It was a mitigation of the sinful sides of human nature, combined with increasing restraints on brutality and vulgarity, that helped make possible the material conquest of this earth. Gentler manners developed in common with growing peaceful competition. MONTESQUIEU was interpreting history with essential truth when, in the middle of the eighteenth century, he wrote in his great book, *De l'Esprit des Lois:* – "Wherever there is commerce there are gentle manners and wherever there are gentle manners there is commerce."

So industrial civilization, as it evolved until the twentieth century, was far more the child of relative peace than the child of war. As a part of the new reasonableness and gentleness introduced during the seventeenth and eighteenth centuries, ideological warfare – which had marked the religious conflicts following the Reformation – largely disappeared from Europe. Wars for the sake of total conquest were ruled out of practical political considerations. Men believed the world was becoming civilized for the first time. That is why the word "civilization" was coined – apparently in the mid-eighteenth century. As GIBBON expressed it some years later, the price of becoming civilized was to cease to want to conquer. In the early nineteenth century BENJAMIN CONSTANT considered the spirit of conquest, introduced by NAPOLEON, an anachronism, explained by the fact that, as a Corsican, NAPOLEON was a barbarian outside the main stream of civilization.

Whatever validity there may be in the prevalent notion that, in the twentieth century, war has contributed more than peace to scientific as well as to technological progress, this was certainly not the case during the first three hundred years and more of rising industrialism, before the era of world wars. And those three hundred years were decisive in setting the world on the course of material progress followed since.

The cold war is unreal because it is founded on an inadequate and essentially false view of the history that led mankind into this unique world.

It was confidence in "civilization" that helped to give wings to scientific discoveries and to their dissemination for practical purposes. In the relatively peaceful Europe which followed the Napoleonic wars for about a century, some men, prominent among them scientists and even some munitions makers like NOBEL, came to feel that the better sides of human nature were winning – and were bound to go on winning – victories over evil. As a result scientists felt increasingly free to give all they had to their discoveries, and to reveal their knowledge with a good conscience, because what they discovered and conveyed was bound, they felt, to be put more to constructive than to destructive uses.

The spiritual forces growing out of fresh beliefs and hopes in human nature were mainly responsible for the material triumphs of recent decades. Humanity reaped its material harvest as a result of generous and disinterested ideas and beliefs and sound moral values sowed generations and even centuries ago.

It is puzzling to understand why different beliefs from those which mainly nourished material progress, beliefs flimsily founded in history as we have seen, should have made such astonishing headway during the late nineteenth and twentieth centuries. Everywhere there are still individuals, among them many of the greatest scientists, nurtured in the generous hopes which originated in the Renaissance, the Reformation and the Enlightenment, who have been shocked by the spreading pessimism and cynicism. Why have they been often inarticulate and, when articulate, almost always ineffective?

Two recent developments in scholarship and the realm of public discourse have contributed to the dismaying success of those unreal interpretations of the past that have engaged our attention.

One is the growing specialization of the scholar, pushed so far that the fields of inquiry have been narrowed sometimes to the point of sterility. Specialization has made it increasingly difficult for any learned man to speak with authority outside his special field, and has diminished his influence even when he has been able to speak effectively. At the very time when an almost mystical value has been attached to the work and the lives of certain scientists – such as EINSTEIN or FERMI – serious discussion in the realm of general ideas has all but disappeared, leaving that realm at the mercy of the cheap and vulgar and even the corrupt.

A second explanation for the present dominance of destructive and unreal beliefs is to be found in the growing currency given to abstractions as substitutes for concrete truths, and for deeper and much simpler moral and aesthetic values, a change mirrored most vividly in recent developments in the arts. For this spread of the abstract, of the unreal, progress in many sciences is to no small extent responsible. Writing a generation ago concerning the origins of modern science, WHITEHEAD had this to say: The whole system of organizing the pursuit of scientific truth which has come to dominate modern learning in universities throughout the world "is quite unbelievable." "This conception of the Universe," he proceeds, "is surely framed in terms of high abstractions, and the paradox only arises because we have mistaken our abstractions for concrete realities."

This desertion of the concrete, this confusion in the realm of the intellect found expression in the historical theories of the cycle historians, of the marxists and the anti-marxists. They plunged into the realm of general discourse and framed their answers to the overwhelming questions, which the specialists avoided, in terms of high abstractions. These answers often seemed convincing to persons seeking for beliefs to replace their ancestors' religious convictions, persons conditioned to the unreal.

The abstractions they were offered were of kinds that appealed especially to the pessimistic and the cynical sides of human nature. Pessimism and cynicism led people to believe that man's capacities for peaceful construction could never become powerful enough to win victories over the human propensities for violence, evil and irresponsible personal power. So the historical theories of recent times bear a heavy responsibility for the two total wars of the twentieth century. They threaten to precipitate a third which would, in all probability, be almost infinitely more destructive than the two some of us have witnessed.

Among the factors leading men to entertain these abstractions, so imperfectly founded in modern history, and even to embrace them with fervor as substitutes for religion, have been the prevalent notions that the scientific methods which had come to prevail in the nineteenth century, for handling data especially in the physical and the chemical sciences, could be utilized in dealing with all human relations and so with history. GOBINEAU considered his theories as strictly scientific. So did SPENGLER and MARX and BÖHM-BAWERK. Human resources came to be treated as unchanging in their nature, much as matter, space and time *had* been hitherto treated by modern scientists.

Science has begun to develop in new ways in the twentieth century. Science is beginning to take account, in the realm of matter, space and time of the relative, the indeterminate and even of the changing. Therefore a scientific approach to human behavior could become helpful in guiding human kind towards the good, the beautiful, the true. But, in utilizing scientific methods in the domain of behavior, it must be recognized that any attempt to lay down *laws in terms of past history*, for the course of future history, is bound to circumscribe human potentialities. Such an attempt would work to block any "new phase of humanity." For if such laws are believed to be binding, they are likely to determine human conduct, as the recent historical interpretations we have considered have partly determined it during the past hundred years.

By such limited approaches to the human sciences, the conditions of the mind and heart would be frozen. Avenues for possible improvement in the human condition, through individual effort, would be blocked by signs reading "no entry."

The coming of modern civilization and industrialism depended on *new* commitments of the mind and heart. If scientific laws, based on what had happened before the Reformation, had governed the behavior of our ancestors afterwards, from the late sixteenth to the mid-nineteenth centuries, the spread of gentle manners, firm devotion to moral values, the advent of an unprecedented economy of delight and commodity, the increasing freedom in France of small property owners (a subject space has not permitted us to explore in these pages) the discovery of limited warfare, and even the rise of modern science with its application to certain kinds of technological progress making for greater productivity, speed of movement and communication – all this would not have been possible.

A realistic view of man's past since the Reformation, suggests that the spiritual resources of the human being are deeper, more varied and more inexhaustible than contemporary politics and scholarship admit. It is necessary to break through both. Renewals in *fresh* forms of the search for perfection, which is at the roots of our present world, alone can save humanity from the menace of total destruction.

The hopes for better human beings and more enlightened leadership, such as made possible our material triumphs, are not dead. Elements for the fusion of mankind, which was part of CHATEAUBRIAND's vision, are still with us. For example, extensive cultural exchanges are being fostered. Men and women are travelling in numbers to an extent unknown before, some of them living, as members of the United States Peace Corps are asked to do, like the people among whom they settle.

It is open to us to discover our neighbors. It is open to us to appreciate and encourage the best in societies other than our own, and, in so doing, to nourish the best in our own, to blend that with the best in others.

The objectives to which the World Academy of Art and Science and the Center for Human Understanding are dedicated, call for an investigation of the real world and the creation of a concrete general universe of discourse concerning that world. We need to focus our attention on solving the new problems of a planet with increasingly interdependent, yet at the same time highly diversified units. We must start fresh and move in original ways. Old habits of creative work and research are not enough. In our efforts to build a world university we must transcend, not only the recent destructive interpretations of history, but also the specialization and abstraction which have helped them to flourish. We must break away from that system of organizing the pursuit of scientific truth which has, according to WHITEHEAD, led university men to cultivate a "quite unbelievable world."

To sum up the relevance of this paper for a world university or for world universities –

It will be worth preparing for such universities only if, in doing so, men's minds are opened to the pursuit of truth in accordance with the most exalted promise of a human nature that is both wary of evil and almost infinitely resourceful in surmounting evil. Hate must go. Mind and heart, reason and love, will have to be reconciled so that emotion becomes explosive for good.

To the preparation of such a program for universities the Center for Human Understanding is trying to contribute.

Conflict Resolution by Peaceful Means

by

MAX HABICHT

Doctor of Laws of the Universities of Zurich and Harvard,
International Legal Advisor, Geneva

Peaceful settlement of conflicts, whether between individuals or nations, requires machinery, not merely declarations of willingness to keep the peace.

Any community of human beings generates conflicts of interests between individuals as well as between nations; and the problem of guaranteeing a peaceful settlement implies the construction of the machinery by which such conflicts can be solved without resort to violence. Such machinery has been in operation for centuries, successfully, within the family, within the tribe, within the village, within the city, and within the nation-state. The community of nation-states, however, is still lacking in satisfactory machinery for the peaceful solution of conflicts.

Within most nations of the 20th Century, recourse to self-help has been eliminated in law and in practice. For instance, in Switzerland even the duel has been made an offence which is punishable by imprisonment up to 5 years. It is indeed a curious fact that citizens of all civilised nations are educated today to renounce recourse to violence for the settlement of their conflicts and are obliged to submit them to third-party decision (parliament, government, judge), while the same human beings, acting as a group in the nation-state, are not fully aware that conflicts between nations can be settled similarly by third-party decision, on the condition, however, that the ultimate aim is justice and order and not the imposition of the will of the stronger party. Every individual, by an intricate system of laws and governmental machinery, has been assigned his proper place within a peaceful national society and, as a rule, has accepted the necessary restrictions to his liberty. The nation-states, however, have not yet been assigned their proper place within the community of mankind and they have not yet accepted the restrictions to their national sovereignty, which are a precondition to the abolition of war.

There is no doubt that mankind is also on the way to introduce compulsory machinery by third-party decision between nation-states. The doctrine of just and unjust wars, and the definition and condemnation of aggression between nations are on the way to be replaced by efforts to set up world courts, a world parliament, and a world government with world police. Since mankind has invented what is called law, it has been able to replace conflict resolution by force with settlement through third-party decision. Moreover, whenever such machinery has been applied the result has been peace, as, overwhelmingly, third-party decisions are obeyed. Peace based on law presupposes the existence of a law making, a law interpreting and a law enforcing machinery. The essence of such machinery is that the parties are not acting as their own judge and policeman but that they are submitting their conflicts to binding third-party decision.

What is the present status of such machinery between nations? The overwhelming majority of governments have subscribed to an obligation in Article 2, paragraphs 3 and 4 of the United Nations Charter which reads as follows:

"All Members shall settle their international disputes by peaceful means in such a manner that international peace and security, and justice, are not endangered."

"All Members shall refrain in their international relations from the threat or use of force against the territorial integrity or political independence of any state, or in any other manner inconsistent with the purposes of the United Nations."

The Statute of the International Court of Justice at The Hague open to Governments provides in Article 36, paragraph 2:

"The states parties to the present Statute may at any time declare that they recognize as compulsory *ipso facto* and without special agreement, in relation to any other state accepting the same obligation, the jurisdiction of the Court in all legal disputes."

Of the 117 Members of the United Nations, only 34 have to-date subscribed to this provision known as the Optional Clause of the Statute. In addition to Members of the United Nations, Switzerland and Liechtenstein are also bound by this clause. Thus less than one-third of the existing nation-states have accepted this legal obligation to appear upon unilateral citation before the Judges at The Hague. There are many reservations attached to the acceptance of the Optional Clause which have further reduced compulsory adjudication. It should also be remembered that compulsory adjudication under Article 36 of the Statute refers exclusively to legal disputes as opposed to other types of conflicts. With regard to conflicts which are not of a legal nature the Statute has a provision in Article 38, paragraph 2 which states:

"This provision shall not prejudice the power of the Court to decide a case on *ex aequo et bono*, if the parties agree thereto."

This opens the way for the Court to settle disputes which are not of a legal nature.

An examination by the author of multilateral and bilateral treaties concluded after the First World War and in existence in 1934 [1] came to the con-

1. See HABICHT: The Power of the International Judge to give a decision *ex aequo et bono*. Constables Co. Ltd., London, page 76

clusion that, at that time, no nation-state had yet accepted compulsory adjudication *ex aequo et bono*. Up to 1966, the International Court of Justice at The Hague has not rendered a decision *ex aequo et bono*. Only a few *ex aequo et bono* decisions by *ad hoc* international arbitral tribunals have been published up to date.[1]

The procedure *ex aequo et bono* is little known outside the circle of experts, and only a small number of governments have concluded treaties providing for compulsory adjudication *ex aequo et bono*. In 1959, the Swiss Government took a new initiative for the conclusion of bilateral treaties for peaceful settlement of international disputes with nearly 100 governments with which it had not yet concluded such treaties. It submitted to them a Model-Treaty which soon thereafter was accepted with only a few modifications by the Governments of Cameroun, Costa-Rica, Israel, Ivory Coast, Liberia, Madagascar and Niger.[2] The new treaties have been signed but have not yet been ratified.

According to these treaties all disputes between the parties, of whatever nature they may be and which cannot be settled by diplomatic means, will be referred to a Permanent Conciliation Commission of five members with different nationalities. Possibly two members of this Commission will be nationals of the disputing parties. This Commission will be set up in advance for all future disputes. Provisions have been made for the members' nomination with the help of the President of the International Court of Justice if the parties cannot agree on its composition.

Conciliation, the first procedure to be initiated, will be an attempt to bring the parties to an agreement. If that fails, the dispute, for any further action, will be assigned to one of the following two classes: legal disputes or non-legal disputes. The definition of the legal dispute in these treaties is the same as the one in Article 36 of the Statute of the International Court of Justice, i.e. a dispute concerning: the interpretation of a treaty, any questions of international law, the existence of any fact which, if established, might constitute a breach of an international obligation; or the nature or extent of the reparation to be made for the breach of an international obligation. These legal disputes will be submitted to the court at the Hague upon the application of one party, and will be decided by a majority vote of the Court on the basis of law as explained in Article 38 of its Statute.

1. See f.e. the *ex aequo et bono* decision on the Free Zone Case between France and Switzerland in United Nations, Reports of International Arbitral Awards, Vol. III, 1949 p. 1457–1476.

2. See Message du Conseil fédéral à l'Assemblée fédérale du 23/11/65 No. 9359; Switzerland and Great Britain have also, on July 7, 1965, signed a treaty on conciliation, judicial settlement, and arbitration which however does not follow the Model-Treaty. The other treaties mentioned have been signed:
with Cameroun on January 22, 1963, with Costa Rica on January 15, 1965 ,with Ivory Coast on October 22, 1962, with Israel on August 2, 1965, with Liberia on July 23, 1963, with Madagascar on May 11, 1965, with Niger on August 2, 1963

All other conflicts will be submitted to a Permanent Arbitral Tribunal of five members of different nationalities to be set up in advance. Two of the members can be nationals of the disputing parties. The conflicts are to be settled by a majority decision of the Tribunal, which shall decide *ex aequo et bono*, "being guided by the general principles of law and taking duly into account the just interests of the two parties." Thus it is the aim of the Swiss Model-Treaty to introduce a compulsory settlement for all legal and non-legal conflicts through conciliation, judicial settlement, or arbitration. However, there is a provision at the end of each of the treaties (See Article 25 of the Model-Treaty) which creates some ambiguity. It reads as follows (translation):

"The provisions of the present treaty shall not be applicable:

(1) to disputes which have arisen before the entry into force of the present treaty between the Parties to the dispute

(2) to disputes concerning questions which international law leaves to the exclusive competence of states."

This reservation raises no problem with regard to legal disputes. If it means that a legal dispute which has already arisen and which has been referred to peaceful procedures before the coming into force of the treaty is excluded, then it is a mere "clause de style" and is not an exception to general principles of law. Furthermore, if international law determines that a matter falls within the exclusive jurisdiction of a state, it is evident that a legal dispute with regard thereto is excluded from settlement by international procedures. But what about disputes of a non-legal nature? There is no generally accepted rule of international law which would prevent, at any time, the application of international arbitration *ex aequo et bono* or conciliation to a dispute on the question whether a matter should continue to fall within the exclusive jurisdiction of a state. This is a dispute on the change of law.

The message of the Swiss Federal Council to Parliament of November 23, 1965 (p. 15) calls this Article 25 of the Model-Treaty a "clause de style," a statement which leads one to believe that it was not the intention of the Swiss Government to exclude any dispute on the change of law from compulsory *ex aequo et bono* settlement. Legal disputes, previously settled by law, and legal matters reserved for the domestic jurisdiction of a state are, by general principles of law, excluded from peaceful procedures. But this is not the case for non-legal disputes. Perhaps the ambiguity in Article 25 is a mere oversight in drafting. The intention of the Swiss Model-Treaty is, evidently, to provide an all-embracing pacific procedure for all kinds of disputes to the extent that existing general principles of law do not exclude them from such procedures. Compulsory peaceful settlement can accordingly be achieved under the new Swiss treaties by conciliation through a permanent conciliation commission, by judicial settlement through the International Court of Justice at The Hague on the basis of law, or by a permanent arbitral tribunal deciding *ex aequo et bono*.

The author, who made a study of the *ex aequo et bono* provisions of bilateral treaties signed after the first world war, concluded in 1935:

"The architects of the pacific settlement of international disputes realized that, to preserve peace, it does not suffice to apply the law, but that every perfect system of judicial settlement must allow the realization of objective justice – even in cases where the law deviates from it. For this reason, they have provided, in addition to the ordinary judicial procedure, a settlement *ex aequo et bono* which permits the judge to set aside existing rules of law, if they are inequitable." [1]

Legislation is usually the task of parliaments by statute or of governments by decree. In the absence of such parliamentary or governmental machinery, courts have legislated in the past. To amend the still imperfect peace keeping machinery between nation-states provision has now been made for legislation by tribunals *ex aequo et bono*. It seems unlikely that the Judges of the International Court of Justice at The Hague would act under Article 38, Paragraph 2, if at some stage of the procedure one party should contend that it did not agree to the adjudication by the Court *ex aequo et bono*. Therefore, as already concluded by the author in 1935, arbitration treaties provising for an *ex aequo et bono* decision by that Court could not be considered compulsory. This has now been changed by referring the task of *ex aequo et bono* settlement to arbitral tribunals. The Swiss Model-Treaty has certainly made an interesting contribution to further development in this field.

The Swiss treaties discussed above introduce compulsory adjudication of non-legal disputes. World Federalists, at their Copenhagen Conference of 1953, already discussed this problem. They advocated the setting-up of a Permanent World Equity Tribunal, but they added that the decision of the World Equity Tribunal should only be advisory unless the parties to the dispute had consented in advance to its being binding. The proposals by GRENVILLE CLARK & LOUIS B. SOHN in their publication *World Peace through World Law* [2] plead for the creation of a permanent fifteen member World Equity Tribunal giving decisions *ex aequo et bono*. This new World Equity Tribunal would not only advise but under certain conditions also could give binding decisions. In case the parties did not accept the proposal of the World Equity Tribunal, the proposals of CLARK & SOHN provide for an imposition of its findings under the following conditions: (See Second Edition page 339)

"Under certain conditions, the World Equity Tribunal would also have jurisdiction without regard to the agreement of those involved in the dispute or situation. This jurisdiction could be conferred by the General Assembly pursuant to Article 36 of the revised Charter with respect to any questions which in the judgement of three-fifths of all the Representatives in the Assembly: (a) cannot be satisfactorily decided on the basis of applicable legal principles; and (b) relate to a dispute or situation the continuance of which is likely to endanger the maintenance of international peace and security.

1. See HABICHT cited above, page 88.
2. Harvard University Press, Cambridge, Mass. First Edition 1958, Second Edition 1960.

If the Assembly should in this way refer a dispute or situation to the Tribunal, the Tribunal would conduct public hearings and make all necessary investigations.

Thereafter, the Tribunal could adopt such recommendations as it deems reasonable, just and fair for the solution of the whole dispute or situation, or of particular questions involved therein, which had been referred to the Tribunal; provided that the recommendations are approved by a two-thirds majority of all the members of the Tribunal.

Recommendations of the Tribunal (pursuant to Article 36 of the revised Charter) would become binding on all concerned only after they had been approved in their entirety by the General Assembly by a three-fourths majority vote of all the Representatives, including two thirds of the Representatives then in office from the member Nations entitled to fifteen or more Representatives in the Assembly; provided that the resolution of the Assembly approving the recommendations had included a finding that the dispute or situation was likely to continue unless the recommendations of the Tribunal were carried out and that such continuance would constitute a serious danger to peace."

This opens the way to international legislations by majority vote.

The world community is still far away from compulsory third-party decision by the application of peaceful procedures in case of international conflicts. Switzerland, when the new treaties are ratified, will have introduced, with about one half of the existing nation-states, compulsory adjudication of legal disputes and with some ten states compulsory adjudication of non-legal disputes. Most Governments are, however, still reluctant to submit their disputes to compulsory settlement by third-party decision. The small states have been leaders towards the introduction of such compulsory settlement.[1] The new Swiss treaties mention in their preamble that it is not only the desire of the parties to strenghen their ties of friendship but also "to favour in the general interest of peace the development of procedures leading to the pacific settlement of international disputes." This progress, little known outside the circle of specialists, deserves to be brought to the attention of a wider public.

1. Cf HABICHT: Post-War Treaties for the Pacific Settlement of International Disputes. Harvard University Press 1931, pp. 552 et seq. Treaty between Belgium and Danemark of March 3, 1922; pp. 562 et seq. Treaty between Belgium and Finland of nov. 19, 1927 pp. 422 et seq.Treaty between Belgium and Sweden of September 27, 1927; pp. 544 et seq. Treaty between Chile and Italy of December 2, 1927.

The Christian's Role in Transforming Society

by

W. A. Visser 't Hooft
General Secretary of World Council of Churches, Geneva

There are two ways in which this theme can be dealt with. First to take just one aspect of this vast problem. Second to deal with the problem as a whole but then of course in almost stenographic form. The second way is followed here, because we are today in a period of confusion about social ethics and we can therefore take almost nothing for granted. Let us call attention to the fundamental points which a very short catechism of social ethics should contain, realising how impossible it is to do this adequately or satisfactorily.

(1) Christians are sent into the world in order to witness in word and deed to the Lordship of Christ. The world's life is largely shaped by social and political factors. Christians are called to serve their Lord within this realm of life as in any other realm.

This may seem an obvious point. Unfortunately the old heresy that politics is a worldly realm which has nothing to do with the Christian faith is not yet dead. The Christian Church is itself largely responsible for the growth of this heresy, because during long periods it has not proclaimed the Kingship of Christ in its fullness and comprehensiveness. It has interpreted the scriptural "not of the world" as if it meant "outside the world" or as if it gave Christians the freedom or licence to act in the world as they pleased.

It is one of the great gifts which God has given to us in our time that we see more clearly that our Lord is Priest, Prophet and King and that His actual Lordship, which we do not see, but recognise in faith, must be proclaimed in every realm of life.

(2) To render witness in the political realm does not mean merely that the Christian as citizen or as statesman defends the personal Christian virtues such as honesty, equity, incorruptibility, but also that he seeks to evaluate the structures of society in the light of the Gospel of Christ, to oppose such structures as embody injustice and to work for a transformation of society so that men may be able to fulfill their entire calling as responsible creatures of God for whom Christ died.

This again seems to be obvious. But in fact the Church has so largely concentrated on the ethics of personal life and personal relations, that it has given the impression that the structures are either sacrosanct or immaterial. We owe it largely to the combined impact of national socialism and communism that the churches have at last begun, only begun, to elaborate a Christian critique of the social and political structures. It is clear that this task cannot and must not be accomplished by church administrators and theologians alone. Christian laymen have far too long waited for the professional churchman. The rediscovery of the role of the laity in our time must express itself in pioneering by layman in rethinking the social and political structures in the light of the Gospel.

(3) The Christian's armour as he enters the life of society does not consist of a code of laws, of general moral recipes or of a system of social ethics based on immutable orders of creation or on natural law.

For God has not revealed His will in the form of legal prescriptions applicable to all situations. And if we create a legal system we are in danger of obeying the system rather than God. In the history of the Christian Church such legalism has often made the Church unable to deal imaginatively and creatively with new situations. Its basic weakness is that it makes the Christian life impersonal and finally irresponsible. For if all that is asked from me is to follow a code I have no longer to decide in faith what God's will is for me here and now. Instead of a person responding to the present call of God I have become what St. Paul calls a slave of the law.

(4) The Christian task in society is to represent the divine history within the secular history. The decisions which he takes in the concrete and changing context of his daily life must be inspired by the eternal, unchanging context of God's plan as revealed in the great divine deeds recorded in the Scriptures.

In this sense the Christian ethic is a contextual ethic. The Christian lives within two contexts, that of the world and that of the history of salvation. But the decisive context is not the concrete situation in which I find myself, but the context of the divine history. To use the terminology which G. B. Shaw uses in one of his plays: "We play the small game. But the big game is played upon us." The Christian seeks to play the small game in the light of the big game.

(5) From the divine history as recorded in the Old and New Testament the Christian receives a perspective on the design of God for the world and pointers or signs as to the nature of Christian obedience in the life of society.

What he learns from God's revelation is not a precise recipe for his behaviour. What he learns is something much more important, namely how the realities of human life look "sub specie eternitatis," in the light of God's eternal will. The Deuteronomic law concerning the way to treat one's servants is not meant to be copied by a modern factory manager in his relation with the workers. But that law contains a perspective on human relations which is as valid today as it was in the times when the Book of Deuteronomy was composed. Similarly we are not expected to imitate the primitive communism of the early church described in the Acts of the Apostles, but that story has an important bearing on our understanding of the limits of the right to private property. But more important still, what we learn from the Scripture about God's dealings with men gives us an outline of the life of the new creation or new humanity, of the exemplary community, which we are called to represent in this world. That is also true of the sermon on the Mount. It does not tell us exactly how to behave in each situation. It tells us about the nature of the Kingdom to which we belong, about the quality of life, about relations between men in that Kingdom. It is, as has well been said, the Speech from the Throne, announcing the constitution of the new Kingdom. It is literally impossible to use it as a blueprint for society in our dispensation. Those who, like Tolstoi have tried to use it in such a way, have failed. But that does not mean that we can neglect that central message of our Lord, for when we follow Him we are members of the Kingdom He describes. And we must ask again and again: How must I live and act as a representative of such a King living in a world, the structure of which is so totally different from the Kingdom of God? In other words, we are never liberated from the duty to decide in each moment how we can best be true to this Kingdom within the hard realities of the old world.

To know the Will of God in a concrete situation I must do three things. First, seek to understand the full implications of my choice and decision, particularly as they affect other people. As this point I must use all the resources of knowledge and of intelligence which are available. Next, seek to discover what light the revelation concerning God's dealings with men and his design for humanity throw on the situation; at this point study of the Bible is indispensable, but a study which takes seriously the interpretation of the Scriptures in the life of the Church. Thirdly, pray for insight into God's will and readiness to obey. At this point everything depends on the reality of my faith.

(6) Christian political action is characterised by the fact that it is not influenced by utopianism or by defeatism. It is not utopian because it must consider all attempts in this world to solve the problems of society as temporary and relative solutions. It is not defeatist because it is sustained by the faith that under all circumstances it is true that work for the cause of justice and peace is not vain in the Lord.

Utopianism is dangerous because it leads to self-righteousness or ultimately to totalitarianism and because it engenders cynicism, when the utopia does not materialise. The utopian by making his ideology or socio-political dream into the measure of all things makes the relative absolute. Now since there cannot be more than one absolute, he is forced to treat the true absolute, that is the superhuman, as something merely relative. (And if the absolute as embodied in the Christian faith refuses to be relativised, the utopian becomes anti-religious). Christians see all social structures as historically conditioned answers to concrete situations. They are not equally bad or equally good. Choices must be made. But none of them is the once-for-all answer to be imposed on men everywhere.

JEAN PAUL SARTRE reports a conversation with a Soviet author who is often used as an official spokesman for communism. The author said: "On the day when communism will reign (that is to say: the welfare of all) the tragedy of man will begin: namely his finitude." That is a most remarkable admission. Here is an official advocate of Marxism who says that the ideology leaves the deepest, the essential question unanswered. But SARTRE makes a different and surprising comment: "It is not yet the time to make that discovery. The spirit, freedom, morality come afterwards. All men must become men by the improvement of their living conditions, *before* a universal ethic can be elaborated." The statement of the Russian author and the comment of SARTRE show also how a utopian ideology can lead to the putting of first things last. As if the revolt of the masses were not a fight for dignity and true freedom as well as a fight for a larger share of material goods.

But the Christian can never become a defeatist either. Just as he knows that the battle against sin in his own life is not hopeless, so he continues to fight hopefully against social sin. When all the appearances are against him, he does not become frustrated, because his point of orientation is the victory of Christ, not observable historical progress. MAX HUBER, the former President of the International Court of Justice and of the International Red Cross, was asked once whether he observed any difference between Christians and others in the life of international affairs. This was in the tragic days before the second world war when the whole fabric of international life was breaking down. He said: "Only at one point. The Christians continue to fight for peace when the situation seems hopeless. The others just give up."

(7) For Christians the criterion of social and political action is not the success of any system, any party, any national or racial or even religious group, but the common good. The crucial question is always: will this or that decision or action help or hinder men to fulfil their human calling?

Our Lord died for men and for all men. As it is put today: Christians live the life of "pro-existence." If in the course of history they have to oppose or resist the actions of any group, they do not write off their opponents as if they were the incarnation of evil; they keep their concerns and interests in mind, they do not preach hatred; they keep the way open for a solution of the conflict and for a true reconciliation.

The leadership of the "Freedom Movement" in the U.S.A., which seeks to gain for the Negroes the enjoyment of full civil rights, gives us a remarkable example of the attitude which combines realistic opposition to injustice with a positive Christian attitude to the opponent. I quote from a recent report: "In the way the movement is given expression it is clearly inspired by the vision of the new humanity in Christ. We see the Christian content even more clearly in the methods being promoted for movement towards the goals – the non-violent method of forgiving love, looking to the winning of 'the enemy' as a brother in the knowledge that each cannot be free without the other." The Church is the reconciled community which manifests the power of reconciliation over all forces which divide men from one another. Churches which instead of showing the reconciliation of the races in God and in Christ, accentuate the racial division, deny the very truth of the gospel of reconciliation.

If the Church fails to bring Christians of different nations, races and classes deeply together, it misses its opportunity to demonstrate the transforming power of the Cross, and makes it harder for the world to understand what the message of reconciliation is all about. Here lies the importance of the ecumenical movement which exists to manifest the reconciling power of the Cross.

Those who are truly reconciled can never see any man, or group of men as the total enemy, as the enemy in any full or radical sense of that word. Christ died for all. Christians can therefore never completely write off any human being.

(8) Since God deals with all men as responsible beings Christians stand for a society in which all relationships are governed by responsibility. The government must recognise that the state is not an aim in itself, but has responsibility towards that which transcends the state and it must be responsible to its citizens. The citizens must be free to act as responsible beings who are responsible for the welfare of their fellowcitizens and for the common life in society.

(a) The Christian faith with its strong emphasis on the call of God that comes to every man and that demands a personal response, is inevitably a ferment in history which tends toward the transformation of purely authoritarian and collectivistic societies into societies in which all men share as persons in the common responsibility for the common life.

(b) The ultimate responsibility of man is not towards the state but to God. States which make loyalty to the state the final norm make the state into an idol and are on the way to totalitarianism. The self-limitation of the State must find expression in its recognition that the state is not the creator, but the servant of justice and that its action must be judged in the light of norms which transcend the state. That is why it is so vitally important that the judiciary has genuine independence.

(c) Citizens must be able to participate in the common decisions affecting the life of their society. At the 1960 Cottesloe Consultation in South Africa more than 80% of the participants of the churches which were at that time members of the World Council of Churches, said rightly: "It is our conviction that the right to own land, to participate in the government of his country, is part of the dignity of the adult man, and for this reason a policy which permanently denies to non-white people the right of collaboration in the government of the country of which they are citizens cannot be justified."

No pattern of social relations, no policy with regard to race-relations can therefore be acceptable to Christians unless it is freely accepted by the major groups concerned. However good the intentions of a group in power may be; if it does not submit its plans to the judgement of those most affected, it implicitly denies that the members of those groups have the right and ability to determine their own destiny.

(d) The corollary is that the citizen accepts to be his brother's keeper, that the welfare of his fellow-citizens and of the whole society is his concern.

(9) Christians must repudiate all use of power in the spiritual realm. But they must realise that in the realm of society the use of power is inevitable and necessary.

For power resides not only in the government or in wealth, but also in the press, the trade-union, in the ballot box and in public opinion. The question is therefore not whether power is to be used, but how it is to be used.

It is often true that power corrupts and it is always true that absolute power corrupts absolutely. But power which accepts to be placed under the control of the freely accepted law and of the expressed will of the people provides its own antidote and so need not have a corrupting influence. The Christian doctrine of man does not teach that men are good and that therefore the will of the majority is good, but rather that no man, no group of men is good enough to resist the temptation inherent in uncontrolled power and that therefore the life of the state and of society can only be healthy if effective checks and balances are provided. For this reason democracy is, in spite of all its weaknesses, still the least dangerous form of government.

(10) By its very nature the Christian Church is obliged to take its stand for the poor and the oppressed and against exploitation and tyranny in all its various forms.

In the Old Testament both the prophetic voices (as in Amos) and the priestly voices (as in the Deuteronomic law) plead for justice to the underprivileged. In the New Testament St. LUKE and St. JAMES make it very clear that the poor who are blessed and who are to be defended are those who are not only poor in spirit, but also the poor "tout court." The classical words of the Magnificat are not to be interpreted in an abstract spiritualised manner:

"He has scattered the proud in the imagination of their hearts. He has put down the mighty from their thrones, and exalted those of low degree. He has filled the hungry with good things and the rich he has sent empty away."

For long periods the Christian Church has forgotten or neglected this essential part of the Christian message. But it has lived on in the witness of prophetic Christian men and women and re-awakened again and again the conscience of the Church.

It is a curious fact that Jean Calvin who has so often been portrayed as a great authoritarian and as the father of capitalism states so very clearly that the Church belongs on the side of the poor and the oppressed. He says even that the criterion by which a government should be judged is whether it deals justly with the poor (Bieler, p. 297). And he goes farther still. The sense of revolt which is born in the hearts of the oppressed comes from God. Since many followers of Calvin, but also many who dislike him, will find it difficult to believe that Calvin should have uttered such seemingly revolutionary language, which in some circles today is considered as "communistic" I will give the precise quotation. Calvin says in his commentary on Habacuc (2:6 see Bieler p. 305): "When one sees that the poor people cannot stand it any longer, but are thus violently oppressed, then everybody cries: 'How long?' And that cry, since it is natural and has its source and rule in equity, is heard by God. For what lies behind the fact that men in trouble cry out: 'How long?' That they know that such confusion and such a subversion of all order and justice cannot possibly be tolerated. *Now that sentiment and insight is given us by God.*"

That was written 300 years before there was such a thing as a social gospel. Those who in our day interpret the demand of the masses all over the world for a place in the sun of justice, as a phenomenon which has not only political and social, but also religious significance, stand in a great and, in the deepest sense, orthodox Christian tradition.

(II) Since Christians stand for justice and for the free exercise of responsibility by all men, they are called to resist injustice and oppression. When injustice and oppression are institutionalised in political or social systems this resistance may have to take the form of resistance against the authorities.

Christians know that government is God's servant for the good of man. The authorities are therefore entitled to be obedienced in everything that is just and equitable. Christians will therefore not resist authority unless it is clear that in vital matters it does not serve God's will and acts against the good of man.

This doctrine of the necessity and limits of resistance has strong credentials in church history. Calvin developed the notion of the resistance against tyranny and injustice, not by individuals, but by the "lower magistrates" chosen to represent the people. John Knox went further. When he was asked whether it was not dangerous to teach that authority could be defied, he answered: "And what harm should the commonwealth receive if the corrupt affection of ignorant rulers be moderated and bridled by the wisdom and discretion of Godly subjects so that they would not do violence to any man?" The tension between the duty of obedience to the state and the duty of resistance to the state under specific circumstances comes out most clearly in the Scottish confession of faith of 1560. It says on the one hand that such as resist the supreme power, in so far as it does that which belongs to its charge, resist God's ordinance and therefore cannot be guiltless (cap. 24). But on the other hand in its interpretation of the good works which Christians are to undertake for the sake of their neighbours it lists the repression of tyranny and the defense of the oppressed. And it adds that it is evil to suffer innocent blood to be shed, if we can prevent it (Article 14).

This puts the problem in the right setting. Resistance must never be undertaken for selfish reasons, it can only be justified, if it will help the neighbour in his need. And the criterion to avoid the shedding of innocent blood is valid for both the defender of authority and the resister.

In our time the deeply serious and responsible Christian men who took a leading part in the resistance against Hitler and the Christians in the resistance movements in the occupied countries have based their actions on the same convictions.

It is however necessary to distinguish between four forms of resistance:

There is first of all the spiritual resistance which will find expression in the prayers, the preaching, the confession of the Church or, if the Church remains passive, of spiritually sensitive minorities in the Church. This is the basic form of resistance. Where the Church does not fulfil its role as watchman and as prophetic advocate of the exploited and oppressed, resistance is bound to deteriorate into a destructive nihilism.

There is next the resistance which takes the legal form of political opposition at the points at which such opposition is still possible. Such opposition must always be positive and constructive. It must show what specific alternatives exist to the governmental policy.

Where opposition in legal forms has become impossible it may be necessary to resort to illegal means either by refusing to apply unjust laws or by organising resistance in ways which are not permitted by the law. Christians will never choose this way without serious and prayerful reflection. They will never engage in illegal activities in order to embarrass the government. They will only do it, if they become convinced that is the only way left to work against manifest injustice and the only remaining possibility to help men in deep mental or material need. And they will not complain if they have to bear the consequences as so many churchmen had to do in the years of the second world war.

There is finally the resistance by force. At this point Christians have been and are deeply divided. Calvin warned against the use of violence, but left the door open for what he called "providential saviours" called by God to overthrow unjust governments. And we know how a remarkable group of

Christians in Germany in our own century came to the conclusion that the disorder created by the government in power was worse than the harm which intervention by force would do.

It must certainly be said that the difference between violent and non-violent resistance is not as absolute as the radical pacifists make it out to be. Both are forms of pressure or rather counterpressure. Both are ethically dangerous in that they make use of power and the use of power is never wholly pure. But it must be added that violence has its own specific momentum, in that it breeds more violence. Violence between national, social and racial groups generally creates such a deep chasm between such groups that it becomes almost impossible to arrive at any form of peaceful co-existence. The deepest separation between peoples is that of a river of blood. We cannot absolutely exclude the possibility that in certain situations Christians may have to participate in violent resistance, but we must insist that they should never do so when they have not counted the heavy cost and become convinced that this is the one and only possibility to serve the cause of justice. In most situations there exist far more possibilities for non-violent resistance than most people realise. There are the basic forms of resistance on which all other forms of resistance depend, that is the spreading through systematic education, training and positive propaganda of the basic concepts about man, about human relations, about society, about politics which give a real content to the will for the transformation of society. And if it is asked whether this is really possible under governments which have the latest techniques of police surveillance, I say that it has been abundantly proved that it is possible to develop an equally perfected technique in the realm of underground literature and periodicals and the preparation of the masses for a new day. During the struggle against national socialism ordinary people, not only young men, but also old ladies, suddenly developed an amazing ability for spreading remarkable and constructive underground press which did so much to build morale in those years and in helping people who were in danger. But it takes imaginative thinking and action to find such possibilities. And it requires much patient spiritual preparation.

It is inevitable that in this delicate matter Christians will not all take the same decisions. For they will not all agree in their analysis of the concrete situation. And we may go further. It is by no means certain that all have the same task and receive exactly the same divine commandment. There is a variety of callings. But two things are clear. No one who is not himself in the concrete situation in which the decision must be taken, can tell those inside what their duty is. And if it does happen that Christians within the same situation come after serious reflection and prayer to differing conclusions about their duty, they must not judge each other, but maintain their fellowship.

(12) In our day and generation it is necessary to choose between two

world views, the one according to which the civilisation dominated by the white race must hold the fort and defend its interests at whatever costs against the other races; the other according to which the world must now become a multi-racial international society with equality of opportunity for all.

Such a moment represents a "disclosure-situation," a time when we are to learn something decisive about the will of God for man. The ecumenical movement has definitely chosen for the second world view. It does not stand for the defense of a particular civilisation, e.g. a white, Western and so-called Christian civilisation. The Oxford Conference of 1937 spoke of the unrealistic and mistaken view that the Churches should seek to maintain as much as possible of the old ideal of the Corpus Christianum and of the privileges and authority which that implies. And since 1937 it has become increasingly clear to church leaders all over the world that the defense by political means of a Christian civilisation, which means in practice the defense of the interests of racial or social groups considered as the bearers of that civilisation, is not only spiritually wrong, but also strategically self-defeating. The identification of Christianity with privileged classes or races is surely the strongest and most effective argument of anti-Christian propaganda and closes more doors for mission and evangelism than any other factor.

The ecumenical movement has chosen positively for the multiracial world society because there is an inescapable analogy between the truly ecumenical church in which all nations and races are at home and make their full contribution and a world society which gives equal room and space and opportunity to all nations and races. By its very nature the ecumenical movement rejects all forms of racial or national narcissism and refuses to recognise any claims to racial or national superiority.

(13) In relation to the issue of race-relations, the churches in the countries where that issue is now the crucial problem of the present and of the future are "in statu confessionis," that is to say their integrity as representatives of the new humanity and as bearers of the divine word of righteousness and reconciliation, in short their obedience to their Lord, are at stake.

They must become confessing churches, churches concentrating on the particular confession or witness demanded in this hour of decision, until the offense of racial discrimination is removed in church and society. And if the official churches are not ready for this and remain mute or even support the system of a privileged race, then groups within the churches have to be formed which will accept the task of making the concrete confession within the church and for the church. Such pioneering groups within the official churches are not created in order to break up the existing churches. They accept provisionally the vicarious role of doing what the official church cannot or will not yet do. In this they must be able to count on the full support of the Christian community in all other countries. Because the race problem is a world problem in which all churches have been and are involved by action or inaction and also since we have been made aware of the cohesion of the cause of Christ and the solidarity of the churches *all* churches in the world share in the responsibility to render a clear witness in this respect.

A confessing church is a prophetic church. It does not say to its members and to the nation in which it lives: this question of race belongs to the political sphere and in that sphere many different choices are possible and the church leaves its members completely free to take whatever attitude they feel bound to take. A confessing Church speaks with regard to the decisive issue of the hour in the language: "Thus saith the Lord." It will say this with regard to the essential choice, not with regard to technical applications. The essentials are: the recognition of the fellow-man as a responsible human being, the recognition of his right to have his full share in the determination of the common destiny of the nation, the rejection of the racial criterion as a decisive criterion for human relations, the demand for true human solidarity and social justice, the calling to the ministry of reconciliation. On those matters the church dare no longer say: "Maybe" or "These are matters of private judgement," but it must speak humbly, but with unmistakable clarity, the language of confession – stating on the basis of God's revelation in Holy Scripture the divine commandment for this hour is clear and that therefore Christians must say individually and together: "Here I stand, I can do no other."

Does this mean that in certain circumstances the Church should advocate resistance to the established authorities? In the light of the experience of the last decades in Europe the answer is that the only resistance which the church actually advocates is a spiritual resistance. The Church resists a heretical ideology or a non-Christian or sub-Christian conception of man, but it does so by its positive witness in preaching and teaching. If this brings it into conflict with the government, it accepts the consequences without bitterness, because it has been warned that this is what the church should expect in the world.

On the other hand, the church should never advocate political resistance, whether violent or non-violent against a specific government, because that is not the role of the church. To propagate political resistance against a specific state would mean that the church has become tantamount to a political party. The issue of the right or even the duty of resistance to the authorities is one which Christians individually or in groups must answer for themselves in each concrete situation. They should analyse the position in their country, ask themselves whether it is really clear that there is no other way to reach the objectives which Christians most pursue, except the method of direct resistance, listen to the voices from the past, learn from the experiences of Christians in other countries, seek to measure the consequences which their choice may have and finally decide with prayer for enlightenment and courage.

In this, as in all other realms of life, we must then learn to accept our responsibility as Christians, who cannot endorse that responsibility over to others; Christians who do not live under the law but in the freedom with which Christ has made us free, but at the same time bound us to Himself.

Some Notes on War and Peace Research

by

M. JANE STROUP

(The following notes are from a book in progress entitled *The Gates of Janus:* A Guide to the Study of War and Peace)

In the face of the so-called "knowledge explosion," it has become increasingly difficult, if it were ever possible, for one individual interested in a specific problem to attempt to find out what others have thought, or what others are currently thinking, before he makes his own effort to contribute.

If one were at leisure to pursue the vast literature on war and peace, one might well start with the *Great Books*, and using their excellent Syntopicon as a guide, follow the thoughts of the many poets, dramatists, historians and philosophers who have written on man, his nature and his problems in a language, if not more illuminating, generally more pleasing, than the language of modern social scientists.

Such a perusal would lead one to discover some of what might be called the "classic" literature on war and peace. For example: the poetry of HOMER and VIRGIL; the plays of AESCHYLUS, EURIPIDES and ARISTOPHANES; the histories of THUCYDIDES, HERODOTUS and GIBBON, and the philosophies of PLATO and ARISTOTLE. In addition: the writings of such men as KANT, HOBBES, LOCKE, HEGEL, AUGUSTINE, ROUSSEAU, AQUINAS and MILL; MARX and ENGLES; the Federalists; MACHIAVELLI's *The Prince*, TOLSTOY's *War and Peace*, and FREUD's *War and Death* and *Civilization and Its Discontents*.

One might also wish to include in this category CLAUSEWITZ *On War*; the selected writings of MAO TSE TUNG; William JAMES' "*The Moral Equivalent of War*," and the exchange of letters between FREUD and EINSTEIN entitled "*Why War?*"

Much of this classic literature on war and peace is based on two assumptions; one, that war is inevitable, i.e. bound to occur although for a variety of reasons: and two, justifiable as the only possible method of resolving international conflicts. While one finds here considerable evidence of war's folly and futility, one finds also considerable support for the necessity, and even the desirability, of war.

Although the mutilated body of a soldier must have looked as horrible to an ancient warrior as it does to his modern counterpart, it appears that the scope and devastation of World War I provoked the first broad efforts to seriously seek out the causes of war in the hope and expectation that the discovery of cause would lead to the discovery of remedy. There was implicit in this concept a tendency to see war as a disease which would be cured when the cause was found and eliminated. This attitude was apparently in keeping with the growing faith of the time in the ability of science and reason to contribute to unending progress in the solution of man's social problems. Thus there exists a vast "causes of war" literature which ranges between two extremes: a seemingly endless listing of probable causes of war, and stout declarations that there is only one cause of war.

Causes frequently cited were classified as psychological, economic, political, social or cultural, religious, moral and dynastic; motivating factors frequently mentioned included fear, anxiety, hate, aggression and the desire for domination and power. To eliminate the causes of war as they were often presented in this early research, seemed to mean the elimination of most of mankind's social activities, if not the elimination of man himself.

Both the values and the defects of this "causes of war" literature were inherited by the developing social sciences as they began to increase their research on problems of war and peace.

One of the earliest and most comprehensive efforts to survey what the various scholarly disciplines had to contribute to the subject, was a project initiated in 1927 by the Social Science Research Committee at the University of Chicago, under the direction of Quincy WRIGHT. It began with members of the departments of political science, economics, history, sociology, anthropology, psychology, geography and philosophy meeting together to discuss topics for research on the causes of war, and it culminated in a two-volume work, published in 1942, entitled *A Study of War*. One conclusion reached by WRIGHT was that while each of the disciplines had considered the problem, there had not been developed a logical analysis of the subject acceptable to the scholars within the various disciplines, much less to those in related disciplines.

World War II tended to interrupt such research as had been instigated on the general subject of war and peace, but the various disciplines continued to press forward on research in areas that seemed relevant; such as aggression, hostility, group dynamics, prejudice, attitudes, opinions, semantics and inter-group relations.

The establishment of the United Nations in 1945, and more specifically, the establishment of the United Nations Educational, Scientific and Cultural Organization, gave a renewed impetus to research into what WRIGHT once termed the causes of war and the conditions of peace. In 1947, UNESCO adopted a "Tensions" project, in an effort to encourage social scientists in every country to work together on the investigation of the psychological and social bases of peace. In 1950, a volume entitled *Tensions That Cause Wars* was produced, and in 1957, UNESCO published *The Nature of Conflict:* Studies on the Sociological Aspects of International Tensions.

In 1952, the formation of a group of psychologists concerned with research on problems of war and peace was suggested by several members of the American Psychological Association, and this group subsequently met and organized the Research Exchange on the Prevention of War. The primary purpose of the organization was to provide a means of communication among interested individuals, and to this end it commenced publication of the *Bulletin of the Research Exchange on the Prevention of War*. The first issue of the *Bulletin* appeared in November 1952, and it ceased publication in November 1956 because of the contemplated publication of a new journal, but this modest effort was, in a very real sense, the birth of a vital exchange among the disciplines imperative to the search for a meaningful analysis of the phenomenon of war.

The new journal, which appeared in March 1957, was the *Journal of Conflict Resolution*. The proposal for this journal was first developed at the Center for Advanced Studies in the Behavioral Sciences in 1955, and the editors put forth two compelling reasons for the venture: the threat to mankind of global war, and the need to make the study of international relations an interdisciplinary enterprise.

The monumental task of organizing and analyzing the vast material on the causes of war was brilliantly undertaken by Kenneth WALTZ in a book published in 1959 called *Man, the State and War*. In it he observes that the answers to the question of where the causes of war are to be found are bewildering, both in their variety and in their contradictory qualities, and he proceeds to develop and discuss the following three images: the causes of war are to be found in the nature and behavior of man: the causes of war are to be found in the internal organization of states; the causes of war are to be found in the anarchic state system. In so doing, he not only considers the nature of cause, but carefully examines the many cures that have been advanced, and discusses the difficulties involved in effecting change even if one assumes one knows what needs to be changed.

The renewed impetus of the 1950's to undertake war and peace research produced considerable controversy over the contribution to be made to such study by each of the many disciplines concerned. The behavioral scientists charged that the political scientists had ignored their findings in the area of psychology, social psychology and cultural anthropology, and the political scientists charged that the behavioral scientists did not adequately comprehend the significance of the political framework of international relations. Into this arena came the economists, charging that every body had ignored the important models of conflict which arise out of economic theory. The concept of conflict began to emerge as a focal point for interdisciplinary communication on the problem of war and peace.

Needless to say, the concept of conflict was not new, but the effort to examine war as merely another example of a social process that had already been studied in considerable depth by people in many fields seemed at least a minor "breakthrough". It appeared to provide a reciprocal arrangement whereby the study of conflict in general could contribute to the study of war, and the study of war could, in turn, contribute to the study of other forms of conflict. It further implied that methods of analyzing conflict and methods of resolving conflict in one area might be transferable, or at least applicable, to other areas.

The chapter by Jessie BERNARD on "The Sociological Study of Conflict," in the previously mentioned book, *The Nature of Conflict*, provides an excellent guide to research in this area, and the volume itself contains a useful and well organized bibliography. BERNARD cites the existence of two rather basically different conceptualizations of social conflict. One is social-psychological and sees conflict as essentially nonrational; the other is sociological and sees conflict as often quite rational.

Another work of interest is Lewis COSER's *The Functions of Social Conflict*, published the same year (1957) and based, in part, on the theories of Georg SIMMEL. Recent emphasis on the constructive aspects of social conflict tends to give a more realistic picture of the phenomenon than did some early research which concentrated wholly on its destructive aspects.

My own search for methods of analyzing social conflict and social conflict situations in the area of international relations (undertaken in connection with a doctoral dissertation completed in 1962) led me to set up the following eight categories:

(1) The methods of history
(2) The political analysis of international conflict
(3) The case study method
(4) Kurt LEWIN and field theory
(5) Conflict episode analysis (as originated by Dr. H. Harry GILES, New York University)
(6) Economic theory and models of conflict
(7) Decision-making theory
(8) Game theory

Exploration of these methods revealed that there has been considerable concern over the formulation of theory in the fields of political science, economics and international relations, but relatively little concern with the development of methods of analyzing specific interstate conflict situations.

The purposes of current research were discovered to be as follows:

THEORY

A. To formulate a theory of social conflict applicable to all social conflict, including social conflict in international relations.

B. To formulate a theory of international relations or politics. This would presumably cover all interstate interaction, cooperative and conflictful.

Both have as their purpose the organization of existing data in order to make predictions concerning future data.

CASE ANALYSIS

A. To develop more adequate methods of analyzing specific social conflict situations in the area of international relations:

(1) in order to find practicable solutions to immediate international disputes;

(2) in order to formulate practicable foreign policy solutions to pending or potential international disputes;

(3) in order to develop a method of analysis which will make possible the comparison and classification of cases:

(*a*) in order to test theoretical hypotheses against facts;

(*b*) in order to derive principles regarding the nature and treatment of social conflict;

(*c*) in order to be able to make predictions on the basis of a typology of conflicts.

RELATION OF THEORY TO CASE ANALYSIS

A. To bring together the theoretical and empirical approaches in a more fruitful way:

(1) in order to avoid theorizing that is abstract and bears no relation to empirical data;

(2) in order to provide a theoretical framework which makes possible the selecting and relating of relevant empirical data.

Thus it appeared that although research activity in this area has been diversified and largely uncoordinated, it does have a common concern – the desire to be able to predict; and this in turn is related to the desire to make the study of social conflict and the study of international relations more scientific.

A considerable literature now exists on game theory, decision-making theory, and economic theory and models of conflict. While much of it is still to be found in professional journals, several books are representative: Morton Kaplan, *System and Process in International Politics*, 1957; Thomas C. Schelling, *The Strategy of Conflict*, 1960; Richard Snyder et al., *Foreign Policy Decision-Making*, 1962; and Kenneth Boulding, *Conflict and Defense*, 1962.

The increasing use of advanced mathematics by social scientists is a source of excitement to some and frustration to others who are finding it more and more difficult to understand much of the more recent research. One can only observe that this is a problem of the computer age not limited to the area of social science. Some assistance may be found in a book by James S. Coleman, *Introduction to Mathematical Sociology*, 1964.

Kenneth Boulding, in a Memorandum on Organization for the Advancement of Peace Research and International Studies (dated 3/17/65), suggests that four movements, intersecting and with overlapping personnel, may now be identified. They are as follows:

(1) The Conflict Studies Movement (The study of conflict as an abstract system)
(2) The International Studies Movement (The study of the international system)
(3) The Peace Research Movement (as distinct from the peace movement)
(4) National Security Research.

What has been discussed to this point is primarily pure research and as such is concerned with the first two movements. Much of the material relating to them is to be found in the professional journals of such fields as economics, sociology, psychology, social psychology, anthropology, psychiatry, political science, history and international relations, and in unpublished doctoral dissertations, generally available on microfilm. In addition, there are many interdisciplinary journals such as; *The Journal of Social Issues*, *Social Problems*, *The Journal of Educational Sociology*, now *Sociology of Education*, UNESCO's *International Social Science Bulletin*, the Carnegie Endowment's *International Conciliation*, and the previously mentioned *Journal of Conflict Resolution*. Three publications which serve as guides to current material are *Current Thought on War and Peace*, *War/Peace Report*, and the *Peace Research Abstracts Journal*.

Information may also be obtained from several organizations established to do or to support research on war and peace: e.g. The Center for Conflict Resolution, University of Michigan; The Committee on Research in International Conflict, Washington University, St. Louis; The Institute of War and Peace Studies, Columbia University; The Institute for Social Research, Oslo, Canadian Peace Research Institute, and the recently formed International Peace Research Association. The Carnegie Endowment for International Peace and the Peace Research Committee of the Institute for International Order, both in New York, also promote valuable related research.

In addition, as a result of the increased interest in war and peace literature in general, many earlier works have been brought forth in new editions, and numerous collections of essays, articles and conference papers have appeared. Two recent examples are *War: Studies from Psychology, Sociology and Anthropology*, 1964, and *International Conflict and Behavioral Science:* The Craigville Papers, 1964.

It is easy to become impatient with great thoughts on war and peace, and with pure and theoretical research on conflict and the international system. The threat of thermo-nuclear war is here and now, and the eternal paradox of disarmament looms larger than ever. How can we retreat from the brink?

National Security Research, as defined by BOULDING, is financed out of national defense budgets and puts a high priority on national power, national defense and survival. The RAND Corporation and the Hudson Institute are examples of research organizations in this area. Herman KAHN's book, *Thinking About the Unthinkable*, 1962, perhaps best reflects the premises on which such research is based, one of which is the ancient maxim that to have peace you must prepare for war. Once prepared, the weapons of war can be utilized through processes of threat and bargaining to deter war. To many this armed truce seems a regrettable but necessary position in a world that has found no new or better solution to international conflict than the use of force.

Among those most apt to be distressed by this position are the pacifists, some of whom are to be found in the peace movement, who oppose all war and all killing on the ground that it is immoral. There exists a considerable literature on pacifism and nonviolence, a recent work is entitled

Instead of Violence: Writings by the Great Advocates of Peace and Nonviolence Throughout History, and under certain circumstances nonviolence has proved an effective strategy. Pacifism has been attacked as an attitude or posture which encourages aggression, and as a ready tool for those who wish to pursue aggression. It is perhaps less a strategy than a moral position, difficult for many to sustain when pushed to its ultimate conclusion – peace at any price.

The serious question arises, is war caused by "evil" men and "evil" states, or does it arise from a faulty system which traps good and evil alike? To many it seems to be growing increasingly evident that the primary cause of war is the existence of separate, sovereign states, of whatever persuasion (see e.g. John STRACHEY, *The Challenge of Democracy*) in a world that has not provided any means of resolving international conflicts except the use of national force.

If this is indeed true, and it is certainly not a new idea, the problem which still exists is what can be done about it. The solution, as is so often the case in human affairs, raises more questions than it answers. Among them are questions of domestic and foreign policy, of disarmament and arms control, and the difficult and delicate problems of designing a world government based on world law and rendered effective through the utilization of some form of world police.

The Peace Research Movement, as BOULDING describes it, is essentially a movement in applied social science and is primarily concerned with the application of such knowledge as we now have to these difficult problems. It seeks in effect to know what specific policies will be effective.

What domestic and foreign policies are conducive to world peace? The answers to this question are as bewildering in their variety and as contradictory in their qualities as are the answers to the question of what causes war, to which they are, indeed, closely related. The feeling that the power to make war, regardless of the form of government, may rest in the hands of a relatively small but powerful policy-making elite, has prompted research on the decisionmakers and on the decision-making process. Early studies in this area were often concerned with what values *should* govern policy makers. Recent efforts to study foreign policy decision-making tend to stress what values *do* govern them and *how* they do. The Foreign Policy Association and the Council on Foreign Relations, both in New York, and the Brookings Institution in Washington, D.C., are sources of information, as is a work edited by James ROSENAU entitled *International Politics and Foreign Policy*, 1961.

The Peace Research Institute in Washington, D.C., which has transferred its resources to the new Institute for Policy Studies, is another important organization concerned with research on problems of public policy related to peace, and with the application of such research. Arthur WASKOW's book, *The Worried Man's Guide to World Peace* 1963, is an excellent and comprehensive guide for the peace researcher as well as the "peace actionist" to whom it is addressed.

Disarmament is felt by many to be the first step needed toward rendering the world more peaceful, but even to those who feel this way, the dangers of disarmament in a condition of international anarchy are apparent. The Office of Disarmament in the Defense Department, and the more recently created Arms Control and Disarmament Agency in the State Department, are two government organizations concerned with technical and political problems of disarmament. In addition, the Institute for Arms Control and Peace Research in Ann Arbor, Michigan, which publishes the *Journal of Arms Control*, is devoted to research on arms control and to research on the social, political and economic consequences of disarmament.

The question of arms control and disarmament is, of course, closely tied to the question of what can be substituted for the use of force in international affairs. Over the years, many proposals have been put forth for some form of effective world organization. The Covenant of the League of Nations, the Charter of the United Nations, and a volume by CLARK & SOHN called *World Peace Through World Law*, are three notable examples. The assumption that all nations, threatened as they are with the possibility of nuclear extinction, want to search for a way of resolving conflicts without resort to arms may be erroneous, but assuming that they do, what kind of world organization might be designed to provide both acceptable laws and an acceptable method of enforcing them.

Certainly there exist within the history of some nations, and within the history of the United Nations, some clues as to directions which might be taken. But, again, assuming that one envisions the desired end design, the question that MILLIS raises of "how do we get from here to there" remains. Mr. MILLIS' latest book, *An End to Arms*, provides some provocative thinking on the subject, and a hopeful note on which to conclude.

REFERENCES

BERNARD, JESSIE, T. H. PEAR, RAYMOND ARON & ROBERT C. ANGELL, The Nature of Conflict. New York: UNESCO, 1957.

BOULDING, KENNETH, Conflict and Defense. New York: Harper and Brothers. 1962.

— , Memorandum on Organization for the Advancement of Peace Research and International Studies (Mimeo. 3/17/65) University of Michigan, Ann Arbor, Michigan.

BRAMSON, LEON & GEORGE GOETHALS (eds.), War: Studies From Psychology, Sociology and Anthropology. New York: Basic Books, 1964.

CANTRIL, HADLEY (ed.), Tensions That Cause Wars. Urbana, Ill.: University of Illinois Press, 1950.

Some of this material previously appeared in an article entitled "Problems of Research on Social Conflict in the Area of International Relations," *The Journal of Conflict Resolution*, Vol. 9, No. 3, September, 1965, pp. 413–417.

CLARK, GRENVILLE & LOUIS B. SOHN, World Peace Through World Law. (2nd ed. rev.) Cambridge: Harvard University Press, 1960.

CLAUSEWITZ, CARL VON, On War. New York: E.P. Dutton and Co., 1940.

COSER, LEWIS, The Functions of Social Conflict. Glencoe, Ill.: Free Press, 1957.

COLEMAN, JAMES S., Introduction to Mathematical Sociology. Glencoe, Ill.: Free Press, 1964

EINSTEIN, ALBERT & SIGMUND FREUD, "Why War?," Readings in World Politics (Vol. I). Chicago: American Foundation for Political Education, 1951.

Encyclopaedia Britannica, Inc. Great Books of the Western World (54 vols.), 1952.

FISHER, ROGER (ed.), International Conflict and Behavioral Science: The Craigville Papers. New York: Basic Books, 1964.

JAMES, WILLIAM, The Moral Equivalent of War, *The Popular Science Monthly* (October, 1910), pp. *400–410*.

KAHN, HERMAN, Thinking About the Unthinkable. New York: Horizon Press, 1962.

KAPLAN, MORTON, System and Process in International Politics. New York: John Wiley and Sons, 1957.

MAO, TSE–TUNG, Selected Works. London: Lawrence and Wishart, Ltd., 1954.

MILLIS, WALTER, An End to Arms. New York: Atheneum, 1965.

ROSENAU, JAMES, N. (ed.), International Politics and Foreign Policy. New York: Free Press of Glencoe, Inc., 1961.

SCHELLING, THOMAS C., The Strategy of Conflict. Cambridge: Harvard University Press, 1960.

SNYDER, RICHARD, H. W. BRUCK & B. SAPIN (eds.), Foreign Policy Decision-Making. Glencoe, Ill.: Free Press, 1962.

STRACHEY, JOHN, The Challenge of Democracy (1963). As reprinted in The Great Ideas Today. Chicago: Encyclopaedia Britannica, Inc., 1965. pp. *524–589*.

STROUP, M. JANE, A Comparative and Critical Examination of Methods of Analyzing Social Conflict Situations in the Area of International Relations. Unpublished doctoal dissertation, New York University, New York, 1962.

WALTZ, KENNETH N., Man, the State and War. New York: Columbia University Press, 1959.

WASKOW, ARTHUR, The Worried Man's Guide to World Peace. New York: Doubleday and Co., Inc., 1963.

WEINBERG, ARTHUR AND LILA (eds.), Instead of Violence: Writings by the Great Advocates of Peace and Nonviolence Throughout History. New York: Grossman, 1963.

WRIGHT, QUINCY. A Study of War. (2 vols.) Chicago: The University of Chicago Press, 1942.

Toward a Theory of the Dynamics of Conflict

by

ROGER L. SISSON & RUSSELL L. ACKOFF
Management Science Center, University of Pennsylvania, Philadelphia

BACKGROUND

The purpose of the research [1] reported herein is to develop quantitative theories of escalation and de-escalation of conflict. This research, although emphasizing theory, is grounded in the basic needs of practicing foreign-policy makers. The potential value of an adequate theory to a practitioner is that it predicts the consequences of a contemplated policy. A more powerful theory tells him more precisely when and what actions to take in order to affect its outcome in a desired direction. For example, modern economic theory permits the U.S. Treasury and the Federal Reserve Board to predict the effect of various monetary and tax policies and to determine when to take fiscal and monetary action, so as to at least partially control economic conditions. The ultimate goal of this research is to develop a theory which will provide similar guidance to statesmen who can affect international conflict situations by diplomatic, trade and military action.

More specifically the goal of this research is to help achieve a better understanding of the basic processes of escalation, de-escalation and control of conflicts between large groups through systems-oriented, quantitative techniques.

Before even partial control of conflict situations can be achieved, theories which *predict* the effects of changes in policy are needed. Thus, the initial goal of the research is to formulate a quantitative theory which will

A paper presented at the 3rd North American Peace Research Conference, Peace Research Society (International) University of Pennsylvania Philadelphia, Pennsylvania, U.S.A. November 16, 1965

To be published in *Papers*, Peace Research Society (International), Vol. 5, 1966. Permission to reproduce this paper granted by the Editors.

1. This research is sponsored by the United States Arms Control and Disarmament Agency.

predict the occurrence and intensity of escalation and de-escalation phenomena as a function of policy decisions.

The development of a quantitative theory of escalation and de-escalation is a complicated task. Such an effort follows centuries of efforts to understand conflict – largely, however, by non-quantitative approaches. The research team for this project, therefore, felt it necessary to devote considerable attention to the formulation of a sound methodological approach to quantitative and systems-oriented research on such a well-studied and complex phenomenon. The approach is summarized in this paper and is exemplified by the results reported.

Nature and Measures of Conflict

Detailed definitions and measures of conflict are provided in Appendix I. A brief summary of this discussion is presented here.

One party, A, is in *conflict* with another, B, if A affects the outcome of B's behavior and the value of this outcome to B is less than that of the outcome that would have occurred if B had not affected it. If the value of the outcome to B is increased because of A's intervention, A is *cooperating* with B.

The degree of A's cooperation with B is the difference between the values to B of the outcomes "with" and "without" A's intervention, if this difference is positive; if it is negative, it is a measure of the *degree* of A's conflict with B. Thus conflict is the negative of cooperation. These concepts are presented formally in Appendix I.

Conflict and cooperation are not necessarily symmetrical: A may conflict with B while B cooperates with A, or they may conflict or cooperate with each other in different degrees. The difference between the degree of A's conflict (or cooperation) with B, and B's conflict (or cooperation) with A, is a measure of the amount of the *degree of exploitation* in the interaction.

There is nothing in this definition of conflict or cooperation that requires that either party be aware or conscious of the conflict. Hence, the emergence and increase of awareness of a previously undetected but existing conflict may be a major factor in its escalation.

When we consider continued interaction of two or more parties, another dimension of conflict becomes relevant. Each action of each party can be classified as conflicting, cooperating, or independent.

The percentage (i.e., relative frequency) of acts that are conflicting (or cooperative) is a measure of the *propensity* for the conflict (or cooperation).

Escalation of conflict occurs when there is an increase in either the degree of, intensity of or propensity for conflict. Hence, escalation is a three-dimensional concept. This multidimensionality is a cause of much confusion in its common usage because the intensity and degree of conflict may move in opposite directions, and hence be perceived differently by different observers. It will be observed in later discussion that these two measures have been kept separate in the conceptual and experimental work reported herein.

Measurement of the degree of conflict requires measuring the relative value or utility of possible outcomes of action. Although our ability to make such measures has increased significantly in recent years (see FISHBURN, 1965), it remains a difficult and costly type of measurement. For this reason differences in value of outcomes are usually indirectly measured by using some more-easily measured property of outcomes; for example, *gain or loss* expressed in monetary units. Such substitution can be shown to be justified if certain assumptions concerning the utility of monetary units (or other units used) are valid; for example, if the utility of money is a linearly increasing function of the amount of money. In using a substitute measure of the value of outcomes, as we do in our experiments, we must continually be aware of and justify the value assumptions which justify their use.

Some possible indicators of *loss* which have been used in the literature are given below. An increase in one or more of these indicators is often considered an indirect measure of escalation.

(1) Overt destruction in process or not (a two-value indicator).

(2) The monetary value of resources (materials and men) contributing to the creation of destructive systems plus the overt losses. (RICHARDSON uses a measure similar to this).

(3) The total destructive power of weapons capable of hitting a geographic area under question, (this seems to be the implied indicator when the phrase "escalation" is used in reference to such conflicts as Viet Nam).

(4) A related indicator would be the average destructive power over the area.

(5) A discontinuous indicator which indicates the state of the situation (similar to KAHN's definition), might take this form; possible states are:

- no weapons exist (in the area)
- weapons exist but not operative
- weapons in position and operative
- sporadic weapon use
- continuous weapon use
- complete mobilization

(further states can be defined by increasing the power of the weapons; the destructive power per unit of resource used to create the weapons)

- nuclear war

In the experimental situations used in this research, we have used these as indicators: the total losses of resources to all parties, the relative frequency of cooperative moves, the pattern of resource losses to each party.

A goal of the research is to predict increases and decreases in loss-indicators, such as these.

The Methodology Developed

The problem, in summation, is one of determining how to control large-scale social conflicts such as hot and cold wars, strikes, and racial and religious uprisings. Such control requires understanding of the dynamics–that is, the escalation and de-escalation of social conflict.

This type of conflict cannot be brought into the laboratory for experimentation. Nor can we experiment on these conflicts in their natural environment because either we do not have the right or capability of intervening, or, if we do, we cannot run the risk of intensifying such conflict by experimental manipulation. We cannot perform quantitative analyses on past conflicts, since histories and descriptions of these conflicts have not been maintained in a quantitative form. Available data are not of a type that permits us to find dynamic regularities or consistent causal principles in past conflicts.

In one sense, then, the researcher into the dynamics of large-scale social conflict is in the same kind of situation as was the astronomer in the early days of his inquiries; the system he studied seemed to be infinitely complex and yet incapable of being experimented upon. In astronomy, however, it was possible eventually to develop mathematical representations (models) of the system under study and to analyze them or to conduct experiments on the models (simulate).

In order to proceed as the astronomer has, however, it is first necessary to have precise, accurate, quantitative descriptions of the system under study. NEWTON's work depended upon KEPLER's, and KEPLER's upon BRAHE's. Without BRAHE's detailed and fastidious accumulation of relevant facts, Keplerian laws and the Newtonian theory could not have been developed. The required quantative descriptions are not yet available in the area of large-scale social conflict. Most of the attempts at description of such conflicts are so value-loaded that they are better described as editorials. Different observers seldom come up with the same set of facts. One could, therefore, legitimately start to create a science of the dynamics of large-scale social conflict by trying to develop accurate descriptions of real conflicts. This, however, is not the only method open to science. We have developed an alternative method in which the problem of preparing quantitative descriptions of real conflicts is postponed.

There has already been extensive study of conflict. This work falls into three classes. The first involves study of very small groups in laboratory situations. Such work is exemplified by the researchers of Anatol RAPOPORT on very simple two-person (Prisoner's Dilemma) conflict games (1965). RAPOPORT has succeeded in developing a mathematical model, a theory, which explains play of a particular simple conflict game. But, as he recognizes, he cannot legitimately draw inference from his highly controlled but simple conflict situations to the very complex uncontrolled ones found in reality. He can only use his work to provide what he calls "insights" into real large-scale social conflicts (1960 and 1965). This is not a meagre accomplishment by any means. However, if we can learn how to infer from conflict situations that can be studied in the laboratory to real situations, the possibility of developing a scientific theory that applies to the dynamics of real conflicts is considerably enhanced.

A second approach to the study of large-scale social conflicts involves the use of relatively complex experimental situations such as international political games where correspondence to reality is less difficult to establish but where precise quantitative analysis and explanation of behavior is extremely difficult. Such an approach is exemplified in the work of Harold GUETZKOW (1963) and BLOOMFIELD (1965).

A third approach involves analysis of real conflict situations. These either involve the traditional form of historical analysis, or more recently developed techniques of content analysis of communications between conflicting parties, or regression analysis of political, social, and economic variables. Such analyses have not yet produced a body of scientific knowledge, only hypotheses and conjectures which are frequently internally inconsistent. However valid some of the conclusions may be, their validity cannot be established in any objectively reproducible way. Nevertheless their relevance to the real world cannot be questioned. Exemplifying the more rigorous efforts of this type is the work done at the Foreign Policy Research Institute of the University of Pennsylvania, and the work of Yale's Dimensionality of Nations Project.

In the method that was developed for this project we tried to incorporate the strengths of each of these three approaches while excluding or minimizing their difficulties.

The method is shown schematically in Fig. 1.

First a relatively complex experimental situation (which we call an "artificial reality" or "rich game") is constructed which is the simplest one that we can conceive that satisfies the following conditions:

(1) It is rich enough to test a large number of hypotheses that have been formulated about the real phenomena under study in this case, the dynamics of large-scale social conflict. Clearly, such test cannot confirm any hypothesis, but they can define limits on the generality of hypothesis or show how they should or can be generalized. The purpose here is to design an experimental situation that is as simple as possible and yet be realistic enough so that most assertions made about real conflict are applicable to it.

(2) There must be an explicit formulation of the variables, their measures and the way in which simplification of reality has taken place, (e.g. holding a variable constant). This makes it possible to design successively enriched experimental situations, by the addition of complexities one at a time or in controlled combination.

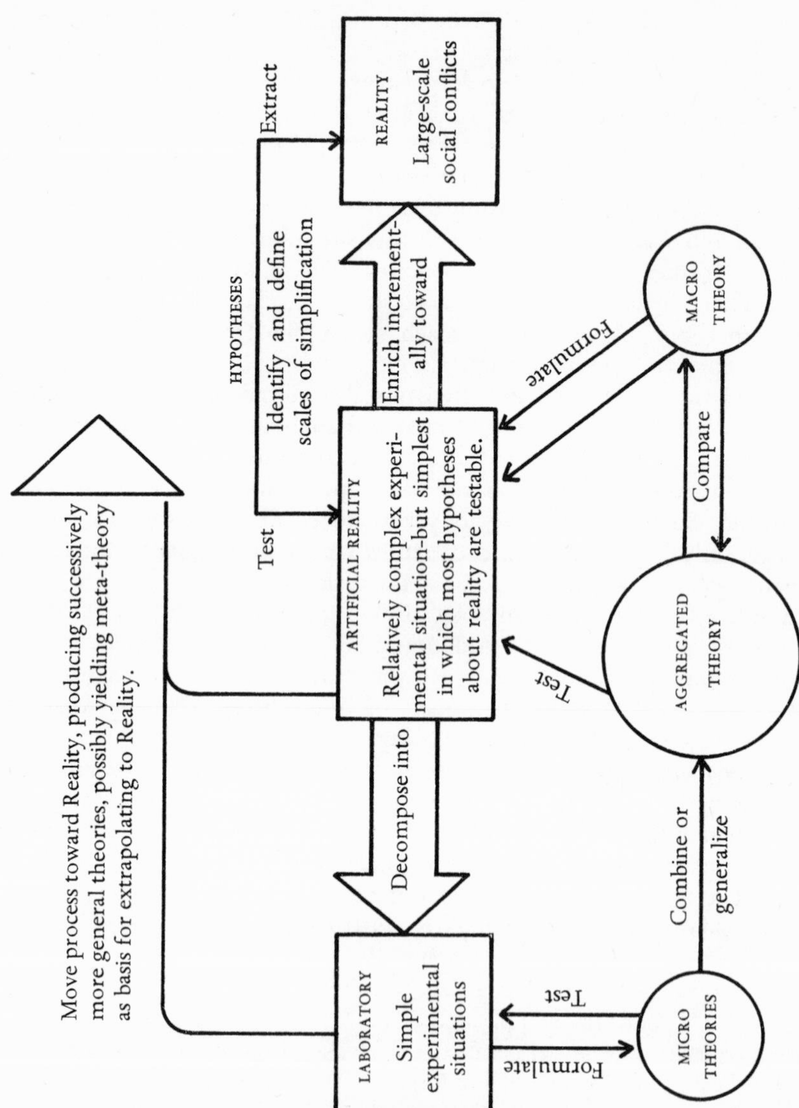

Fig. 1. Schematic diagram of methodology

(3) The relevant behavior in the experimental situation must be describable in quantitative terms.

(4) The situation must be decomposable into a set of simpler experimental situations and, where possible, these simpler situations should be ones which have already been experimented in, or closely resemble situations on which work has been done.

The experimental situation which satisfies these conditions *is not used as a model of reality, but rather as a "reality" to be modelled;* hence its name, "artificial reality". This situation is used to generate a history which is to be explained by the first theory to be constructed. The history is generated by experimentation – by playing the rich game.

Experiments are also conducted with the decomposed parts of the artificial reality, that is, with simple conflict games. Either separate "micro" theories for each of these simple games are developed, or a general "micro" theory of simple games is developed in which game characteristics enter as parameters. An effort is then made to aggregate or generalize these theories into a theory of the "artificial reality." (See lower left in Fig. 1.)

A simultaneous effort is made to formulate a "macro theory" of the "artificial reality" by direct analysis of the history which it generates. These two theoretical efforts interact until a satisfactory theory (call it T_1) is developed.

The "artificial reality" (call it S_1) is then modified in a well-defined manner in the direction of reality to provide a more realistic conflict situation S_2. Efforts are then made to generalize the earlier theory, T_1, so that it applies to S_2. The output is a more general theory T_2 of which T_1 is a special case. T_2 is tested against "history" generated by experimentation in S_2. This procedure is continued, hopefully producing a sequence of successively more general theories, $T_1, T_2, \ldots, T_n$.

As this set of theories expands it is analyzed in an effort to find principles to explain how the theories must be generalized as the "artificial reality" approaches reality. That is, a *meta-theory* is developed. The meta-theory is a procedure for producing T_{n+1} given $T_1, T_2, \ldots, T_n$, and the way in which S_{n+1} is to be an expansion of S_n. The development of such a *meta-theory* should make it possible to take larger jumps toward theories of real conflicts; hopefully to a theory applying to reality in all its complexity.

A principle benefit of the methodology is that it provides a framework for organizing and integrating diverse studies of conflict and escalation.

To accomplish such a research program we have found it useful to divide the initial research effort into three parts, each carried out by a separate (but coordinated) team.

(1) *The Reality Team* is responsible for analyses of actual, past conflicts and for the interpretation of analyses which have been made by others. This team summarizes, classifies, and provides operational translations of hypotheses. That is, it reformulates these hypotheses so that they are testable in

experimental situations. It is also this team's responsibility to identify and define the variables, and their measures, necessary and sufficient for accomplishing the operational translation of relevant hypotheses. These variables also provide the basic measures of simplification. Ability to deal explicitly with these variables is an essential requirement incorporated into the design of the "artificial reality."

(2) The *Artificial Reality Team* designs and carries out experiments in order to test the relevant hypotheses and, thereby, to generate the required "history." By analysis of these results it formulates generalizations about conflict behavior which must be accounted for by theory. It also attempts to construct a "macro" theory to explain the results which it obtains.

(3) The *Micro Team* deals with very simple experimental situations obtained by decomposing the artificial reality, or with games suggested by such decomposition. It attempts to develop a micro-theory to explain these games. Then, by generalization and aggregation of the micro-theories, it attempts to develop a theory to explain the history of the "artificial reality".

As work proceeds the tasks of the Teams will change as more effort is directed toward the development of mathematically based theories (T_1, T_2 ...) of artificial realities and of the meta-theory to explain theory generalization in the sequence of increasingly complex situations which are developed.

For the past year we have used this methodology to conduct research on the escalation and de-escalation of large-scale social conflicts. We have only taken first steps down the long path just described.

SUMMARY OF RESULTS

The Reality Team has made an extensive survey of the conflict literature and has completed its work on hypotheses analysis. After extracting a large number of vague assertions and conjectures and translating them into operational terms it was able to reduce them to a relatively small number of hypotheses. In the process more than thirty relevant variables were identified and defined. Here we cite only a few of what appear to be the more important of these variables.

(1) *Communication:* type, mode, frequency, and amount.

(2) *Technology:* the maximum capability per unit of cost of any party to inflict loss on another.

(3) *Parity:* the ratio of technology (these capabilities) among interacting parties. [An important related variable is a measure of parity at various levels of technology. This variable may be central to the military escalation process.]

(4) *Number of interaction Parties.*

(5) *Amount of Resources* available to the parties and their distribution.

(6) *International Organizational Structure* of the conflicting parties.

The first three of these variables – communication, technology, and parity

– have been studied in some detail in the research reported here, and designs for proceeding with studies of the others are well along the way.

The initial artificial reality that was developed involves two players who compete for resources. The players do not see or know each other, but in some cases they may communicate by telephone. All conservations are recorded and used in subsequent analysis. The play involves the following steps:

(1) Allocation of earned resources by each player to either a "developmental" or "military" stockpile and reallocation between stockpiles at limited rates.

(2) The selection of a strategy (i.e., cooperative or competitive in the developmental sector, and defensive or offensive in the military sector) and the choice of the amount of resources used in that strategy from the appropriate stockpile. The developmental sector consists of a prisoner's dilemma, in which payoffs are proportional to the amount invested in a play. The military sector consists of a two-by-two payoff matrix in which payoffs are proportional to the joint investments. The players can "defend" themselves against attack by investing in defense. There is a cost associated with such an investment. In an attack-defend situation the payoff depends on the difference between the amounts played. If both players attack in a move, both lose heavily. The game environment is not simple, but is completely, quantitatively defined.

(3) Payoffs are made in accordance with the joint, but independently made, choices.

(4) Communication takes place (when permitted). In open communication either part can initiate conversation (over an intercom) and the other must listen, but need not respond. With "agreed to" communication, each party can indicate to the referee that he wants to communicate, but they actually converse (over a telephone), only if both so indicate for that move. In some games, no verbal communication is allowed.

This cycle is repeated until either one player loses all of his resources, or the referee intervenes.

Twelve types of experiments have been run. These have involved three variables. each at two levels. The table shows the number of experiments run of each type.

Communication Channel

	Open		Agreed to		None	
Technology	Low	High	Low	High	Low	High
Parity = 1	5	5	10	10	10	10
Unequal Parity	5	5	10	10	10	10

Results of these experiments have been used to analyze the effects of these variables on escalation as indicated by the number of conflict choices (related to intensity of conflict) and amount of losses (related to degree of conflict) that occur in each run. The histories generated by experiments can be grouped into three patterns:

(1) *Mutual Destruction:* escalation to a destructive equilibrium; both lose.
(2) *Domination:* one player destroys the other and benefits.
(3) *Mutual Cooperation:* no conflict or rapid de-escalation after initial conflict.

Some initial generalizations extracted from these plays which must be accounted for by the theory are as follows:

(1) Mutual cooperation is very likely with open communication channel, less likely with "agreed-to" communication, and unlikely with no communication.

(2) Mutual cooperation is likely after a communication act.

(3) Mutual cooperation is more likely with an agreed to communication channel than with a closed channel even if communication does not take place.

(4) Domination is very unlikely under low technology (weak weapons). When either no communication is available *or* technology is low, mutual destruction is more probable.

(5) When technology is high: players tend not to communicate, even if they can, and domination is the most likely outcome.

The elementary (micro) experiments involve the identification and quantification of the decision procedures used by players in very simple conflict situations. This experimentation is directed toward producing an accurate computer simulation of players' behavior. Such simulation forces quantitative formalization of the hypothesized procedures used by players. The simulation produced in thus way is a microtheory. Preliminary formulations of such a theory have been developed and are currently under test.

The conceptual model underlying the simulation hypothesizes that the player proceeds as follows:

At the start of the experiment he combines his internal goals with those he perceives to be given by the rules to get an operating set of goals. He recognizes alternatives, usually the obvious ones. He chooses (from his past experience) a way of predicting future moves of his opponent. Prediction schemes can include the process of mentally "playing ahead" a few moves. Using the prediction scheme he evaluates the alternatives and makes a choice most appropriate to his goals.

When the results of that move are given to him, he evaluates the situation. If he feels he is attaining his goal he continues to play using the same procedure. (He may "learn," however; his prediction scheme may use past move data to improve his prediction of future moves.) If he is not meeting goals, and becomes sufficiently dissatisfied, he restructures his thinking. He may choose new alternatives, a new prediction scheme, or even modify his goals. The choice of a new structure is based on his previous experience in decision-making situations similar to this one. After restructuring, he uses the new procedures to make a choice.

This conceptualization appears to explain all phenomena observed in micro-experimental runs.

The computer simulation-model developed and tested to date incorporates all of the features just described except the full re-structuring process. The player is assumed to be attempting to maximize either the joint return, his total return, the difference between his and the other player's return, or some combination of these. A variable called "competitiveness" is used to describe the combination. Two other variables indicate the player's weighting of past history in predicting future moves (his "hindsight") and the extent of his planning horizon (his "foresight"). It was found necessary to incorporate a fourth variable to represent the extent to which the player would change his interpretation of the other's play (his "rigidity"). If he is not rigid, he goes through a form of restructuring in which he partially ignores past data and redesigns his prediction process. Appendix II presents the flow chart for this simulation.

We have been able to find sets of parameters to permit the simulator to reproduce 20 games (of 35 moves each). Thus there is preliminary evidence that the model has validity. Further validation and testing is necessary.

It should be clear that the methodology described is not intended to provide a quick or easy way to understanding of complex conflict phenomena. To the contrary, it provides a basis for an extended programmatic and accumulative build-up of knowledge in an area of ignorance. It involves large and continuing expenditures of time and effort. It is possible, however, for a number of research groups to collaborate effectively within a program so formulated. Thus the results to date, while not trivial, are just a beginning of the accumulation of theories leading toward a quantitative theory applicable to real conflicts. In the long run, this methodology should produce usable results at a lower cost than the uncoordinated pursuit of knowledge by the three approaches described earlier.

CONCLUSIONS

The principle findings of this study may be divided into two parts: findings in regard to the process of escalation and de-escalation and suggestions for further research. These may be summarized as follows:

Theoretical findings: (1) Perhaps the most dramatic finding, although not counterintuitive, is that, in an experimental conflict situation, the probability that a conflict will escalate decreases significantly as the availability of communication increases. In particular, conflict is less likely to escalate as the form of communication tends towards one in which the principals can communicate directly with each other and in which either can initiate the communication.

As explained above, our methodology does not extrapolate findings from these experimental situations to the real world, so that we are not prepared to make policy recommendations. It is interesting to speculate, however, on the effect of the nature of communication on the progress of real conflict. Does common language, frequent visits among members of elites, or informal contacts between principles effect de-escalation possibilities? (In the real world, the nature of the communication channel is a controlled, not a given, factor).

(2) In a particular experimental conflict situation, once communication does take place the probability that the conflict will de-escalate or never escalate is quite high as compared to situations in which communication does not take place.

(3) There seems to be less inclination to communicate when the level of technology (the power of the weapons) is high.

(4) The behavior of people in a simple conflict situation can be explained by a model which assumes the player is maximizing his utility function through a learning process. This model has been made precise by a computer simulation. It illustrates the process of escalation. When the player perceives an advantage in non-cooperation in terms of improved utility, escalation occurs. De-escalation occurs when the estimated utility of non-cooperation becomes less than that of the estimated utility of cooperation.

Methodological Conclusions: The principle conclusions as to the best methods for developing a theory of escalation are as follows:

(1) It is possible to model the behavior of people on simple conflict situations by means of computer simulation. The simulation exposes the process by which the human decisions are made. This, for the first time, offers the possibility of observing and measuring precisely the behavioral variables. It is felt that this simulation approach will provide a data base upon which a mathematical theory of conflict situations can be built.

(2) Carefully controlled experimental situations are good vehicles for isolating key variables and testing hypotheses about the processes of escalation and de-escalation.

More generally, our methodological conclusion is that the overall approach should be continued. We are beginning to develop predictive models of the processes involved in conflict in simple games. We believe that these models can be generalized to apply to the artificial reality; for example, to include communication and resource allocation. If this generalization can be carried out successfully, there is hope that the overall methodology will lead to theories of escalation and de-escalation in the real world.

Suggestions for Continuing Research

As a result of our research to date it appears that the following programs should be undertaken:

(1) Continue to develop and test the simulation model of the prisoner's dilemma player. Specifically: further test the model, add elementary communication facility, add resource allocation, attempt to design a player who plays optimal games.

(2) Attempt to develop a mathematical theory to explain the micro results.

(3) Continue the macro experiments in order to further identify key variables. These experiments would include the following additions to the situations: situations with a spectrum of technology levels, situations with more than one person on each side, and situations with more than two sides. The latter will allow us to study alliances.

Appendix I

CONCEPTS AND DEFINITIONS

Conflict and cooperation can be given operational definitions and can be measured along one continuous scale. This has been done in detail by ACKOFF (1964). A brief summary of this work is given here.

The definitions are based on the concept of a *purposeful state* of a decision maker (individual or group). Let

I = an individual or group whose behavior is observable.

N = the environment of the individual or group.

$C_i(1 \leq i \leq m)$ = the courses of action available to the individual or group in environment N, defined so as to be exclusive and exhaustive.

$O_j(1 \leq j \leq n)$ = the possible outcomes of the courses of action, defined so as to be exclusive and exhaustive.

$P_i = P(C_i|I, N)$ = the probability that I will select C_i in N.

Note that

$$\sum_{i=1}^{m} P_i = 1.0$$

$E_{ij} = P(O_j|C_i, I, N)$ = the probability that O_j will occur if 1 selects C_i in N; the *efficiency* of I's use of C_i for O_j in N.

Note that

$$\sum_{j=1}^{n} E_{ij} = 1.0$$

V_j = the relative value (utility) of O_j to I in N.

An individual or group can be said to be in a purposeful state if:

(1) there are at least two courses of action, C_1 and C_2, for which P_1 and P_2 are greater than zero: I has at least two potential courses of action in N;

(2) there is at least one outcome, O_1, for which $V_1 > 0$ for I; and

(3) relative to at least one outcome, O_j, for which $V_j > 0$, that $E_{1j} > 0$, $E_{2j} > 0$, and $E_{1j} \neq E_{2j}$ i.e., I's choice can make a difference.)

In ordinary English these conditions state that I is in a purposeful state if I wants something and if I can pursue it by alternative means which have some, but unequal, efficiency with respect to the outcome(s) that I desires.

The expected value of a purposeful state (S) is

$$EV(S) = \sum_{i=1}^{m} \sum_{j=1}^{n} P_i E_{ij} V_j,$$

if the V_j's are independent, as they would be if the outcomes are exclusive and exhaustive. (They can be made so by use of a Boolean Expansion.)

If $\Sigma_j V_j = a$, then max $EV(S) = a$, since $\Sigma_i P_i = 1.0$ and $\Sigma_j E_{ij} = 1.0$.

Let I_1 and I_2 represent two individuals or groups and

$EV_1(S|I_2)$ = the expected value of S to I_1 if I_2 is present in N.

$EV_1(S|I_2')$ = the expected value of S to I_1 if I_2 is not present in N.

The *degree of cooperation* of I_2 with I_1 (DC_{21}) is now defined as

$$DC_{21} = EV_1(S|I_2) - EV_1(S|I_2'),$$

and the degree of cooperation of I_1 with I_2 as

$$DC_{12} = EV_2(S|I_1) - EV_2(S|I_1').$$

These quantities measure the difference in the expected value of the state to one party with and without the presence of the other party. If max $EV(S) = a$, max $DC_{kj} = a$, and min $DC_{kj} = -a$. Negative values of the degree of cooperation are *degrees of conflict*. If $DC_{kj} = 0$, the value of the state to I_k is independent of the presence or absence of I_j.

DC_{12} and DC_{21} are not necessarily equal; that is conflict or cooperation is not necessarily symmetrical. Therefore, the *intensity* of conflict (in contrast to the *degree* of conflict) increases as

(1) $DC_{12} + DC_{21}$ approaches $-2a$ (its minimum value), and as

(2) $|DC_{12} - DC_{21}|$ approaches zero

If $DC_{12} \neq DC_{21}$, one of the parties is *exploiting* the other. If $DC_{12} > DC_{21}$, then I_2 is exploiting I_1; if $DC_{21} > DC_{12}$, then I_1 is exploiting I_2. The *degree* to which I_1 exploits I_2 is $DE_{12} = DC_{21} - DC_{12}$.

If this is negative, then I_2 exploits I_1. In general, $DE_{12} = -DE_{21}$.

In negotiation and bargaining the conflicting parties are frequently more concerned with removing exploitation (asymmetry of conflict) than with removing conflict itself. Each party does not want "to be taken advantage of." The result of such negotiation is conflict equilibrium, not resolution, and may, of course, be very temporary.

Finally, *competition* is defined as conflict *regulated* with respect to a "third party." Consider three individuals or groups (I_1, I_2, and I_3) of whom two (I_1 and I_2) are in conflict with each other. Now if this state of conflict increases I_3's expected value, then I_1 and I_2 are competitive relative to I_3. I_3

may be the group formed by I_1 and I_2, or a separate entity (e.g., I_1 and I_2 may be two tennis players in conflict relative to winning the game and in cooperation relative to a mutual or collective recreational objective; or they may be two industrial firms whose conflict serves the interests of their consumers, I_3).

As RAPOPORT (1960) has shown there are essentially three levels at which a conflict can be waged:

(1) *Fights:* The objective is actually or effectively to remove the opponent from the environment (by destroying or incapacitating him). Therefore, fights involve the use of *force* directed toward eliminating the opponent (*hot wars*). (That is I_1 tries to remove I_2 from the purposeful state.)

(2) *Games:* The objective is to "win" the conflict and have the opponent "lose" by outwitting him, without eliminating him (*cold wars*). (That is, I_1 tries to increase DE_{12}).

(3) *Debates:* The objective is to change the opponent's desires so that the conflict is resolved. (I_1 tries to change I_2's efficiencies or values.)

There are a number of properties of a conflict situation which are causally connected with the type, degree, and intensity of conflict. For example in conflicts between groups the following may be a few examples of many such characteristics:

(1) The number in (or percentage of) each group that are directly involved in waging the conflict.

(2) The destructiveness of the instruments of conflict which are available and are in use.

(3) The degree of commitment to superordinate goals by each group, i.e., shared goals.

(4) The presence of 'stereotype' judgments of other groups.

Appendix II

SIMULATION FLOW CHART

Fig. 2 is a flow chart of the computer simulation program which plays the Prisoner's Dilemma. Further details may be found in EMSHOFF's thesis.

The matrix used was this.

		Opponent C	*Opponent* D
Computer	C	10, 10	−50, 50
	D	50, −50	−10, −10

Payoff's are computers, then opponents.

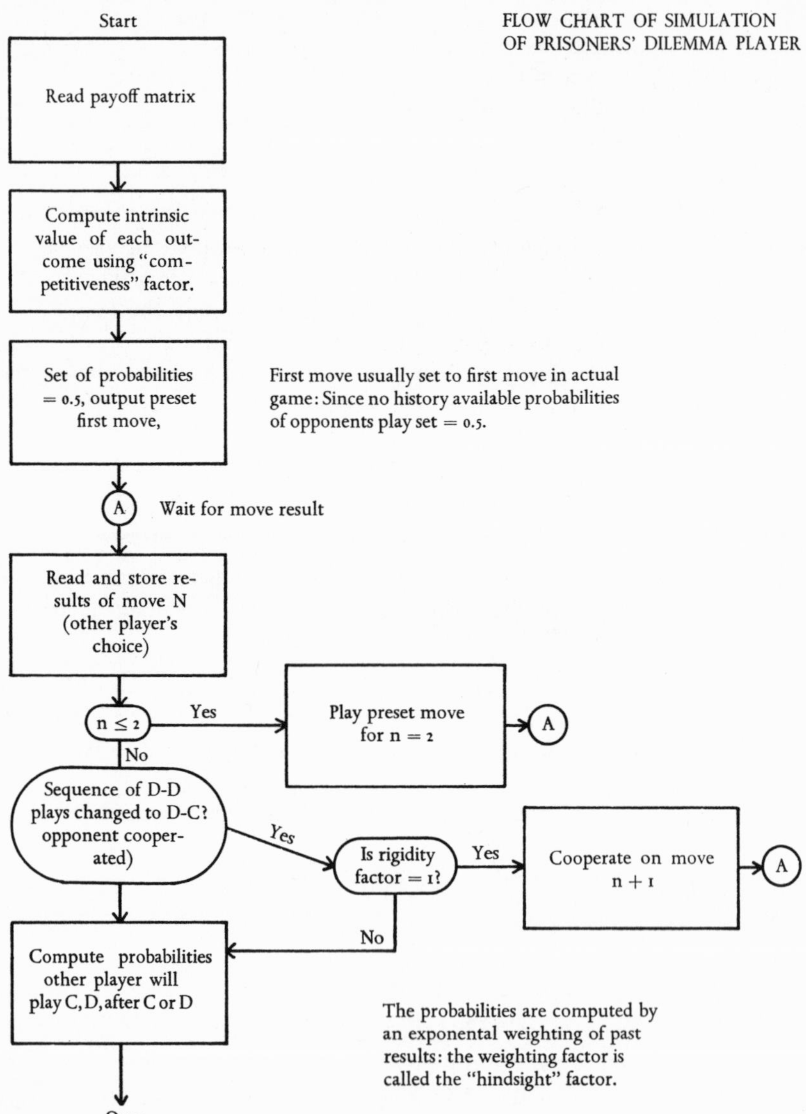
Start
FLOW CHART OF SIMULATION OF PRISONERS' DILEMMA PLAYER
Read payoff matrix
Compute intrinsic value of each outcome using "competitiveness" factor.
Set of probabilities = 0.5, output preset first move,
First move usually set to first move in actual game: Since no history available probabilities of opponents play set = 0.5.
A
Wait for move result
Read and store results of move N (other player's choice)
n ≤ 2
Yes
Play preset move for n = 2
A
No
Sequence of D-D plays changed to D-C? opponent cooperated)
Yes
Is rigidity factor = 1?
Yes
Cooperate on move n + 1
A
No
Compute probabilities other player will play C, D, after C or D
The probabilities are computed by an exponental weighting of past results: the weighting factor is called the "hindsight" factor.
Over

Fig. 2, page 1

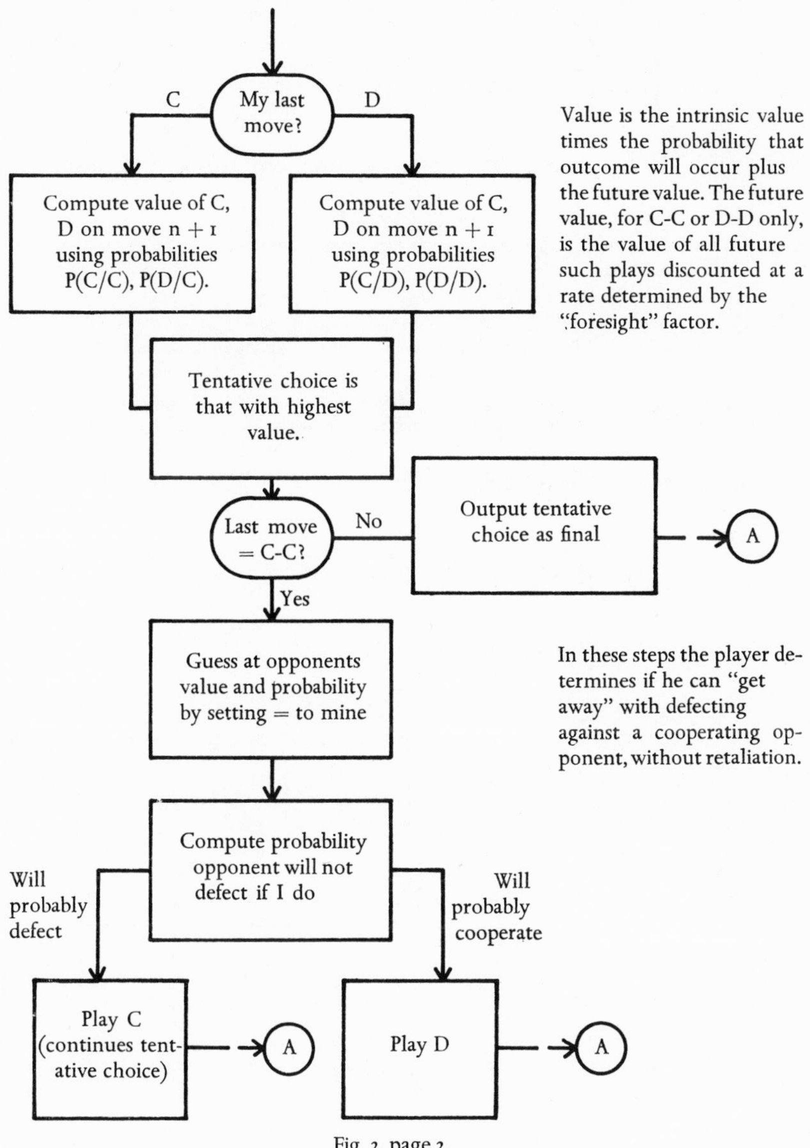
My last move?
C
D
Compute value of C, D on move n + 1 using probabilities P(C/C), P(D/C).
Compute value of C, D on move n + 1 using probabilities P(C/D), P(D/D).
Value is the intrinsic value times the probability that outcome will occur plus the future value. The future value, for C-C or D-D only, is the value of all future such plays discounted at a rate determined by the "foresight" factor.
Tentative choice is that with highest value.
Last move = C-C?
No
Output tentative choice as final
A
Yes
Guess at opponents value and probability by setting = to mine
In these steps the player determines if he can "get away" with defecting against a cooperating opponent, without retaliation.
Compute probability opponent will not defect if I do
Will probably defect
Will probably cooperate
Play C (continues tentative choice)
A
Play D
A

Fig. 2, page 2.

REFERENCES

ACKOFF, RUSSELL L. Conflict, Cooperation, Competition and Cupid, in : Essays on Econometrics and Planning, Pergamon Press, India, 1964.

BLOOMFIELD, LINCOLN P. The Political-Military Exercise; A Progress Report. *ORBIS*, VIII, 4, *854–870*. 1965.

EMSHOFF, JAMES R. An Analytic Model of Prisoner's Dilemma. Master's Thesis, University of Pennsylvania, 1965.

FISHBURN, PETER C. Decision and Value Theory. Wiley, New York, 1964.

GUETZKOW, HAROLD, et al. Simulation in Inter-Nation Relations. Prentice-Hall, Englewood Cliffs, N.J., 1963.

KAHN, HERMAN. On Escalation. Praeger, 1965.

RAPOPORT, ANATOL. Fights, Games and Debates. University of Michigan, Ann Arbor, 1960.

RAPOPORT, ANATOL. The Prisoner's Dilemma. University of Michigan Press, Ann Arbor, 1965. (Preprint)

RICHARDSON, LEWIS F. Arms And Insecurity. Boxwood, Pittsburgh, 1960.

RICHARDSON, LEWIS F. Statistics of Deadly Quarrels. Quadrangle, Chicago, 1960.

Animal Conflict and Adaptation in Relation to Human Conflict

by

J. L. CLOUDSLEY-THOMPSON
Professor of Zoology, University of Khartoum, Sudan

Most intelligent people, and especially those who have experienced it, would say that modern warfare is both evil and undesirable. Beyond this, however, there is little measure of agreement. For while some of us consider cruelty, bad faith and the suppression of freedom to be even greater evils, others think the demands of national or political loyalty should be rated more highly. Our approach is essentially subjective and it changes as we grow older and wiser and more tolerant.

Science does not pretend to include the entire spectrum of human knowledge and experience. It is concerned not with isolated events but with general phenomena from which the laws of nature may be deduced. The views that I would like to express here are therefore a compromise between my feelings as a human being, conditioned by the traditions of the particular society in which I was brought up, and more objective conclusions reached from the study of biology.

CONFLICT WITH THE PHYSICAL ENVIRONMENT

Man has always been interested in and curious about the number and variety of animals that live in the world. This variety results from the innumerable different environments, each of which can be exploited in many ways, that animals are forced to inhabit as a result of conflict and competition of one kind or another.

During the last half century, the biologist's approach to the study of living organisms has changed radically. Modern ideas are permeated by evolutionary theory and concepts of the survival of the fittest. Life is seen to be a dynamic force in which the organism is pitted against an environment that is often hostile and always changing. This environment consists not only of inanimate nature, but also of a host of other animals, plants and micro-organisms whose interests conflict in varying degrees. Resulting from such conflict, natural selection eliminates the less successful so that, with the passing of time, species become gradually better adapted to their environment. A static condition is never attained, however, because the organism is an agent of the geological, climatic and other changes that occur long before any equilibrium has been reached.

The animal exists amid various conditions both favourable and unfavourable. Of some it takes advantage, others it overcomes or avoids. Changes are inevitable – they occur from age to age, from century to century, year to year and even from moment to moment. Each change places some stress upon the living organism, results in some degree of adaptation. I am not thinking of conflict in any narrow sense, but regard it as the automatic consequence of change. Equally inevitable is the adaptive reaction of the living organism to such conflict. The two are inseparable: failure to adapt would result in immediate death. Even comparative failure to adapt sufficiently rapidly and extensively may be a frequent cause of the extinction of living organisms.

The life of an animal is primarily concerned with avoiding unsuitable environments of one kind or another, finding food, escaping from enemies and reproducing its species. Its offspring, with their congenital variations are brought into the world to thrive and themselves reproduce if well adapted or to perish if not. New habitats are colonized, new modes of life assumed, new behaviour patterns acquired, not only during the history of the race but, to some extent, even within the life-time of the individual.

For example, conflict, resulting from crowding and the instability of environmental conditions in estuaries and on the sea-shore, has compelled some kinds of animals to return to the open sea. Thus the ancestors of many teleost fishes, having acquired a lung in response to oxygen deficiency in tropical swamps, recolonised the ocean. Their lungs became swimbladders which enabled them to regulate their density and compete favourably with the heavier cartilaginous skates, rays, dogfish and sharks which had never acquired these organs. A few enterprising forms went on to colonise the land. Some of their descendents evolved into modern lungfishes; others are the ancestors of the terrestrial vertebrates. Therefore conflict with the environment was beneficial and resulted in adaptation and evolutionary progress in various directions.

INTER-SPECIFIC CONFLICT

When inter-specific conflict is considered it can be seen that animal species have become adapted to predation and parasitism and that these are not only beneficial but necessary for continued prosperity.

Predators

Although predation is a universal phenomenon throughout the animal kingdom, it by no means always results in depressing the populations of prey species. Indeed, it may often have the reverse effect if not too intense. For example, until the beginning of this century the deer populations on the Kaibab plateau of Arizona probably numbered about 4,000. This was well below the carrying capacity of the range, but numbers were kept down by predation from pumas and wolves. Between 1907 and 1923, nearly 700 pumas and 11 wolves were shot. As a result of this, the deer population increased very rapidly until it far exceeded its winter food supply. From a peak of 100,000 the herd declined to 40,000 in the winter of 1924–1925. By 1931, it had dropped to 30,000 and continued to decline until it fell to 10,000 ten years later. The normal carrying capacity of the Kaibab plateau has been estimated at about 30,000 deer and this number does not damage the vegetation as do excessive population eruptions. It would seem, therefore, that an optimal number of predators would have kept the deer population adjusted to its food supply at this level, and far too many were eliminated by man for the benefit either of the deer or of the vegetation.

The potential birth rates of all animal species are extremely high. Even the slowest breeders, such as elephants, would soon reach fantastic numbers if a large proportion were not killed off in some way or another long before death from old age, which must be a rare occurrence, intervened. The statement is sometimes made that, if all were to survive, the progeny of a single pair of aphids would, within a season, produce a heap of insects as high as Mount Everest. This is really quite meaningless, however, because, from an ecological point of view, the animal does not exist independently of its environment. Not only do innumerable aphids fall victim to various predators and parasites but, even if this were not so, food shortage would impose a check to further increase in numbers long before there were enough to build even a small molehill.

It is quite obvious, from the study of ecology, that there are optimal sizes for animal populations and that these are regulated in nature largely through the activities of predators and parasites. I would like, therefore, to introduce the idea that natural selection may result in the adaptation of a species not only with regard to the morphological and physiological characters of the individuals that comprise it, but also in respect of the size and density of the populations in which they are grouped. Obviously, if a species becomes too numerous, it will tend to outgrow its food supply and if it becomes too sparse it is likely to become extinct. For example, it is now known that the minimum size for a herd of elephants to survive in the Addo Forest is 25 animals. Not all individuals are mature at the same time and some mutual stimulation appears to be necessary for breeding to take place. Once an animal population has been reduced below a minimum threshold value, it may become extinct even if no further action is taken. Unfortunately, we are ignorant of this threshold for almost all animals, which makes it very difficult to fix limits for exploitation. The whale fishing industry provides an example: nobody knows to what extent whale populations can safely be reduced for, as soon as whales become really scarce, the chances of a male meeting a female are suddenly much decreased. The survival of such valuable animals as whales ought not to be allowed to drift at the mercy of immediate economic expediency.

In the fishing industry, it is well known that as intensity of fishing increases there comes a time when the total weight of the catch decreases. A very intense fishery may actually yield less than a moderate one, both being well under the possible maximum. The important question is, what level of population safely permits the greatest rational exploitation?

Of course the effect of predation by animals other than man can sometimes be quite dramatic but this is often more apparent than real. It is said that when the Mormons established their earliest settlement in Utah, their first crops were almost destroyed by myriads of black crickets. In the following season the crickets again appeared and the settlers were in despair, because the failure of their second crop would have meant starvation. Fortunately, at the critical moment, thousands of sea-gulls appeared and ate up all the offending insects. The settlers regarded this as a miracle and commemorated the event with a monument, costing $ 40,000 in Salt Lake City.

In actual fact, other more efficient but less obvious factors such as parasites and disease must also have been in operation. The numbers of crickets, as of locusts, are usually far too great in a large swarm to be affected substantially by the predation of birds. In one plague of grass-hoppers, for example, it was estimated that insects reached a density of 20–30 per square yard. It was calculated that predation by birds probably accounted for over 120,000 grass-hoppers per square mile per day. This means, however, that birds could only have eaten one grass-hopper out of every 5,000! They cannot therefore have been very effective in controlling the swarms.

When a prey species increases in numbers, predators will increase at its expense until numbers decline. This, in turn, will result in a decrease in the numbers of predators owing to starvation and, as the pressure of predation is released the prey species will again increase in numbers. This type of interaction between species may result in regular cyclical changes in population numbers, provided that the environment is otherwise relatively homogeneous. Since natural environments tend not to be stable, it is probable that when cycles appear at regular intervals in nature they are usually environment-dependent and not due to the inherent rhythmicity of the system. Nevertheless they are more likely to occur in simple rather than complex environments.

It has long been assumed that the number of offspring produced by a species bears a relation to the death rate. Larger and less vulnerable species tend, on the whole, to have a lower reproductive rate than weaker and more vulnerable animals. When parental care eliminates much of the mortality among eggs and young, fecundity is correspondingly smaller.

An analysis of the mean number of eggs laid annually by the species of birds which regularly breed in Britain has shown that larger birds lay fewer eggs than smaller birds. Generally speaking, colour varies with size, smaller species being less conspicuous, and the number of eggs laid decreases in relation to powers of offence and defence. In the case of sea-birds it is found that long-lived species with a lower adult death rate have compensated for this by a number of physiological adaptations resulting in depressing the rate of recruitment. Indeed, many kinds of animals show elaborate social and territorial systems whose function is to disperse the population to a density suitable to the particular habitat and thus avoid overcrowding. This, like migration, is an adaptation of behaviour directly concerned with the regulation of numbers. The fittest are not necessarily the most fecund, and natural selection tends to favour populations whose reproductive rate enables them to live in harmony with their environment and eliminates those whose balance gets out of control. The birth rate does not however play such a dominant part in determining the number of a population as might appear on cursory reflection. In species with a high rate of reproduction there is automatically a higher death rate resulting from greater environmental resistance.

Parasites

In the case of parasites, prolific reproduction compensates for the excessive hazards of the offspring in finding a new host. An exception to this general rule afforded by the louse-flies or Hippoboscidae is correlated with the retention of the larva within the genital tract of the mother fly until it is fully developed. Thus, although the number of young is greatly reduced, these are well cared for and have a low mortality rate.

Parasites are organisms that live on, or within the body of another living organism, the host, on which they depend for sustenance and shelter. The consequences of the dependence of a parasite upon its host may have a considerable biological significance, for both host and parasite become more or less adapted as a result of their association.

Man sees this conflict between one species and another from his prejudiced point of view and tends to regard as "degenerative" the evolutionary simplifications of structure that occur to varying degrees among parasitic organisms. These, however, are more properly regarded as specializations and represent adaptations to this particular mode of life. At the same time, parasites may induce considerable physiological and morphological changes in their hosts, for example, by upsetting the secretion of the hormones that regulate development, or by interfering with the reproductive glands and causing "parasitic castration" and the production of intersexes.

When a parasite is first introduced into a new kind of host, the reaction of one upon the other is extreme and usually either the parasite or the host succumbs. Naturally it does not benefit a parasite to kill its source of food and shelter and consequently, as a result of selection, its effects tend to become more benign with the passage of time. An example of this is afforded by the venereal disease, syphilis, a new strain of which is said to have been introduced by Christopher COLUMBUS's sailors on their return to Europe after discovering the island of Haiti where it was endemic. On their discharge, many of these adventurers promptly joined the army of King CHARLES VIII of France in its invasion of Italy in 1494; soon afterwards, the triumphant forces were ravaged by a terrible epidemic and retreated almost in a rout. During succeeding centuries, the disease has become less acute and now takes very much longer to kill.

The various species of *Trypanosoma* also exhibit the phenomenon of tolerance. *T. rhodesiense* in man causes a toxic disease that is rapidly fatal, while *T. gambiense* produces chronic sleeping sickness which may take years to kill. *T. brucei* is non-pathogenic to game animals but causes 'nagana' in cattle while *Trypanosoma lewisi* of rats and *T. duttoni* of mice are non-pathogenic. The last two are transmitted by the bites of fleas, the others by tse-tse flies. *T. lewisi* increases in numbers for about four to seven days after infection. An antibody is then produced by the rat which inhibits further reproduction of the parasites but does not kill them. After about ten days of infection, specific trypanolysins are acquired which kill the parasites. In this instance the host is less tolerant than the parasite! In any case, the insect vector does not appear to suffer and it has been postulated that trypanosomes have been adapted to insect hosts much longer than to vertebrates, and to the wild game animals of Africa longer than to man or cattle. Natural immunity may have evolved in some instances, while in others there has been an evolution of mechanisms producing acquired immunity.

Tolerance is not only found in parasite-host relationship, it also occurs in the natural balance between predators and their prey and even between herbivorous animals and their food plants. It is an interesting idea that plants may have slowly become adjusted to grazing herbivores through various regenerative and protective devices. Grasses grow from the base of the leaf and therefore can withstand grazing that would destroy any plant whose growing point was at the apex of the stem. Grass can also survive regular mowing and is therefore suitable for making lawns.

Again, the cacti, euphorbias and acacias of desert regions may be protected from overgrazing by their bitter flavour and defensive spines, though there is some evidence that spines are also a physiological response to conditions of drought. Such defences, of course, are not absolute, but afford relative protection, enabling the plants to survive when otherwise they might well be eliminated.

Tolerance is therefore a fine example of the mutual adaptation of two or more types of organism resulting from their inter-specific conflict. But, whereas predation may actually benefit a species as we have seen, this is less often true of parasitism, unless such a degree of tolerance has been reached that the interaction is better regarded as symbiosis. On the other hand, the development of hyperplastic tissue as a reaction to the liver-fluke *Fasciola* actually enables the parasite to survive in the bile duct of its host. This is paralleled by gall formation in plants as a response to nematode infections. The adaptation of the host thus compensates for damage caused by the parasite and the interaction of the two should be regarded as a single system.

From this discussion it will be apparent that my approach differs from that of the average medical or veterinary textbook whose author regards the parasite merely as something to be eliminated. In general, I think that control is more desirable than the elimination of parasites because it leaves a reservoir of the resistance and tolerance that, in the past, has enabled the host species to survive. Nor, in a parasitic relationship, does the host invariably suffer in all respects. By adapting to the conflict with its parasites, the host may benefit in quite unexpected ways, such as the development of social habits through mutual grooming, or by increased resistance to other parasites.

INTRA-SPECIFIC CONFLICT

Cannibalism

Perhaps the simplest way in which two members of the same species may come into conflict is when one preys upon the other. At first sight, it might seem strange that a species could become adapted to cannibalism, or that this trait could ever have beneficial results. On further consideration, however, it will be seen that the phenomenon is no exception to the general law that I have been propounding. Animals do become adapted to conflict within members of their own species and benefit from it. Even when such conflict reaches the extreme of cannibalism, the species becomes adapted and puts it to good use.

Cannibalism among human beings is generally regarded with abhorrence, and even in animals the trait is often looked upon as an expression of the lowest depths of utilitarian turpitude. To the zoologist, however, this view appears not only anthropocentric but to be based upon misconception. When cannibalistic actions are considered objectively, it becomes necessary to modify such preconceived notions for, in nature, the sole valid criterion is that of efficiency. Moral judgements can apply only to man, and the actions of other animals must be judged entirely in relation to their function.

Animal populations are largely regulated by their death rates – only in some civilized communities are populations to any extent controlled by reduction in the number of births. From a biological point of view, perpetuation of the species takes precedence over survival of the individual whose importance is merely that of a reproductive unit.

It is therefore logical to expect that, through the ages, carnivorous animals will have evolved behaviour patterns that tend to offset the loss by death of the proteins, etc., concentrated in their species. Consequently the occurrence of limited cannibalism amongst predatory animals is not surprising. On the other hand, if the habit were to become too widespread it would naturally be disadvantageous to the species; for this reason cannibalistic proclivities tend to be controlled.

Cannibalism as a form of population control is not confined to invertebrates and lower vertebrates, but occurs also in birds and mammals. Juvenile cannibalism is a common phenomenon among birds of prey such as buzzards, eagles, falcons, goshawks, harriers and owls, in which a gradation of nestling size is found. This not only prolongs the period during which the young are dependent on their parents for food, but also permits cannibalism to reduce the family to a feedable size when food is short.

Many birds such as eagles and penguins lay two eggs and normally rear only one. In some cases, as in penguins, eggs of different sizes are produced. An early decease of the second nestling through cannibalism usually occurs in cranes, terns, cockatoos, herons, etc., and, if the second young does live, a dominance hierarchy is soon established. Crows, ravens, rooks and other Corvidae also show juvenile cannibalism. Peregrines, kingfishers, terns and other birds at times destroy their own eggs. This is no unnatural perversion as was at one time thought, but a positive act that regulates the effective output of the population.

Cannibalism is a common response to over-crowding in voles, mice and rats, and its homoiostatic function cannot be doubted. Along with stress-disease and infanticide, it is an important density-dependent form of social mortality. Likewise, intra-uterine absorption, litter-size, pregnancy and neonatal mortality are all capable of density-dependent variation in mammals.

Even where cannibalism does not take place, juvenile mortality probably increases with overcrowding as in fur seals. At times of food shortage, weaker lion cubs are known to die, but information regarding most mammals in the wild is fragmentary. Nevertheless it may be concluded that juvenile mortality is a method by which population numbers are controlled in nature, and cannibalism, when it takes place, is also concerned with protein economy.

Among animals, therefore, cannibalism is related both to protein shortage and to population control. When we consider the eating of human flesh by man, however, a more complex situation is revealed.

The word cannibal is a Latinized form of "Carib", the name of a South American tribe originating from the West Indies. Herodotus and Strabo described people like the Scythian Massagetae, a nomadic race of the Caspian regions and the Troglodytes of Fezzan who killed and ate old people, while Marco Polo attributed cannibalistic tendencies to the wild tribes of

China and Tibet. Indeed, until comparatively recently cannibalism was prevalent over a large part of Central Africa, New Guinea and the East Indies, New Zealand, Australia and the Americas.

In many cases this anthropophagy was related to food shortage and the struggle for existence, and is therefore directly comparable with much cannibalism among animals – human flesh was at one time regularly sold in West African markets. More frequently, however, it played a part in ceremonial rituals, burial feasts, skull-worship and various magical rites. For instance, many savage tribes believed that a person assumed the mental or physical characteristics of the man or beast he had eaten. The custom of tearing in pieces the bodies of men and animals and of devouring them raw was often practised in religious rites. Doubtless the evident benefits derived from a diet supplemented in this way lent circumstantial support to these beliefs.

Other savages thought that if a man were murdered and a small part of his body devoured, his ghost would not trouble the murderer. These types of cannibalism, comprising many forms of diverse origin, require anthropological rather than biological consideration. Cannibalism has certainly played a most important part in the social organization of many savage tribes. Clearly there can be no justification for maintaining that it is a sin against the laws of nature. On the contrary, it should be regarded as another form of conflict that has adaptive value.

Fighting

Fighting among animals is generally concerned with territorial behaviour and mating: it is therefore largely seasonal. Its biological function, in fact, is economic. It ensures that the members of a species are well dispersed and prevents, among other things, excessive competition for food. This is especially important in birds such as sparrows and starlings which hatch in a naked, defenceless state so that their parents cannot leave them for long. Obviously it would not benefit a species if its members were invariably, or even frequently, killed or injured as a result of combat. Consequently, it is not surprising to find that threatening gestures and ceremonial displays frequently replace actual fighting. In this way, conflict tends to become ritualized and adapted, so that its function may be achieved without harm to the rivals.

Thus, in many animals the bark is far worse than the bite. Two dogs may be excessively rude to one another when separated by a gate or a fence. But, if the gate is opened, a fight does not necessarily develop. They may discover that they have other matters to attend to! Fierce and dangerous species usually have some instinctive gesture of surrender which inhibits the attack of an adversary. Dogs and wolves adopt an attitude of humility in which they expose their vulnerable necks to a stronger rival. However enraged that rival may be, he cannot overcome his inhibitions and bite his opponent. In the same way, ravens, crows and other birds with formidable beaks are inhibited from pecking at each other's eyes, which might otherwise cause serious injury or death.

Human beings hold up their hands in token of surrender. The Homeric warrior discarded his helmet and shield, falling on his knees as he offered his bare head in surrender to the enemy. Men, however, are less compelled by instinct than are other animals and until the days of chivalry it was not unusual for prisoners to be killed without mercy. Even so, it is probably easier to kill millions at long range with bombs, explosive shells or botulinus toxin than it would be to slaughter a single defenceless prisoner with a knife. The more that remote control is employed in warfare, the less are cruel and bloodthirsty actions inhibited by instinct.

Conflict between human beings is as inevitable as intraspecific conflict in other animals. Before the invention of long-range modern weapons it was almost certainly beneficial. Even modern warfare is not wholly bad in that it brings out the qualities of courage and endurance, comradeship and initiative which are not always apparent in times of peace. Instead of investigating the causes of conflicts, which are largely irrelevant, politicians and statesmen might do better to concentrate their efforts on negotiating just, compromise solutions, recognising that no single view can be entirely correct and that tolerance in nature is beneficial to all sides. At the same time constant efforts should be made by education to channel natural human competitive instincts into harmless and productive fields, such as sport or the race to the moon, which can also bring out the finest of human qualities.

The value of education in this respect is often overlooked. Not only do educated people tend to be less biased, more understanding and tolerant of the views of others, but it has been shown experimentally that frustration and conflict lead to actual aggression only among individual animals that have acquired the habit of being aggressive. Curiously enough, boys appear to be more aggressive in their imagination than in real life. Whereas they will make dolls or toy animals behave aggressively 100 per cent more often than girls do, actual quarrels are only 30 per cent more frequent among boys than among girls.

In an attempt to study the development of group aggression, the members of a boys' camp were set co-operative tasks of such a nature that they did not lead to competition, frustration or conflict within the group. A similar camp was established nearby whose occupants also had a well-developed team spirit, and the two groups were managed in such a way as to produce bad feeling between them. All contact was prevented except in competitive situations, and a tournament organised in which one side won all the prizes. Frustration led to aggression and the boys soon began to raid each others' camp and to fight if they met accidentally.

When, however, a situation occurred that provided a threat to both groups – the water supply to each camp failed – the two groups worked together and mutual aggression was greatly reduced. The results of this and other experiments do suggest that man's aggressive nature may be curbed by cultural methods that reduce the social causes of aggressions or direct them into harmless and creative channels.

PROBLEMS OF MANKIND

Change engenders conflict, conflict poses problems that must be solved by adaptation. It is no accident that many of the chief medical, agricultural, social and economic problems of the human race result from maladjustment in one form or another.

Animal population sizes are directly controlled by environmental influences of one sort or another. If these are sufficiently complex, no one species can become too numerous: but where they are simpler, it is easier for plague proportions to be reached. For instance, Arctic animals, such as snowshoe rabbits and lemmings, show marked cycles in numbers at the upper limits of which mass emigrations occur. The regularity of the cycles may be because the basic predator-prey oscillation is little disturbed by other factors. In contrast, the equatorial rain-forest, because of its extreme complexity, has the greatest inherent stability of any biogeographical region. A tremendous richness of species tends to give a buffering effect to any unusual population change.

Man's activities tend, on the whole, to create simpler conditions than would normally occur in nature. The growing of crops, the herding of animals, bulk storage, urbanization – all these result in a relative lack of natural checks to sudden population increases. For economic reasons man destroys complexity and replaces it by large tracts of uniformity. Consequently conditions conducive to plagues of one form or another are inevitably created by the activities of human beings.

As long ago as 1907, E. Ray Lankester wrote: "But it is not only by his reckless mixing up of incompatibles from all parts of the globe that the unscientific man has risked the conversion of paradise into a desert. In his greedy efforts to produce large quantities of animals and plants convenient for his purposes, and in his eagerness to mass and organize his own race for defence and conquest, man has accumulated unnatural crowds of his own kind in towns and fortresses. Such undiluted masses of one organism serve as a ready field for the propagation of previously rare and unimportant parasites from individual to individual."

The major problem of mankind today is one of adaptation: to accomodate the rising world population without war, pestilence or famine. There are some who think that the human race is doomed to early extinction: yet the threat of the hydrogen bomb, with its universally devastating potential, has probably done more to preserve world peace than centuries of diplomacy. Others fail to appreciate that grave problems exist. I do not believe either of these views to be correct. The one underestimates human resourcefulness and adaptability, the other is based on ignorance. Of course we will pull through in the long run. The people who live in underdeveloped countries will, however, long continue to suffer from malnutrition and disease. At the same time a lucky minority will acquire even bigger television sets and cars and have even less space in which to drive them. They will also suffer increasingly from stomach ulcers, obesity and stress syndromes caused by unnecessary competition with their neighbours.

Common sense dictates that world population increase should slow down without tyranny, misery or vice, a trend which is already beginning in many countries. Perhaps it is not too much to hope that eventually people will begin to plan in terms of optimum rather than maximum population numbers.

Let us hope that international co-operation from the countries with an economic surplus over their immediate needs will help to tide over the severity of the population crisis during the next fifty years. In any case, population pressure will, during the next few years, become so important as to override all other political and economic problems. It is encouraging to know that, if all the land suitable for farming were exploited to the full with present techniques, it could support 10–25 times the present population. A single Canadian wheat farmer with modern machinery can produce enough food for 800 people. With simple tools an able-bodied man in the tropics can only produce enough for six.

Throughout this discussion we have seen how wild animal species become mutually adapted both to their environments and to their enemies and even acquire tolerance to their parasites so that inter-specific conflict is reduced. Mankind is not so rational as is often thought. The two ruling motives of our behaviour are pain and pleasure and we do not consciously adapt ourselves to the environment from which technological knowledge partially shields us. Nevertheless, although so greedy, man is also strangely unique in being naturally compassionate. By exercising this quality towards other human beings as well as to the fauna and flora of our world, we can surely overcome the dangers inherent in our temporary escape from the laws of nature. If we do not succeed, these will eventually catch up with us: but there is no reason why, before then, we should not achieve an economic and balanced compromise that could last for centuries.

Science cannot always provide a guide where problems of an ethical nature are concerned. Each of us, in the last resort, is compelled to be subjective in deciding his course of action. We possess two incompatible drives; the one self-centred, the other altruistic and social. Freed from the tyranny of instinct, we are unique in that we can look upon ourselves as the objects of our own thoughts.

Consequently, we are forced to test every impulse by conscious thought, to find out if we can yield to it without harming the cultural values of our society. Hence there is a conflict between our simple, but often by no means ignoble, instincts and our deeper insight. To some extent freedom is inevitably surrendered as the price of the security and the aesthetic and cultural advantages of civilisation. Despite instinct and environmental influences there is much scope for free will. Naturally this is limited; just as we cannot drive a car everywhere yet can select between the high road and the low, so we can use our instincts creatively in the best sense, or we may consummate them crudely and selfishly. The choice lies with everyone.

SUMMARY

This paper is an exposition of the hypothesis that animal conflict is inevitable. It is also necessary for the evolution of variety. Conflict is not treated in a narrow sense, but is regarded as the automatic consequence of changes to which organisms must adapt themselves or perish. This applies to morphological and physiological problems of adaptation that confront living animals as a result of conflict, in its widest sense, with their environment. Turning from this to more direct forms of conflict – inter- and intra-specific – I suggested what may have seemed surprising, that such conflict is not only advantageous but is actually essential to survival. Finally, and somewhat pragmatically, I applied the idea to human problems and suggested that many of them result basically from faulty adaptation and lack of restraint. Nature leads and science points the way – to the conservation of variety, to the rational exploitation of fisheries and game populations, to the control rather than the elimination of pests and parasites, to educating people so that their competitive instincts are channelled into useful cultural activities, and to the stabilisation of human populations at an economic level. I have tried to outline the justification for such views.

REFERENCE

The subject has been discussed more fully, with bibliographical details in

CLOUDSLEY-THOMPSON, J. L. (1965) – Animal Conflict and Adaptation. London: Foulis.

Features of a World Capable of Achieving Peace under Law

by

STUART MUDD
Professor Emeritus of Microbiology, University of Pennsylvania, Philadelphia

While we are meeting in Rome, a World Conference on World Peace through Law is being held in Washington. World Law is, indeed, a necessary condition for World Peace; but is it also a sufficient condition?

With improving communication and awareness have come rising expectations. Disease, undernutrition and malnutrition, lack of housing, lack of education, lack of hope for better conditions of life, are no longer accepted passively as the inevitable lot of mankind. In consequence we see political instability, coups d'état, civil strife, little wars and the looming horror of major wars. We see the emergence of sovereign states, too small and too poorly provided with resources and with leadership to be economically and politically viable, too competitive to be willing to associate themselves into groupings which can be viable. We see the population in particular of the developing countries increasing at rates out of all proportion to the feasible rates of development of human and material resources, and the already miserable standards of living in consequence deteriorating even further.

Cardinal SUENENS in commenting on the magnificent Encyclical "Pacem in Terris" has written: "No man of good will can accept the fact that two-thirds of the world – two million of every three million men – do not attain the level of normal human development that technology places at the disposition of privileged peoples. This disproportion, this disequilibrium, hangs with all its weight on the peace of the world."

There is profound need that there be widespread understanding and passionate feeling that the unit of survival has become the human *species*, all of mankind. It no longer suffices that the goal of great religions should be individual Enlightenment and release from the suffering of this world. It no longer suffices to seek individual, corporate or national wealth and power for the fortunate at the expense of the less fortunate.

To remake a world that is capable of peace under law will require all the love and compassion, all the vision and leadership, all the knowledge, skills and resources of which modern science, technology and art are capable. No less a goal than the good of all mankind will serve.

A world capable of permanent peace will need to have been modified in at least the five following categories:

(1) Development of human resources through education, technological training, and public health measures.

(2) Development of material resources of agriculture, energy sources, forests, minerals, river basins and the riches of the seas.

(3) Control of population growth to realistic proportion in relation to available resources.

(4) Economic, political and legal association of states so as to become viable units.

(5) The development of skills in interpersonal communication and understanding, of mutual good will, and of capacity for compromise and conflict resolution. The development of leadership with the vision and the will to achieve a world peaceful under law.

Of course it is possible to conceive of a world unified and pacified by despotic force, a sort of *Pax Terrestris*, under some hypothetical tyranny. It is hardly necessary to say that this is not the sort of world the Academy aspires to.

The intuition of OMAR KHAYYAM, written centuries ago, has present relevance:

> "*Ah, Love, could you and I with Him conspire*
> *To grasp this sorry scheme of things entire,*
> *And, shattering it to bits,*
> *Remold it closer to the heart's desire.*"

The word in this quatrain to which I would direct attention is "*entire*". For the human state is now determined by a nexus of economic, demographic and political factors so complex as to negate the value of any *partial* solution of its problems.

It is, indeed, dangerously misleading to suppose that the ingenuity of science and technology can lift the burden of poverty and hunger in disregard of the demographic facts of life. The very same applications of public health measures which have and are so dramatically increasing life expectancy in the developing areas of the world, in the absence of corresponding measures to control fertility, have precipitated the tragic disproportion between population growth and the development of resources. This disproportion is increasing the gap between the more fortunate and privileged parts of the world and the less fortunate. This disproportion unquestionably increases the misery of a large segment of mankind, is a basic factor in economic and political instability and is a menace to the peace of the world.

Happily a wave of understanding of the necessity for controlling population increase is now traversing the thoughtful and responsible leaders of the world. Great institutions of government, of education and of philanthropy are concentrating on questions of motivation and of the operational realities of fertility control. The Economic and Social Council of the United Nations on July 29, 1965, took an epochal step by voting to "request the Secretary General to provide advisory services and training in action programs in the field of population at the request of governments." Unexpected technical advances within the last few years, specifically the anovulatory pill and intrauterine contraceptive devices, have changed the whole prospect for the better. There is now hope that the age-old proportionality between fertility and mortality can be reestablished through reduction of fertility rather than through increase of mortality.

To gain time for this demographic revolution in the developing areas of the world, development of human and material resources must be energetically pursued. The subject is too vast to be discussed in this talk except in the most general terms. It may be stressed, however, that introduction of modern methods of agriculture, discovery and efficient utilization of new sources of energy and of mineral wealth, multipurpose development of the great river basins for flood control, irrigation and hydroelectric power, involve operations which far transcend national political boundaries. A relevant example is the Mekong River Basin development, in which many nations are participating, and which if the area could be pacified, would contribute enormous resources to the political units of the area.[1]

The fragmentation of empires into small sovereign states, the civil strife within those states, may represent necessary stages in the evolution of human self-determination and freedom. However if these states are to become economically and politically viable, counter-trends must somehow be established toward cooperation and association into mutually supportive regional groupings. Tribal and national rivalries must become subordinated to common interests.

With many aspects of these world problems great agencies are at work: the Special Agencies of the United Nations, numerous national governments, philanthropic foundations, educational institutions and private organizations. What contribution is it possible, then, for the World Academy of Art and Science and the proposed World University to make? The fellows of the World Academy have been selected because of their eminence in their own vocations and because of their concern for mankind. You have been chosen as individuals free from the obligations to special interests that inhere in representation in international organizations. You are influential citizens of many countries. Surely your intellectual and moral

1. WHITE, GILBERT F., The Mekong River Plan, *The Scientific American*, 208: *49–59*, Apr. 1963, *Bull. Atomic Scientists* 20: *6–10* (Dec.) 1964.

PHILLIPS JOHN, Certain Criteria for Application to Large-scale irrigation Projects in the Developing Countries, this Monograph, pp. 259–274.

influence can play a part in the evolution of concepts, motives and actions appropriate to the modern world.

There are vital tasks peculiarly appropriate to a World University. Leaders must be trained for many lands and many special undertakings; such men and women should be dedicated to the welfare of mankind; they should also be trained to high competency in one or more essential operational areas: professional, technological or political, as the case may be. Researches should be undertaken with regard to the manifold necessities of a world changing at an unprecedented rate.

His Excellency ABBA EBAN has referred to the tendency of those with great political power to become preoccupied with small issues, and the opportunity of those with small political power to concern themselves with great issues. Surely not the least of the challenges to the World Academy and the nascent World University is the evolution and refinement of the image of a world in which people can live together in good will and mutual cooperation, at peace under world law.

PART II: CONFLICT RESOLUTIONS

A. The Idea of a World University

Some Comments on the Idea of a World University

by

HAROLD TAYLOR
Chairman, National Research Council on Peace Strategy, New York

The argument for the establishment of a world university can be put quite simply. The scholar and the intellectual hold their allegiance to the ideal of full intellectual enquiry and exchange among all men, in all fields of knowledge. National systems of university education limit by their nature the possibility of such enquiry and make demands for allegiance to certain local values and truths which are assumed rather than explored. The lack of opportunity for the continual confrontation of these varieties of truth with each other has meant the consolidation of intellectual blocs which roughly parallel the political blocs now in existence between East and West, North and South. In the case of the African and Asian universities, much of their intellectual and social force is dissipated because of a continuing reliance on forms of organization and content derived from British and European models no longer relevant to post-colonial needs.

Certain inroads have of course been made – through international congresses of scholars, the Pugwash meetings between Eastern and Western scientists, collaboration among world scientific groups on specific projects such as the International Geophysical Year, the increase of exchanges between students and scholars of the seven continents, and the internationalizing of trade and transportation. The World Academy of Art and Science is an example of an organization designed to meet the need for treating the world as a single entity and its intellectuals as men and women with a common set of intellectual values and a universal community of interest. However, full recognition of the necessities and possibilities of internationalism in cultural and intellectual affairs has lagged behind the facts of the world situation, and the world's educational system is presently in danger of becoming less, rather than more, internationalized as the political divisions and antagonisms multiply and coalesce into opposing institutional forms. In one sense, the educational institutions of East and West have become parts of the ideological structure of the cold war.

There are various ways in which the situation can and should be changed. Among the most promising conceptions are the following:

(1) The concept of an international network of scientists and scholars, a network similar to that proposed by the World Academy of Art and Science through which existing groups of intellectuals in the world's universities can be brought directly in touch with each other through a central headquarters. The variations in this concept are the Pugwash Conferences, meeting once a year with continuing work throughout the rest of the year on issues of disarmament, world peace and scientific collaboration. A variety of suggestions for this kind of network, and in fact for a world university, were made during the early days of the League of Nations, both in its Committee for Intellectual Cooperation and in Assembly discussion.

Special projects undertaken as part of the International Cooperation Year provide another means of linking the world intellectual community on specific tasks. There are countless variations of such projects, some of them already in motion. The practical possibilities are great in expanding such projects and linkages into regional centers around the world, where groups of scientists and scholars can be organized on a six month or yearly basis to carry out tasks of the kind suggested by members of the World Academy of Art and Science, for example, a school for brain research, a team for educational problems in prodigy children, a team for research on human understanding, etc. UNESCO serves the function of acting as one center for such enterprises and has administrative facilities which can be used more widely in the future.

(2) The establishment of institutions deliberately designed to bring together an international community of scientists and scholars to deal with specific problems in science, technology and social change.

The example of the CERN laboratories in Geneva for research in physics carried on by scientists from 13 countries with students added as an extension of the research, is one model which suggests many variations in other areas of knowledge. The financing is on a pro-rated basis by the participating countries who pool their resources to provide laboratory facilities, staff and administration.

The United Nations Institute for Research and Training, which began its operations last year, provides another model, this one directly connected with the UN and designed to act as an educational and training institution for international diplomats and members of the UN Secretariat. The financing in this case comes not only from Governments who volunteer for inclusion in the project, but also from private foundations and individuals. This concept could be expanded into that of a UN University by the addition of faculty and programs ranging more widely than the political, social and economic subjects. Whether or not this is a development which will occur over the next ten years is in part a question of how well the present organization works and whether or not the Soviet Union and the

Eastern Socialist Republics become interested in joining in the effort. It would be my hope that at some point Mainland China could be persuaded to join such an organization, although at the present time the Chinese have refused to join even the intermediate programs such as those of the Pugwash conferences, and the prospects are relatively dim of a change in Chinese policy over the next four or five years. This of course will depend to some extent on whether or not the Chinese are invited to membership in the UN and whether or not they accept that invitation.

(3) The establishment of an international educational institution for the development of Peace Corps Volunteers from a variety of countries. There is already in existence an international secretariat for voluntary services with headquarters in Washington, with participation by 41 countries. Until now, the Soviet Union and the Socialist Republics have not been represented in the organization, although it is possible that they may wish to join in the future. In the meantime, there have been suggestions made that an international training center be established, manned by an international faculty and supported by a larger number than the present 41 governments. The curriculum of such an institution would naturally include areas of economic and social planning, science and technology, education, and languages. I believe that were such an institution to be established it would be a major step toward an eventual world college attended by a representative cross-section of world youth whose aim would be to achieve a variety of forms of international cooperation.

(4) There are in existence several international universities and research centers sponsored by governments which, provided political decisions were made, could be expanded to include a greater cross-section of ideological and geographical blocs. The two most important of these are Friendship University in Moscow, the East-West Center in Hawaii. Brief accounts of these institutions are included in the summaries attached to this memorandum, pp. 191–207.

(5) International projects, sponsored by UNESCO and other organizations can provide the basis for a future institutional framework, for example the UNESCO International Tensions project and the World History project, various efforts to develop texts in history from an international point of view, capable of being used in the Soviet Union, the United States, China, and anywhere else. The World Academy of Art and Science has already moved in this direction and a series of collaborative projects could be developed in the field of education, science and the humanities. There already exists a substantial international peace research community which publishes a newsletter with the intention of keeping scholars who are interested in world war/peace problems in touch with each other. There are also a number of international education organizations with the secretariat and facilities for undertaking an expanded program of international intellectual effort.

At the present time, according to the findings and research presently available in this area, the general inclination of UNESCO and UN officials is to believe that it would be more profitable to work at the task of further internationalizing the existing universities rather than striking out on the path of establishing a completely international university. My own judgment is that both things should be pressed as hard as possible, and that action in the one field lends support to action in the other. One specific task for the World Academy of Art and Science might be to make suggestions and proposals to the existing world organizations of scholars through which regional research and teaching centers with a world point of view might be established, at least in embryo, by special institutes based on approaches to specific problems. Another possibility exists in establishing truly international communities within the framework of existing universities. I am at present involved in a feasibility study of establishing such world institutes, or possibly UN academies, in Africa and Asia, and over these coming four months will be conferring with African and Asian scholars about possibilities of this kind.

In the meantime I believe that a review of the materials attached to the present statement will show that some progress has been made toward the ideal of world institutions and that there are a considerable number of possibilities for the extension of present proposals and institutions in the fully international direction.

Thoughts on World Education

by

Morris R. Mitchell

Director, Committee on a Friends World College, East Norwich, N.Y.

Is it not basic to all assumptions, whether deity be interpreted in personal or in cosmic terms, that we are all creatures of the central principle of the creative process of the universe, hence rightful heirs of some measure of that very impulse: all men, all women, all children, all races, all creeds. It is with such reverence I address you all as friends.

There might be no need, however, of education of any kind were there not the contrary axiomatic assumption that there is in each of us also that of evil.

It is the eternal tension between these two that has caused conflict and constant need of adjustment, achieved now by love and reason, now by hate and violence, from first emergence of life on this planet. Among humans these tensions expressed themselves first between individuals in families, then tribes, states, nations, empires. And as the arena enlarged, so did the consequences.

We meet in the city called "eternal" when no one knows what hour may bring that thud that would mark the end of the contest between human love and hate, the end of human life; and that at just the time when the creative powers, harnessing science, could drain the swamps, irrigate the deserts, blend opposite extreme temperatures the world over, ameliorate storms, feed all, clothe all, shelter all, heal all on such a plateau of existence as has hardly been imagined.

In such a crisis culture then we must achieve an education equipped to deal with this paradox. And that means two basic changes.

First, education must outgrow all traces of tribalism. We must nurture the impulses of respect, sympathy, love, that were inherent binding forces in tribal structure and deliberately outgrow the counterbalancing hostilities toward other tribes by accepting the reality that we are all of one family and all interdependent. Specifically we must accept into our affection all we now regard as enemies, those we may now fight, those we may now fear, those against whom we arm at such cost, with such danger, such folly

We must realize that, tragically, we have been confusing cause and effect. We have made men our enemy when our real enemy was enmity. We have fought through fear when fear was our foe. We have reacted to individual and group responses to poverty, hunger, degradation, by fighting those made desperate, thus further victimizing the victims.

World Education must replace this inverted perspective with a true one built on the knowledge that all men want the same basic values as, sufficient nourishment, adequate dress, suitable shelter and privacy, sexual expression, emotional and physical health, economic security, mutual devotion, recognition and appreciation, recreation, education, the experience of growth, the sense of sharing, the sense of purpose, and optimum freedom; and that we all subordinate these values according to the circumstances, so that all hungry men are alike in subordinating freedom, if necessary, to the demands of hunger. So we must learn that the only moral equivalent of war is the war on the causes of war.

Second, we must accept a revolutionary change of attitude toward the nature and function of the educational process. For in content, too, we must outgrow the universal provincial pattern of employing education as a tool to transmit tribal beliefs, tribal attitudes, tribal structures, tribal skills, tribal habits, and tribal knowledge. Education must undertake a loftier purpose, an aim of new qualities, new dimensions. It must become for now a tool for human survival, and that assured, must assume its ultimate goal of individual and social growth as an end in itself. Then education on a world scale will be the social counterpart of the creative forces that shape our destinies. Then we shall have achieved PLATO's dictum that education is "process not product." Indeed man may find such education the means of so identifying with the progressive evolution of his environment as to share, through his inherent creative ability, in the primal processes of change. Then, creature of environment that he is, man might rise to the nearest possible approach to the longed for freedom of will, by deliberately changing the environment for universal human betterment. This would call for the discovery for each time period of universally applicable concepts by which a creative cycle might come to replace the past downward spiral of destructive exploitation leading to further destruction. Already there are inklings of this prospect as those revealed in the purposes and program of the World Academy of Art and Science.

Let us call this new form World Education, and seek to describe it. The task is made easier by the emergence over the world of a surprising number of proposals. There are believed to be a thousand or more of these plans, some dating back to the turn of the century. Most have been put forward in the last twenty years. Some result from individual concern. Others have come from various types of organizations. Some presume one large central institution. Some are schools afloat. Many are fairly traditional in educational approach. Several involve two radical changes:

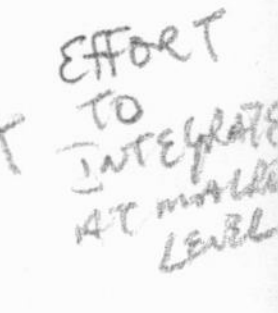

One, the world itself becomes the campus, with study centers in selected regions. At these centers the students enjoy study, work, recreation. From these centers they go out to experience at first hand the problems and resources of the region.

In one such plan for an undergraduate college there are to be seven regional centers: East Europe, East Africa, South Asia, East Asia, North America, Latin America and West Europe. When in full operation about 100 students will enter each regional center from the region of that center every six months. The faculty will remain at each center, but after six months the students will move by chartered plane to the next center in sequence. Local transportation of many kinds will be used intra-regionally. But travel by chartered plane is to cost less than $ 700 per student to encircle the globe with half-year stops at each center. And since there are eight periods of six months each, each student returns for the last period of study to the center of the region of his origin. From this brief description it will be seen that in three and a half years there would be seven groups of 100 each at each center, making a polycultural group of 700 students from seven regions, living, working, studying, travelling together. And the total enrollment around the world would be approximately 5000.

In this case there will be no language entrance requirement but by graduation each student will be expected to have a working knowledge, written and spoken, of three of the following five languages: Spanish, Russian, Chinese, Japanese, English.

The tuition in dollar equivalency will be, except for personal extras, $ 2,625.00, including food, lodging, tuition, use of books, intra-regional and inter-regional travel. In regions where such a charge would be prohibitive, special plans are being studied, as use of counterpart funds to cover the expenses of all students of all seven regions in India in return for the expenses of Indian students around the world. And grants are hoped for.

Two, bolder than this plan of employing the world as a campus is the curriculum approach. Several of these planned World Colleges or World Universities have independently arrived at the conclusion that our stereotype program of texts and lectures and quizzes and examinations and grades and graduation, all dovetailing into the socio-economic status quo, fail to meet the challenge of our world-in-crisis and tend to provide the student with a false sense of security. For knowledge changes so rapidly in its present explosive manner and in consequence of this factor and such others as cybernetics, that jobs keep changing too.

And so in the plan being outlined, all these traditional paraphernalia are to be replaced by a program of study based on the recognition and definition and attempted solution of the critical problems that now so dangerously divide mankind. Actually this shift to the problem approach will be accompanied by a further important change: that from primary emphasis on teaching to central emphasis on learning. As a corollary there will be a shift from assignments by faculty to a joint search by student and staff.

The first six weeks of each student's participation, wherever his initial center, will comprise an effort largely by the students (but students and staff together) to list the world's major problems, as perhaps: the danger of total war, the cost of armaments (said to be about $ 100 billion per year), race prejudice, waste of natural resources, population explosion, hunger, disease, housing, education, disintegration of family life (expecially in industrial societies), blocks to communication (as between the United States and China), pollution of air and water, insufficiency of water in places, at times floods, poverty in the midst of affluence, poverty in vast areas, adjustment of production to consumer needs, unplanned urban development, others.

It is the search for the solutions of such problems the world around that will comprise the heart of the program. And this search will lead toward a philosophy of education, indeed of life, structured about emerging universal concepts of truth appropriate to resolving the terrible tensions of our time.

Out of this problem-solving approach which has engendered all the creative scholarship of the past, now mummified in textbooks, must come a new and more potent scholarship. For such scholarship is inherent in the careful exercise of the thinking process: 1, in the very act of recognizing the problem as a problem, not a mere frustration, we exercise that emotional control that by constant repetition becomes habitual. The violence over the earth today is witness to this need. 2, In defining the problem we exercise our analytical gifts, separating the immediate obstacle from the maze of circumstance. 3, In conceiving possible solutions we exercise the subtle, elusive power of imagination, a precious product of purpose and emotional health. For creative imagination does not flourish on negative emotions of anger, hopelessness, helplessness, rejection, docility, insecurity, disappointment or fear. Education must prepare the seed-bed for creative imagination. 4, In selecting between the imagined solutions we exercise another quality of true scholarship, judgment, judgment rooted in value system. We judge with care because of involvement in the consequences. The purpose is a world of peace and plenty. The obstacle is as real as life itself. The stakes are the highest. 5, We apply the chosen solution whether with ease or with difficulty, and the profounder the difficulties the greater the exercise of determination, will. But this is an exercise in freedom, truly an exercise in freedom of will. For the task is, within widest environmental context, self-imposed; is not assigned by an authority figure. 6, We approach and accomplish our objective. At that moment we experience the exhilaration of achievement. And if the process has involved mental, emotional and physical effort, the reward in the experience of growth is the broader. The earned sense of well-being and increased self-confidence rightly has moral overtones. For the problem met was met creatively, not evaded, not attacked with irritation, anger or violence.

If the thinking process was a joint one we learned further the art of constructive cooperation.

Out of this process of problem solving, then, comes knowledge, knowledge most broadly speaking, including, importantly, but not chiefly, factual knowledge. Thorough and well documented study proves that even factual knowledge is thus acquired and retained even more effectively than when factual knowledge is made the chief object of learning.

The daily program these first six weeks will include, under guidance, group preparation of food, a work program, general study, and language study, recreation, art experience, documentary films, meetings for business. But the heart of the day will be given, each day, to the consideration of one of the problems proposed and accepted by the group. The approach will be in the mood of seeking, a seeking beyond the immediate problem to the nature of reality, and, further, seeking beyond the immediate problem for a cohesive complex of emerging concepts that all men would find acceptable. Reverent meditation will precede each group meeting, for perhaps half an hour. The silence will be subject to interruption for expression of any deep concern. Similarly it is hoped that the attitude of search thus experienced in profound contemplation will permeate the following discussion. Daily there will be large group discussions with a team of faculty members, and smaller group discussions, usually including a resource staff member. Study material will be available and presented for afternoon or evening study. By thus viewing each problem in its general outline and significance the interrelationship of world problems will begin to appear, admittedly at this stage superficially.

The second six weeks will involve travel, usually by car, plunging into the social tension areas and sensing the problems at first hand. The purpose will be to live and work with people at their level, high or low, feeling deeply of reality. The areas chosen will exemplify the problems discussed.

Then will follow at the student's original center two and one half months of less scheduled time for deeper study of these same problems. Meetings will be scheduled as wished, some students spending more time than others in its unprogrammed use. Faculty will always be available as resource persons and as friends and counsellors.

Throughout these five and one half months each student will keep a "journal" describing step by step his intellectual and spiritual journey into the frontiers of truth. On Saturday morning small groups of students with faculty assistance will compare these journals and work on matters of content and expression. On Sunday mornings from 9:30 to 10:30 there will be opportunity for a summary period of meditation, worship. These will be unprogrammed and not required. The early hour will make possible attendance at 11:00 o'clock service in meetings, churches, synagogues, or such other places of worship as may be desired.

There will follow a two weeks vacation after which the entire group at that center will move by plane or otherwise to the next regional center. In four years thus spent in traveling around the world and scouring over seven of its vast regions, meeting everywhere the reality of local problems, always seeking their solutions, visiting various hopeful frontier projects, not only will the students become aware of the repetition of the same problems, even their ubiquitousness, they will perceive, each for himself, as reward for his seeking, a repetitious pattern of seeming solutions. These will doubtless emerge as vast concepts.

For example, in the first regional development encountered he will see related problems of soil erosion, deforestation, unplanned urban development, health, floods, lack of power, monotony of life, needed facilities for transportation and communication being largely answered by a total program in which all the people within a given watershed are seen in their interdependence and their dependence on the natural resources, with consequent measures of conservation and use through dams, vegetative control of run-off, flood control, irrigation, power development, industrialization, navigation, health measures, urban planning, rural community development, housing, road buiding, cooperative transmission of power, extended telephone systems, recreation, all leading to an enriched life, to a heightened plane in art and the art of living. When he has encountered thus the Dnieper, the Volga and Don complex, the Damodar, over-all plans for the Jordan, rivers in China, the T.V.A., and many others, he will perceive that there has arisen in the past 30 years a new manner of attacking many problems with a single bold concept, that of planned regional development.

Similarly with projects of community development which he meets again and again at every level from crossroad hamlet to the United Nations, he senses another concept of seemingly recent origin, and still too little felt, too little understood. So with social planning, initiated with vigor less than 40 years ago, now world wide; and so, too, with other emerging potentially universal concepts as socialism and consumer cooperatives, the latter by its first principle (of the Rochdale principles) being universal, for it is based on the only all-embracing category of humans, consumers, and by prophetic wisdom dating to the 1840s, open to all regardless of race, creed or nationality.

Finally he will realize that the concepts, far from being mutually exclusive are related, indeed overlapping, and that taken together broadly enough with others both old and new comprise for our dangerous period of cultural metamorphosis the germinal essence of tomorrow's design. He will see that it is the cultivation of these potentialities that dwarf the provincialism of present educational stereotypes and if humanity is to survive, reveal the true dimension, the vision, the challenge, the necessity of World Education.

Towards a Dynamic "World" Education

by

JOHN MCHALE
Research Associate, World Resources Inventory, University of Southern Illinois, Carbondale

There is little need to dwell long, or in much detail, on the general magnitude of our present educational problems.

We may focus the urgency of these problems, now on a global scale, as hinging upon the importance of education as the basic determinant of social and individual development in our swiftly changing world.

Now, as never before, the level and quality of formal education largely determines the degree of freedom of the individual, the prosperity of a nation, and, in the final analysis, the survival of human society. In the developing complexity of our present world, lack of education is, on the one hand, a form of dis-enfranchise. The illiterate individual is denied full cultural participation in his society: his economic freedom and social mobility are restricted according to such formal knowledge, skills and techniques as may only be gained, and duly certified, within a formal educational system. On the other hand, it is also a world which is being transformed by scientific and technological agencies whose understanding, service and control demand a high degree of organized formal knowledge and attainment for their continued functioning and development.

It is a world which depends, quite literally, for its physical survival on a highly educated society.

Against these requirements we may place the statement on world education given by the Sec. Gen. of UNESCO last year:

"More than 2/5ths of the adult population of the globe cannot read or write – about 700 million people. In certain countries illiteracy runs as high as 90% of the population and in many the female population is almost entirely illiterate. Schooling is available for less than half of the world's 550 million children between five and fourteen years old. According to the present estimates the number of illiterates is rising by 20 – 25 millions persons each year."

It would be a mistake, however, for us to dwell too closely on the problem of universal literacy – immense though this may be.

Even in the advanced countries the task of educating the bulk of the population to merely adequate standards is proving to be more than our most highly developed educational systems can cope with. Whilst much apparent success may be recorded, statistically, of the numbers of degrees awarded, courses completed and school places available, there is evidence of great strain and inadequacy in even the most progressive countries.

The restricted access of many to higher education, the drop out rates from schools, colleges and universities, and the great wastage of human resources which these represent, can give satisfaction only to those most narrowly concerned with academic excellence.

These inadequacies, both in combatting illiteracy in the lesser developed areas and providing full educational opportunity in those more fortunate regions are certainly related together. Both depend on the failure of traditional outlooks and methods to cope, not only with the vastly greater numbers to be educated but, also, with the larger and more complex body of knowledge, skills, and techniques to be imparted within the educational system.

However, whilst great ingenuity is now being devoted to the development of new systems and devices through which the *content* of education may be conveyed, little or no attention is being paid to the educational content itself. Great progress is being made in how we may present more information, test more rigorously and instruct larger numbers – but *what* and *why* are questions seldom heard.

The magnitude of our present task requires that we re-examine and reorganize the content as well as the channels of education; we re-shape the curricula as well as the buildings and classrooms – that we restore to education its prime concern with the development of whole men – not merely greater numbers of technicians or well stuffed specialists of this or that subject area. It is time to make a comprehensive re-assessment of our educational goals and the means through which these may be attained.

We have touched upon some of the problems. Where may we look for new directions and solutions?

Knowledge itself has exploded exponentially and now constitutes a major overload on the system. Traditionally it has been our concern to attempt to communicate the maximum amount of subject knowledge possible. Now perhaps we need to ask what is *the minimum amount of knowledge necessary* to understand a field or a group of fields. As rote learning was rendered obsolete by the printed book so the intensive specialization of "human books" may now be obsoleted by mechanized data storage.

Science gives a lead here in its trending towards fresh unities and relationships of many fields – in cosmology, atomic theory, genetics, etc. We have gone swiftly from a great number of isolated principles to much simpler models and hypotheses. Education should seek to re-inforce such convergence of knowledge by pacing each accumulation of new detail knowledge with its conscious integration in new concepts and meaningful wholes.

A dynamic education should have as its prime goal the communication of the unity of human knowledge. We can no longer think in terms of static subject division – one thing, one isolated area, one problem – but only in terms of dynamically interrelated processes and relationships.

Where science education may have given a lead in this new understanding of our world, the traditional arts and humanities still lag far behind. Those areas of our education which deal with the transmission of the symbolic and value content of our culture do so almost entirely in terms of the past. They avoid any immediate relevance to the external cultural environment.

Outside the school this environ is that of the film, T.V., radio, the pictorial magazine and the massive advertisement of a mass culture brought into being by our accelerated technology.

It has been particularly pointed out that "perhaps though *politically* the world has never been so sharply divided, *culturally* it has never presented such a uniform appearance."

It is largely within the mass media and through the products of a mass production technology now distributed on a global scale that the main symbolic and value communication of our cultural situation is carried on. A world society is being brought into being and an international culture now exists – largely through these agencies.

Again, though centers for world scientific studies now exist through the various international geophysical and other years, no centers for world cultural studies have been begun. Less than 2% of our present educational time is spent in the study of cultures other than our own, let alone the emergence of the new forms of culture which surrounds us.

We do have various centers for International Studies but these tend to be no more than cold war colleges concerned solely with political and economic positions. Their internationalism is generally of the 19th century imperial variety.

We need, rather, to emphasise the reality of a world which is being made 'one' – not by political and economic notions – but by scientific and technological fact.

Within this world both the formal and informal realms of education are already undergoing extensive *decentralization*. Not only in terms of physical extension – more schools, colleges, training centers etc. but also in dematerialised extension. Wired and wireless, piped and beamed facilities may now extend one teacher, one classroom or one college to possible vast geographical coverage – via telephone, television, air and satellite transmitters, computer linked libraries and information services etc. etc.

One may literally tune-in on knowledge through the radio, T.V. and telephone. With more sophisticated systems now available, one may even select and follow through complex sequences and instructional programs.

Through advances in educational technology it is now literally and technically possible to have the equivalent of the school (or even college) in the home dwelling. This may very well be the indicated direction for development in the emerging countries. It is not really a new concept. The family dwelling for most people in most of recorded history was the prime educational environ, and remains so for almost all in their earlier and crucial years.

The importance of these early years, for example, has always been recognized but has only recently been massively documented.

The study by Prof. Bloom[1] published last year demonstrates "that half of all the growth of intelligence takes place between birth and age four. The next 30% increase in intelligence is made between the ages of four and eight. Between eight and seventeen when the child is of school age, intelligence increases only about 20%. In short just as much intelligence develops in the first four years of life as in the next thirteen and there is very little growth after eighteen years."

Indeed, relative to such findings our input of personnel, funds and energy into education should actually be reversed – we presently expend most effort in the years after eighteen and leave the first four years to happenstance. A case could be made for inverting our educational pyramid – that is to pay the mother or other person responsible for the most important and formative years, more than the college professor – in due ratio to the greater effect and responsibility!

But, to return to the immediate problems of world education, the swiftly emerging capacities of remotely linked educational service networks could enable us to surmount many of our needs if properly employed.

Where conventional educational planning most often begins with static buildings or centralized facilities, we may more effectively employ the newly available "high frequency" technologies to deploy education and to make it more widely available to all men.

These, and other such dynamic means, however, are not the end answer to our educational needs. A central question remains!

How may we engage the imagination, increase the awareness and most effectively communicate the understanding of our emerging new world?

I should like to conclude this discursive essay with an account of one way in which we are trying to do this with students on a world scale.

Our program, which is called the "World Design Science Decade 1965 – 1975." was initiated by Prof. Buckminster Fuller at the 6th Congress of International Union of Architects in London, 1961.

He proposed then that the architectural and planning schools around the world be encouraged by the IUA to invest the next ten years in a continuing problem of how to make the total world's resources which now

1. Benjamin S. Bloom, "Stability and Change in Human Characteristics", 1964.

serve only 44% of humanity serve 100% through competent planning and design.

Each congress of this international body of some 2500 architects and planners from 65 countries meets every two years in a different host countries. It is quite unpolitical, and recent congresses have ranged from Moscow to London, Cuba to Paris.

For these meetings the world students are generally asked to compete on a given theme for showing in the main exposition of the congress. Themes given may range from the design of a mobile theatre to a school or a dwelling.

FULLER suggests that in the world design scheme such competition was inappropriate – rather, that working groups in all the various countries should cooperate to the fullest extent.

The first stage of the program suggests that the world students should undertake a beginning survey of the total resources now available to man on a global scale – a first stocktaking of what man has to do and what he has to do with it. Such an inventory would be the preliminary phase of an overall plan concerned with the "designed" use of our total global capacities in the service of all men.

The first physical problem given to the students is concerned with the "literacy" of world problems. "The Design of a facility for displaying a comprehensive inventory of the world's raw and organised resources, together with the history and trending pattern of world peoples movements and needs." To define the major world problems and to communicate them effectively through dramatic educational tools, in such a manner as to catalyse their possible design solutions.

One such dramatic tool, outlined in the proposal, is the construction of a 200ft. diameter miniature Earth or Geoscope. This display facility made of light metal trussing would be correctly oriented on its polar axis in location with basic geographic data worked accurately on its surface. Linked to an electronic computer, within which would be stored the "inventoried" world data, and wired on its interior and exterior surfaces with closely packed light points under computer control, this would furnish a giant spherical television screen allowing for the flexible display of dynamic world trending patterns of variable display speeds.

"Viewing the stars through the semi-transparent land masses from the center of such a miniature earth would powerfully locate man in his universe and its electronic display facilities would enable him to see and comprehend patterns far beyond his normal training range. Man cannot see the motions of atoms, molecules, cell growth; he cannot see the motions of planets, stars and galaxies; he cannot see the motions of the hands of the clock. Most of the important trends and surprise events in the life of man are invisible, inexorable motion patterns creeping up surprisingly upon him. Historical patterns too slow for the human eye and mind to comprehend such as changing geology, population growths and resource transpositions may be comprehensively introduced into the computer's memory and acceleratingly pictured around the surface of the earth."

In general, you will agree that such a program offers the greatest challenge and most imaginative sweep for students to respond to. They are, in effect, being asked 'how can you make the world work', how can we redesign the world's prime tool networks and environment facilities so as to make the world's total resources, now serving only 44% of humanity serve 100% through competent scientific design and anticipatory planning – despite decreasing available resources per capita. Young people respond to such challenges!

Architects, planners and engineers are now engaged professionally in very large scale undertakings – they have gone from the planning of the village, to the town, the city, now outward to the region; and are in many cases concerned with national planning.

Fig. 1. 20 ft diameter geodesic sphere with translucent plastic skin with world map and resource data applied.(School of Architecture, University of Nottingham, England.) 1965. As exhibited in Tuileries Gardens Exposition of World Design Science Decade 1965–1975.

This call to face up to world planning is the most logical and urgently necessary next step. In terms of architectural and planning education it provides the most comprehensive framework which could be desired; in terms of general education it provides a meaningful basis for a truly dynamic world education.

Such 'Geoscopes' or "Miniature Earths' as outlined above (cf. Figure 1) may function as nuclei for world information centres in universities, schools, libraries, museums, and communities. Within such centres may also be housed, in easily viewable display forms, chartings and graphic compilations of all such information as would afford the viewer a swift and comprehensive awareness of man in the universe. He may thus be able to review and project all past historical and future trending patterns of the human society on earth – the history of invention, of scientific and technological developments, world population and resources, social and cultural trends, the circulation of raw, processed and scrap materials, etc. These would be conveyed in such a manner as to communicate the sense of their interrelations within various overall ecological developments.

No such centres for direct experience and participation in the "global navigation" of world society have yet been directly developed, though the function exists embryonically in the world's universities, libraries, and institutes, and in its international cooperative agencies and communications networks.

Such facilities, once initiated, might eventually evolve into the beginnings of "world" universities in the truest sense. The activities necessary for the design, maintenance, servicing, and processing of such facilities would certainly attract and provide for the education and training of world educators of a unique kind. Their necessary grasp of the fundamentally integral patterns of man's accumulated knowledge would enable them to communicate and engender that awareness, or attainment, of a truly "world view" which is now essential – not only to further development of human society, but to its basic survival.

Educational Problems of Gifted Children in South-East Asia

by

RUTH H. K. WONG
Dean, Faculty of Education, University of Malaysia, Kuala Lumpur

PREAMBLE

The countries with which this paper is concerned are Burma, Cambodia, Indonesia, Laos, Malaysia, Philippines, Singapore, Thailand and South Vietnam. Much of the information on which it is based has been gleaned through observations made on visits to the countries concerned in March and April of 1964 (Indonesia excepted) and through the use of a questionaire sent out in July this year to Education authorities, University departments of education, colleges of education and principals of a sample of primary and secondary schools in each country.

The response to the simple questionnaire is disheartening for two reasons:

(1) Of 109 forms sent, only 51 were returned; Laos and Cambodia did not respond;
(2) The returned questionnaires highlight, in general, a vast area of lack. For, although 52.9% of these did refer to a special programme for the gifted, 21.6% were positive replies from the Philippines; 60% of the replies from the remaining countries indicated no special programme for the gifted.

This paper is necessarily subjective since the sample of replies is too small for firm generalisations to be made and there is but little data from research or experimentation of consequence in the area on which one could draw. Heavy reliance is therefore placed on the observations during personal visits.

WHO ARE THE GIFTED?

Anticipating that the term "gifted" may have varying connotations in different countries, the first question in the form sent out specified possible definitions for the term. Excluding the Philippines, where the Government and educational institutions have begun, in one form or another, to consider seriously the specific needs of the gifted, 37.5% of the responses from the remaining countries favoured the definition, "a child who is in the top ten per cent of his age group in one or more areas of study in school." 42.5% favoured alternative (d) viz., "a child exceptionally endowed with talent, e.g. poetic, musical, artistic or mechanical talent". The rest of the opinion was divided between a combination of (c) and (d), 7.5% definition (a), 7.5% and definition (b), 5 %.

Of the responses relating to 1(d), 33.3% indicated that there was a special programme for the gifted. Yet on comparing these responses with those for Question Four, Six and Seven on the same forms, it was noticed that the usual criteria of selection through examination was followed in the identification of the gifted; that these were then put in accelerated classes or top streams in schools and treated to a specially intensified programme with extra topics given to them for study. In other words, while there was an awareness that gifts varied, the educational systems which admitted the importance for the nurture of these gifts, did not necessarily cater to these gifts severally except in a very small way within the normal class-group structure. Perhaps the absence of a coherently organised programme for the gifted as defined by 1(d) accounts for the nil returns to Questions Four, Six and Seven in the rest of the forms subscribing to this definition (67%).

It is also interesting to note here that the majority of the 1(d) replies and all the combination 1(c)–1(d) replies, excepting those from the Philippines, came from Malaya, a country where the 11+ Secondary Selection Examination has only recently been abolished and Comprehensive Education introduced at the Junior Secondary School level. One of the expressed aims of the new education is to cater to the individual needs and capabilities of pupils. How this is to be done, however, has yet to be substantiated in practice. Grouping and streaming of pupils on the overall results of a battery of teacher-made, non-standardised achievement tests continues to be adopted. Each child, after the initial classification, remains in a group kept rigidly together in a lock-step process.

The acceptance of a particular definition of "giftedness" seems very closely related to the educational system which obtains in a particular country. In Malaya, where a change has occurred in the status quo and a slow transition is being made from an examination-dominated system to one admitting of the need to cater to individual differences, the gifted child is viewed by some in terms of definition 1(c), hitherto the orthodox view, or in terms of 1(d), a more liberal view in keeping with the new aims, or in terms of both. Replies from Thailand, Sarawak, Sabah, Burma and South Vietnam where examination and elimination continue to be twin practices in the control of school cohorts, all favoured 1(c) without a single exception. One respondent added the definition, "a child in the top 30 per cent in the main areas of study." 46.7% of the 1(c) responses, however, indicated that the educational system did not cater to the gifted child.

Similarly, in the Philippines, in which the system of education is less organised as a governmental effort, where more flexibility of organisation within each institution is permitted, and where the pattern of education is rather closely associated with that of the United States, the respondents have tended to favour both 1(b) and 1(d) and have fanned out over the whole range of the choice of alternatives to Question Six. Methods of work with the gifted too cover most of the measures set out in Question 7 with the strongest emphases on 7(b), 7(d) and 7(h), items significantly lacking in returns from respondents in other countries.

The I.Q. definition has not been favoured except by respondents in the Philippines, because, perhaps, of the lack or absence of standardised I.Q. tests suitable for use in the region.

EARLY IDENTIFICATION OF THE GIFTED FOR SPECIAL ATTENTION

Every one of the respondents, except for two, agreed that early identification of the gifted for special attention was necessary. The two who dissented gave respectively the following reasons:

(1) We may find children who seem to be gifted at an early age but turn out later not to be so. Hence it is better to wait a year or two for this.

(2) Early identification is psychologically unwise; it is unnecessary. The geniuses of history were not identified for special attention. They developed despite society and environment.

The first reason against early identification came from an Elementary School principal in Malaya. In this country, children of parents of middle income groups who are relatively well-off are sent at the age of four or five to private Kindergarten schools (Government does not organise pre-school education). Many of these schools incorporate in their curriculum both play and the traditional study of the three R's. Thus children who finish Kindergarten and enter the first year of Elementary School are well ahead of their less fortunate peers who have not had the same opportunities. Because they are more articulate in their speech, more facile in their use of vocabulary, and more advanced in number skills, teachers tend to regard them as "gifted". Such children are generally diverted between the ages of seven and nine to "express" or "accelerated" classes where they do three years' work in two. Their academic superiority is not always maintained as the dissenting reason given above has already implied.

The lack of distinction between pure academic advantage, gained through a better cultural and material environment, and true giftedness may have accounted for the replies from the rest of the Malayan Elementary School principals who responded to this questionnaire positively in respect of Question 3 and elaborated by checking off Item 6(a). At any rate their responses to Item 7 do not bear out the presence of a programme for the gifted.

Associated with the second reason may be the typically Eastern concept of learning. The scholar seeks continually the truth and meaning of life through a philosophical approach to the environment. Historically, the gifted of the East was first and foremost a wise man who could apply his wisdom to the fruitful use of his gift or gifts. These were regarded as similarly available to all men in varying degrees. But the gifted was essentially he who nurtured his gifts; others lost them through neglect. Thus in Chinese history and folk-lore, tales of boy prodigies abound – prodigies who themselves were gifts to men. The gods were no respecters of persons: many of these prodigies were born into the most ordinary of ordinary homes. Among them were young cowherds and slave children. One, for example, was described as studying the logistics of war with the stones he gathered from the wayside; another read by the light of glow-worms. All had great powers for reflection.

From among the scholars of Buddhist temple schools in Burma, Thailand, Cambodia and Vietnam were those of the past gifted in leadership and in the arts of government and peace. Tradition dies hard. This humanistic view of giftedness as potential quite beyond the reach of environmental influence to mar or make good still persists even though most of the South-East Asian territories have been through a period of colonial rule. Its influence persists in the conduct of teaching in the classroom and in the general organisation of activities. He who applies himself to learning will in the end prove his gift-worthiness. Hence the great respect for textbooks and for the teacher's words. The idea of the original remains but the substance has given way to the shadow in practice. For a technological age, this view of giftedness seems inadequate.

It is, however, encouraging to note that all who supported the early identification of gifted children for special attention also agreed that there was no adequate programme for the nurture of the gifted and made suggestions as follows:

(1) Research must be undertaken to study proper motivational devices to help the gifted to respond to their work positively;

(2) Pertinent criteria and instruments for the identification of the gifted should be established;

(3) Existing school curricula should be examined so that special provision may be made to meet specific talents; or

(4) Special schools should be set up for such talents/gifts as mentioned in Item 1(d);

(5) More flexibility in school administration should be allowed; (To appreciate this suggestion, it must be understood that most of the school systems in the newly emergent territories in South-East Asia are Government-determined. In some places schools are not allowed to deviate either from the pattern of organisation imposed or from the given syllabi for the subjects to be taught in the curriculum).

(6) Relaxation of age requirements should be permitted.

(7) Specialist teachers should be trained to identify and meet the needs of gifted children. In general, the standards of teacher-training could well be raised.

(8) A system of scholarships should be instituted to cater to the needs of the gifted poor.

(9) Good guidance and counselling should be made available to the gifted.

(10) A special fund should be set up for the specific purpose of enabling gifted children in schools to develop to the fullest extent of their promise.

(11) More facilities and materials for the improvement of teaching should be made available to schools.

WHY SHOULD THE GIFTED BE IDENTIFIED?

The reasons given for the need to identify the gifted early were generally the following in the order of frequency:

(1) They have to be identified early so that their special talents may be allowed to develop;

(2) The gifted progress much faster than others in the same class. It is not fair to hold them back in the same lock-step process. They should be identified in order to be put in special classes with special programmes;

(3) The gifted should be identified for special attention; guidance and counselling could be given to them to enable them to develop to their fullest potential;

(4) They should be identified lest a non-challenging and unsuitable programme should cause undue frustration on their part so that they become maladjusted beings who do not eventually make effective contribution to society;

(5) They should be singled out for special treatment; this is particularly desired in respect of children from rural areas who not only lack environmental and cultural support but may, for lack of money, be lost to society.

Only five out of the forty-nine respondents, who felt the gifted should be identified early, stressed the need of the country and society for the gifted. Their reasons may be summarised as follows:

(1) The gifted are a country's asset, particularly the developing country's greatest asset. The state with limited resources should give special attention to those who have most to contribute to the welfare and progress of the state and its people;

(2) The gifted should be trained for leadership in the educational, cultural, administrative and scientific fields;

(3) Guidance and help for the gifted will result in the maximum exploitation of their gifts and society will be repaid by being brought closer to the goal for good living.

AGE RELAXATION FOR THE GIFTED

In respect of this the institutions fall into two categories, Government and Private Institutions. In Government-established schools and Universities there is no relaxation in the age requirements for the various levels of education. For Malaya, however, the age requirement is relaxed at Primary level as already explained. Even then there is no fixed policy and not all elementary schools have "express" streams. In order to expedite the education of science and medical scholars at the University of Malaya those who have obtained their Higher School Certificate with appropriate subjects at advanced level may seek direct entry into the second year of the University course. Whether these direct entries can be considered among the gifted depends on the definition accepted. They are certainly those in the top 10% of their age group.

In private institutions, particularly those of the Philippines, the age requirement is waived at one or more levels of school though not at the University.

Respondents generally associated the ages at which the gifted are identified with those at which pupils sit the various selection examinations in the school system.

RESEARCH

No research on gifted children is currently carried out in any South-East Asian country except in the Philippines. In Malaya, a four-year follow-up study of student progress, begun in 1964 and using both the 1964, and 1965 cohorts, examines the relationship between high achievement in school examinations and final success at the University. A derived problem for study is the extent to which high achievement may be accepted as an indication of giftedness.

Studies in the Philippines are being conducted under the auspices of the newly established National Coordinating Center for the Study of Filipino Children and Youth. This institution is charged with conducting and encouraging research among public and private institutions with a view to making a scientific and thorough study of the needs of Filipino children.

At the Philippine Women's University a study is currently conducted on the background of Gifted Children. A particular sample of students in Maquiling School was given the WISC, the Philippine Mental Ability Test (Form III) and the Zafran Culture-Free Test in an attempt to find out the particular needs of these children and to suggest special educational provisions for the gifted. There are limited studies too for the setting up of developmental norms. On the whole what research is being carried out on gifted children in South-East Asia is still meagre, barely informative and hardly worth citing.

The responses to the questionnaire as a whole have given some indication of the highly selective and competitive process which governs the opportunities for education within the South-East Asian region. Giftedness tends to be identified with high achievement in the school. There is a lack of clear and coherent thinking on the needs of gifted children although there is certainly a kind of inarticulate feeling for them. There is the impression too that more organised effort could be made to meet their needs, that officially at any rate, Governments lack an appreciation of the importance of the contribution which the gifted can make to society.

It rests with research not only to indicate how talents may be identified but also how they may be properly developed. In the context of South-East Asia these are crucial problems and difficult to solve. To see them in perspective it is necessary to appreciate the social conditions which seem to militate against rather than nurture the gifted.

PROBLEMS OF THE GIFTED ARISING FROM THE SOCIAL CONDITIONS OBTAINING IN SOUTH-EAST ASIA

1. *Nurture of the gifted is difficult in the context of traditional values held.*

According to traditional thinking, giftedness is a child of "happenstance." Well enough if it grows and manifests itself! It may not even be right to pay overmuch attention to it lest the gods should take the possessor of the gifts away. Thus in families where children, particularly boys, show promise, they are given nicknames such as "Fool" and "Rubbish" so that they may be mistaken for what they are not and thus preserved from the Evil Eye. Among more sophisticated urban peoples of the region there is hardly any of this thinking left and ambitions parents like those in the West push their children hard if there is any indication of ability at all. But only 13% of the population in this region as a whole live in urban areas. A great number are still rural and mentally inhibited by the values and superstitions which have been handed down.

Again in societies which have been mainly feudal, there is an unquestioning acceptance of one's lot. Only education can correct such an attitude and promote social mobility, but for education to work there must first be a rise in the level of aspiration. In the villages of Cambodia, Laos, Thailand and South Vietnam, for example, much has still to be done to bring children in to schools. Such conditions are not conducive to the identification of talent. Besides, talents do not flourish in economically underprivileged homes or a culturally impoverished environment.

2. *The too-rapid rate of educational development cannot ensure sound programmes for the gifted.*

With limited means and scant resources some countries in the region can scarce give four years of free compulsory primary education to all children of the correct school age. But when the goal was set at the Karachi Conference of 1959 for all countries in Asia to reach at least a six-year target, the cost became staggering in respect of teachers and teaching facilities. In trying to establish this broad base to the educational pyramid standards are necessarily lowered. Mass education brings its concomitant problems of strained resources and poor teaching. In Malaya, a further effort is added through making available, to all who demand it, a place in secondary school up to the age of 15+ from 1965 onwards. A programme for the gifted which calls for special facilities and specialist teachers can hardly be expected to thrive in these circumstances, unless new measures are sought for the deployment of teachers and the grouping of pupils. New methods may involve the discarding of the staff-pupil ratio idea and the use of mass communication media for instruction.

There has been mention made also of the establishment of schools for the intellectual elite (in Singapore, for example). If the general tone of education is poor in the average school, the setting up of a special school or schools merely enhances the invidious comparison between the gifted have's and the average have-nots.

3. *The highly selective and competitive system of education causes unnecessary wastage of talent.*

No follow-up studies have been made in any country to establish the validity and the reliability of the selection procedures used at different levels of the schools system. Malaysia has three such selection points – at 15+, 17+, and 19+. Those who go on to the University have to submit to further selection. The attrition rate even at the University level is heavy. The following tables are revealing.

TABLE I

Success of Science Students admitted in 1960/61 & 1961/62

	1960/61	1961/62
No. admitted to first year.	67	86
No. graduate with pass degree after 3 years.	29	22
No. graduated with honours degree after 4 years.	18	14

TABLE II

Success of Science Students admitted by direct entry in to the Second Year in 1960/61 and 1961/62

	1960/61	1961/62
No. admitted to second year.	14	12
No. graduated with pass degree after 2 years.	8	9
No. graduated with honours degree after 3 years.	8	8

Table II gives the numbers of those students who according to the definition of Item 1(c) of the questionnaire may be termed gifted. Yet for both 1960/61 and 1961/62 groups there were those who failed to arrive at the honours degree qualification (six and four respectively) and would never have a second chance at it again. The wastage rate in Table I is quite alarming. Seeing that Science students are much in demand in a developing economy such wastage can scarcely be justified and less so because at each of the previous levels so many have been turned away from completing their progress through the educational system.

In all countries except the Philippines, promotion from one level to the next is determined by a statistic, a practice which assumes that a constant intellectual quantum exists from year to year. Yet this practice, in view of the limited numbers of places available at each higher level, seems to be necessary. The unimpeded escalation of youngsters through the years of elementary and secondary levels of school in the Philippines does not afford a better solution since the general standard of education, excepting that in certain well-endowed institutions, is too low for the educational output to be of value to society.

Aggravating the wastage through failure is the practice of retention of which there is high incidence in countries like Burma and South Vietnam. In the former, retentions average about 50% in the first two years of primary education, rising to nearly 70% in the last two years. In the latter, there is an average retention of 40% of the pupils in primary school. The pupil does not necessarily improve through retention since no remedial work is provided and having been put through the course for a second year he often becomes a bored and disinterested "over-ager."

Wastage also occurs through drop-out. This may be due to lack of aspiration, poverty, lack of the necessary home support, or the need to assist in the work in the fields. The drop-out rate can be very heavy. In Cambodia for example, there was a total primary enrolment of 356,100 with 85,000 entering the first year in 1955. At the end of a year, only 66,000 went on to Grade Two, 19.000 having either dropped out or been retained.

According to the figures supplied by the UNESCO publication, *World Survey of Education*, 1960, there were in 1953/54 90.3 %of South-East Asia's total school enrolment at the first level of school, 8.4 %and 1.3% at the second and third levels respectively. The North American continent with a comparable population had 73%, 20.8% and 6.2%, respectively, at the same three levels. A comparison of the two educational pyramids speaks for itself. The South-East Asian case draws attention immediately to the two causes of drastic elimination and heavy drop-out.

CONCLUSION

I have not so much tried to explain the problems of gifted children in South-East Asia as leave them for inference by referring to the conditions which obtain in the region. Much remains to be done. For the academic, the greatest problem in circumstances of need is how to convince the Government that educational research is not a luxury which can easily be dispensed with and that improvement and development are more likely with proper experimentation and evaluation.

QUESTIONNAIRE ON GIFTED CHILDREN

[Gen. Instruction: For each question below, please place a X in the appropriate box]

1. Below are different definitions of a gifted child.
   Check the definition/definitions which you feel has/have common usage in your country:
   a. A genius □
   b. A child of I.Q. greater than 140 □
   c. A child who is in the top 10% of his age group in one or more of the areas of study in school □
   d. A child exceptionally endowed with talent e.g. poetic, musical, artistic or mechanical talent □
   e. Other definition (if not covered by above)

   ____

   ____

2. Should gifted children be identified early for special attention?

   YES □ NO □

   Why? ______________________________

   ____

   ____

3. Does your government/institution* have a special programme for the gifted?

   YES □ NO □

   *Delete whichever is not applicable.

4. If your answer is YES, check which of the following method/methods is/are adopted for the identification of the gifted.
   a. Selection by Testing □
      (i) on results of examination □
      (ii) by I.Q. tests □
      (iii) by standardised Achievement tests □
      (iv) by aptitude tests □
      (v) by all of the above □
      (vi) other tests (specify) □

      ____

      ____

   b. Use of Cumulative Records □
   c. Through observations and interviews □
   d. Through the help of: (i) guidance counsellors □
      (ii) psychologists □
      (iii) teachers as a team □

5. At what age are they identified?

   Circle *one*: 4 5 6 7 8 9 10 11 12 13 14 15 16 17 18

6. Check the programme/programmes adopted in your country/institution* for catering to the needs of gifted children after they are identified.

a. They are placed in express or accelerated classes ☐
b. They are placed in the top stream on the results of an examination/examinations ☐
c. They are placed in a special ability group within their class ☐
d. They are given individual attention ☐
e. Other programmes, if not covered above: ______

*Delete whichever is not applicable.

7. Which of the following measure/measures is/are taken to ensure the proper nurture of the gifted?

a. Subject tutoring in area of weakness ☐
b. Intensive individual and group counselling ☐
c. Discussion of study methods ☐
d. Special motivational devices ☐ Specify: ______

e. Special problems for the child's individual pursuit ☐
f. Extra topics are given them for study. These are beyond the normal requirements of the curriculum ☐
g. The content of the curriculum is specially diversified ☐
h. Special enrichment materials are used ☐ Specify: ______

8. Do you consider that your government/institution* has an adequate programme for the nurture of the gifted?

YES ☐ NO ☐

*Delete whichever is not applicable.

9. If NO, specify what else you would wish to be done.

______

10. Are age limitations relaxed for gifted children on entrance to

a. Primary School	YES ☐	NO ☐
b. Secondary School	YES ☐	NO ☐
c. University	YES ☐	NO ☐

11. Is any research carried out on gifted children in your country/institution*?

YES ☐ NO ☐

*Delete whichever is not applicable.

12. If YES, please describe briefly.

______

Also, please include available literature with the return of this questionnaire. Thank you.

Existing International Institutions which Approximate, or Might Become, World Universities

selected and described by

HAROLD TAYLOR

At the present time no single institution exists which can properly be called a world university – that is, an institution with a fully international curriculum of the major university disciplines of knowledge, with a student-body and faculty representing every major cultural and geographical area of the world. Some are closer to the concept than others, all are limited in some measure by present circumstance.

In the following summary an effort has been made to judge the degree to which each institution approximates the concept of complete internationality, and to identify institutions which, if developed further, could become genuine world universities. For example, if the East West Center in Hawaii were open to students and faculty from all major continental areas, including Communist China, and a curriculum were planned to include all major cultures and sciences, it would become a world center rather than an American-sponsored Asian-American institute. Or, if a series of regional world centers were established, with completely internationalized curricula in the arts and sciences, open to students and faculty of all countries, the interchange of faculty and students among them would form a global network within the world's present academic community.

On the other hand, there are institutions staffed by scholars which in structure are already world institutions, such as the Economic Development Institute of the International Bank for Reconstruction and Development, or the United Nations Institute for Training and Research, but which serve a more limited purpose than that of a world university. These are extremely valuable as examples of international structure, since they point to a form of organization – international governing bodies, financial subsidy by a variety of nations, research projects of significance to world problems, work by scholars in which graduate students may join – which could be transposed directly into the field of higher education were there sufficient interest in making such a transposition.

The first category consists of institutions some of which are related in some way to the United Nations, and are involved in research and projects, with possibilities for extension into the educational field on a larger international scale.

CERN (European Organization for Nuclear Research), Meyrin, Geneva 23, Switzerland, was founded July 1, 1953, through the cooperation of scientists and officials of thirteen European governments (Austria, Belgium, Denmark, Spain, France, Greece, Italy, Norway, the Netherlands, Germany, the United Kingdom, Sweden, and Switzerland) as a center for cooperative research in high energy physics. The center was designed to provide the necessary equipment and personnel for advanced research, equipment more expensive and complicated than any one country could easily furnish for itself. CERN provides research facilities for approximately sixty-five resident scientists from the sponsoring countries, three hundred visiting scientists, and courses enrolling five hundred and fifty students from a highly selected roster of applicants. Among other activities the center conducts a translation service for its research results, a public information service, and a monthly journal.

The administration includes a president of the international three-man governing council and an international scientific executive committee, each member of which is a practicing scientist in a particular field. Funds are supplied by the governments involved on an apportionment basis, with the larger contributions coming from France, Great Britain, and West Germany. Visiting scientists join the center on a selected basis and include persons from Canada, Brazil, Nationalist China, the United States, Hungary, India, Israel, Japan, Pakistan, Poland, Rumania, Czechoslovakia, and the Soviet Union. All of the work is devoted to non-military research. It is conceivable that the basic idea of CERN could be expanded to include regional world institutes in the natural sciences, to which might be added the social sciences and the humanities, with students drawn from all parts of the world. Participants in the CERN project testify to the great value of the international aspect of work in the laboratories and the scientific community gathered together in Geneva.

European Centre for the Co-ordination of Research and Documentation in the Social Sciences, Bauernmarkt 6, Vienna 1, Austria. In pursuance of the resolution adopted by the General Conference of UNESCO at its twelfth Session, the European Centre for the Co-ordination of Research and Documentation in the Social Sciences was organized in Vienna, following a decision taken by the Executive Committee of the International Social Science Council (ISSC) during its meeting in that city on April 5, 6, 1963. The purpose of the Centre is to stimulate comparative research in the priority areas selected by its directing bodies, to co-ordinate such research, and to encourage the building up of appropriate documentation for the selected areas. The Centre is a permanent external body of the International Social Science Council and has a Steering Committee whose members are appointed by the Executive Committee of the ISSC.

The first Steering Committee, appointed for two years (subsequent nominations will be for three years) was composed of the following individuals: Chairman, Professor A. SCHAFF (Poland); Vice-Chairman, Professor E. A. G. ROBINSON, (United Kingdom); Committee members, Professor A. A. ARZUMANIAN (USSR), Professor S. GROENMAN (Netherlands), Rector L. KERSCHAGEL (Austria), Professor A. KNAPP (Czechoslovakia), Professor J. STOETZEL (France). The Directorate includes a scientific director acting provisionally as Director of the Centre, and an administrative secretary acting provisionally as General Secretary.

The actual work of the Centre began on November 1, 1963, and, for the present, its research program is concentrated on seven main fields: comparative studies of programming and planning, social consequences of industrialization, social and legal aspects of industrialization, the problem of under-developed areas in economically developed countries, time budgets, comparison of concepts and methods of aiding developing countries, and peace research.

Were it possible to expand the research topics and a curriculum into the humanities and the natural sciences, the Vienna Centre would become a fullbodied world university. The model is an appropriate one for other research and educational institutes and for regional world centers, since it includes scholars from the major cultural and geographical areas of the world, with the present exception of Communist China.

INTERNATIONAL ATOMIC ENERGY AGENCY (IAEA), Kaerntnerring, Vienna I, Austria. The statute for the IAEA was approved on October 26, 1956, at a conference held at the United Nations headquarters in New York and came into effect on July 29, 1957, when the United States ratified the treaty. The Agency, while not a specialized organ of the UN, is under UN auspices. In the field of atomic energy, the Agency represents one sector of need for a world research and planning body and, as such, has great educational possibilities for the future. The Agency is concerned with: a) fundamental techniques in the field of nuclear energy, b) theoretical and experimental aspects of the science and technology of nuclear energy; and c) advanced training, including active participation in research work, for persons potentially qualified to carry out research programs in the basic sciences and engineering.

The Agency is supported by pledges from Member States. The countries which presently belong to the IAEA are: Argentina, Australia, Austria, Brazil, Canada, Ceylon, Republic of China, Denmark, Finland, France, Germany, Greece, India, Iraq, Israel, Italy, Japan, Korea, Mexico, Monaco,

Netherlands, Norway, Pakistan, Philippines, Poland, Portugal, Republic of South Africa, Switzerland, Sweden. Thailand, United Arab Republic, United Kingdom, United States, Venezuela, and Yugoslavia.

Fellowships are awarded to nationals of Member States who then go for training in countries with well developed programs in atomic energy. It offers training at both undergraduate and graduate levels, with the more qualified applicants being sent for doctoral studies. In October 1964, the IAEA created the International Center for Theoretical Physics located in Trieste as a contribution to international collaboration in science and to physics in developing countries. During the first year of operation the staff of fifty-two consisted of twenty-eight nationalities the majority coming from Latin America, East Europe, Africa and Asia. The center is established for a period of four years with its continued existence depending on the decisions of the atomic energy commissions of the IAEA's member states.

International Children's Centre, Chateau de Longchamp, Bois de Boulogne, Paris-16, France, is the joint effort of intergovernmental arrangements and agreements. It also cooperates closely with UNICEF and WHO. The Centre is open to nationals of all countries, and it offers training courses in maternity and child welfare, social pediatrics, child behavior and development, nutrition, and all fields related to child welfare. Depending on the particular field of study, courses run from six weeks to one year or longer. These courses are usually at a graduate or post-graduate level, and trainees are generally those whose professions are directly related to the field of child welfare.

In most cases the students are awarded scholarships by the Centre; these scholarships cover tuition, travel expenses during the course, and spending money. The cost of transportation for the participant to travel to and from the Centre is usually provided by the co-operating government or, in rare cases, by the participant himself. A student who is involved in a six-month course is awarded a scholarship amounting to $ 2000, while a one-year course entitles the student to a scholarship amounting to not less than $ 3000.

International Computation Centre, Palazzo degli Offici, Zona dell'EUR, Rome, Italy is an intergovernmental agency and its principal concern is with providing training in the processing of information and in applied mathematics. As of 1964, the member countries of the International Computation Centre are: Argentina, Belgium, Ceylon, Cuba, France, Israel, Italy, Japan, Libya, Mexico, and the United Arab Republic. Courses range from six to twelve months, and the Centre awards scholarships to the trainees.

INTERNATIONAL CONFERENCES ON SCIENCE AND WORLD AFFAIRS (PUGWASH – COSWA) 8 Asmara Road, London N.W. 2, England. The Pugwash Conferences were first suggested by Lord BERTRAND RUSSELL in an appeal he made from London on July 10, 1955. Other co-sponsors and co-signers of the written appeal included ALBERT EINSTEIN, FREDERIC JOLIOT-CURIE, HIDEKI YUKAWA, and other eminent scientists from Great Britain and the United States. The Russell statement follows.

In the tragic situation that confronts humanity, we feel that scientists should assemble in conferences to appraise the perils that have arisen as a result of the development of weapons of mass destruction... We are speaking on this occasion, not as members of this or that nation, continent or creed, but as human beings, members of the species man, whose continued existence is in doubt. The world is full of conflicts; and, overshadowing all minor conflicts, the titanic struggle between communism and anti-communism.

Most of us are not neutral in feeling but, as human beings, we have to remember that if the issues between East and West are to be decided in any manner that can give satisfaction to anybody, whether Communist or anti-Communist, whether Asian or European or American, whether white or black, then these issues must not be decided by war. We should wish this to be understood, both in the East and the West.

We invite this congress to be convened, and through it the scientists of the world and the general public should subscribe to the following resolution:

"In view of the fact that in any future war nuclear weapons will certainly be employed, and that such weapons threaten the continued existence of mankind, we urge the governments of the world to realize, and to acknowledge publicly, that their purposes cannot be furthered by a world war, and we urge them, consequently, to find peaceful means for the settlement of all matters of dispute between them."

Though the appeal was made in 1955, there was no perceptible movement in the direction suggested by its initiators until Lord RUSSELL gained the interest of the American industrialist CYRUS EATON. With Mr. EATON's financial backing, a group of scientists from East and West met at his summer home in Pugwash, Nova Scotia, for the first of what later proved to be a series of conferences of scientists from the two major ideological blocs. This conference, which took place July 6–11, 1957, was attended by scientists from the United States (seven), the USSR (three), Australia, Canada, Great Britain, France, Nationalist China, and Poland. The second conference, which took place in Lac Beauport, Quebec, from March 31 to April 11, 1958, had the active participation of scientists from the United States, the USSR, Canada, Australia, Great Britain, West Germany, and Communist China. Although invited each year, Communist Chinese scientsits have not attended during the past five years. Beginning in 1958, there have been two COSWA conferences every year.

COSWA has been officially endorsed by the Soviet Academy of Sciences, the American Academy of Arts and Sciences, and comparable organizations in the participating countries. By 1962, when the ninth and tenth Pugwash Conferences were held, participation – both in terms of individuals attening and countries represented – increased markedly. The ninth conference, which took place in Cambrige, England, was attended by sixty scientists from eighteen countries; the tenth, in London, brought together two hundred scientists from thirty-six countries, including an eighteen-member Soviet delegation and some top experts and government advisors from the United States and Great Britain.

To add permanence to the conferences, a Continuing Committee was set up at the third conference in Kitzbuehel, Austria. The composition of the Committee shows a degree of cooperation between East and West;it consists, at present, of three Soviet scientists, three Americans, three British, and one scientist each from Italy, France, Poland, and India. The efforts of COSWA members to achieve a solution to the problem of atomic bomb testing are considered to have had an important part in bringing about the test-ban treaty in 1963. Were it possible to develop a year round program of research, study, and education in science and society through COSWA at a central place, the world university idea would be achieved in considerable measure.

International Schools Examination Syndicate, 62 route de Chene, Geneva, Switzerland. In collaboration with the International School of Geneva, the International Schools Association has developed a pilot project in international examinations for the graduates of secondary schools, with the intention of providing international standards of entrance to universities throughout the world. Such an international system, if carried out on a large scale, will have great significance in the creation of new forms of world education in the universities.

Should it prove possible to establish a network of universities which recognize the international examination, and to link it with a network of the world's secondary schools which agree to develop curricula adapted to the standards of the examination, it will be possible for students educated in one national educational system to move easily to the universities of other countries. The circulation of the world's students would then become infinitely more possible and potentially more desirable.

Already progress has been made in this direction with the development of an examination in Contemporary History 1913–1963, administered for the first time in June, 1963, at the International School in Geneva. Subsequently, the syllabus and examination papers were sent to all ministries of education and departments of education throughout the world, with some forty favorable responses. With the cooperation of UNESCO, curricula and examinations are being developed in all areas. An international board is in the process of formation to supervise further work and to continue the analysis of existing syllabi of national educational systems, to select what is appropriate, and to broaden the conception of the various disciplines, categories, and teaching methods into world dimensions.

INTERNATIONAL SECRETARIAT FOR VOLUNTEER SERVICE (ISVS), Washington, D.C. 20525 was created by forty-one governments attending the International Conference on Human Skills in the Decade of Development (Middle Level Manpower Conference) in Puerto Rico, October 10–12, 1962. Its purpose is to support and assist national volunteer service programs by serving as an information exchange and clearing-house, by encouraging more programs of this kind and helping to set up and operate them, and by cooperating with other interested organizations with a view to increasing "the supply and quality of middle level manpower available to developing countries."

The Secretariat is financed by voluntary contributions of member countries and staffed by an international group from Germany, Israel, the Netherlands, and the Philippines. Seven regional meetings have been held in the past two years for discussion of common problems, and meetings were held in Africa, Latin America, and the Far East in the latter part of 1965. Teams of international experts are sent to interested countries on request. Should the Secretariat develop an educational program to prepare youth for voluntary service, "while at the same time promoting understanding between people of different cultures," a genuine world college might emerge from the present organization.

UNITED NATIONS INTERNATIONAL SCHOOL (UNIS), First Ave. and 70th St., New York, N.Y., was established in 1947, in Lake Success, New York, to meet the needs of members of the UN Secretariat and Delegations for the education of their children. From the start, the philosophy of the School called for the preservation of the cultural values of each nationality while practising the ideals of international understanding and cooperation of the UN Charter. An association of parents and friends of the School began nursery-school classes in 1947, in the guest house of the then UN headquarters in Lake Success with twenty children from fifteen countries and a faculty of four teachers, each of a different nationality. By September, 1949, the first elementary class had been started, with a higher grade added each year until the ultimate objective was realized in 1961 – 62 of six years of elementary, four of secondary and three of pre-university education. When the UN moved to its present headquarters in 1950, the School moved into a group of converted apartments in Parkway Village, Jamaica, New York. In 1959, temporary quarters were obtained in Public School 82 in Manhattan to house all thirteen grades. These premises and the Parkway Village feeder school through the fifth grade will be maintained until September, 1968.

During the academic year 1964–65, the School had 568 pupils from sixty-eight countries, including 30 from the Eastern European Socialist Republics, 3 from Cuba and 14 from the USSR. Of these 568 pupils, 310 were children of those working in the UN Secretariat, 50 were children of UN Delegation members, 55 were of international origin not connected with the UN, and 175 were Americans. Children of local U.S. citizens made up approximately 30 percent of the enrolment. There were forty-six full time and three part-time members on the academic staff, nine from Asia, one from the Middle East and one from Africa, one from South America, seven from North America, twenty-eight from Europe, and two from Australia.

The objectives of the School curriculum are to "provide a unique opportunity for the development of international and inter-cultural understanding ... This, however, does not mean that the School is a denationalizing institution. On the contrary, its aim is to maintain each student's pride in and knowledge of his own culture. It aims also at providing for a mastery of the basic skills of communication and calculation, as far as feasible, in the home language of the pupil as well as in the language of his or her environment ... The School tries to ensure that the child develops in harmony with his age group requirements, in harmony with his environment, and in harmony both with his national culture and the wider world community."

Policy for the conduct of the UNIS is set by an eighteen-member Board of Trustees; administration of the School, its management and its operation are the tasks of the Director, appointed by the Board. In addition to managing the day-to-day affairs of the School, the Director is responsible for the establishment of educational methods, curricula, and standards; the administration of the budget, and the making of all appointments. Apart from establishing policy for the conduct of the School, the Board of Trustees is also concerned with its development and with raising funds for the School's advancement.

The importance of the School to the United Nations is recognized in the financial support given to it by the UN General Assembly which has made grants-in-aid since 1949, ranging from $ 7,400 in 1952 to $ 100,000 in 1959 and later years. On February 10, 1965, the UN General Assembly passed a resolution which approved plans for the construction of a $ 7,000,000 building and campus with facilities for one thousand children. The new building at Twenty-fifth Street and Franklin D. Roosevelt Drive, to be completed by September, 1968, is made possible by a gift of up to $ 7,500,000 from the Ford Foundation, conditional on the School becoming self-supporting. A three million dollar fund-raising drive is now under way to ensure that the School can become independent of additional UN contributions.

The United Nations International School is one of the first of its kind in the world, and can serve as an example for the development of similar schools and world colleges on a regional basis on other continents. It can also serve as an experimental center for the development of world curricula and for the creation of an international baccalaureate degree.

United Nations Institute for Training and Research, 801 United Nations Plaza, New York, N.Y. Resolution 1827 (XVII) of the General Assembly proposed the creation of the United Nations Institute for Training and

Research (UNITAR). During the next session, resolution 1934 authorized the Secretary General to take necessary steps to establish the Institute and to explore possible governmental and non-governmental sources of financial assistance. In its broadest terms the purpose of the Institute is to enhance the effectiveness of the United Nations in pursuing its two overriding objectives – the maintenance of peace and security and the promotion of economic and social development. The Institute will provide facilities for certain types of training and research which are of high priority in advancing toward these objectives.

By March, 1965, the Secretary General had appointed and convened UNITAR's Board of Trustees, which is now composed of seventeen distinguished members of international reputation in fields of interest to the United Nations, drawn from different regions of the world and representing different political and cultural backgrounds, two United Nations Under Secretaries and four *ex-officio* members: the Secretary General, the President of the General Assembly, the President of the Economic and Social Council, and the Executive Director of the Institute. Mr. KENNETH YOUNGER of Great Britain, director of the Royal Institute of International Affairs, is the elected Board Chairman; the countries represented on the Board are Belgium, Canada, Chile, Denmark, France, India, Iran, Kenya, United Arab Republic, United Kingdom, United States, and Venezuela.

After consultation with the Board of Trustees, the Secretary General announced in March, 1965 the appointment of GABRIEL d'ARBOUSSIER of Senegal as Executive Director of the Institute, with the terms and conditions of service of a UN Under Secretary. The Board of Trustees is responsible for determining the basic policies of the Institute and for adopting its budget on the basis of the proposals submitted by the Executive Director, who has an overall responsibility for the organization, direction, and administration of the Institute, in accordance with the general policies formulated by the Board of Trustees.

The Institute's envisioned budget for the first five to six years is $10,000,000. As of November, 1965, sixty-five countries in Asia, Africa, and South America had pledged or paid total contributions of $ 5,723,355.

In the field of training an agreement was reached on the transfer to the Institute of certain existing training programs within the UN Secretariat. These are: the Training Program for Foreign Service Officers from Newly Developing Countries, the Training Program in Development Financing, and the Training Program in Techniques and Procedures of Technical Assistance. A Projected program for the training of assistant resident representatives and counterpart personnel, which has been accepted in principle is under preparation.

The Executive Director submitted to the Board at its third session, in March, 1966, criteria and standards to govern the general and special fellowships which are to be established, including the UNITAR Adlai Stevenson Fellowships.

A few preliminary studies are now being carried out in connection with research. The Executive Director has agreed, in principle, with the Director of the World Food Program that the Institute might undertake an evaluation of some of the Program's activities, and technical discussions are now being held on the application of this agreement. Execution of this research project, in addition to being of special interest to the World Food Program, will take the Institute into the general field of evaluation, in which, by means of comparative studies, an attempt will be made gradually to develop a methodology. Preliminary studies are being carried out on two other subjects with a particular effort to avoid duplication. These are language teaching and a directory of existing training and research institutes.

Further research possibilities have been discussed and recommended by the Board of Trustees. These include a survey of existing studies on the instrumentalities of UN peace-keeping, a feasibility study on technological and scientific resources released by disarmament for purposes of economic and social development, and a study of UN methods and techniques for the promotion and protection of human rights. The training and research activities of the Institute will be closely inter-related. It is intended that the training program will benefit from the analysis and evaluations performed in the field of research, and that, in turn, it should be possible for the Institute's research work to profit from the highly qualified personnel participating in the training programs. The value of the group which would be associated with the Institute in both fields need not be limited to the accomplishment of their immediate tasks. Their studies and contacts with the UN may also build a relationship of great potential value.

The Institute's headquarters are located in its own building, opposite the headquarters of the United Nations Secretariat itself, since the range of the Institute's interests will be so closely related to the activities of the United Nations. The Rockefeller Foundation contributed $ 450,000 for a building to house the Institute. Much of its operation, however, will be decentralized; aside from its Geneva office, the Institute may administer various research and training activities in other locations, as appropriate.

The second category includes organizations and institutions based on international concepts although operating regionally.

Albert Schweitzer College, Corcelles sur Chavornay, Switzerland, was founded in Churwalden, Switzerland, in 1950. The College offers the equivalent of a junior year course of study in the liberal arts with emphasis on tutorial instruction. The student body, faculty, and board represent many nationalities, and instruction is tri-lingual. The purpose of the College is described as a "one world college dedicated to the ideals of scholarship, religious freedom, international understanding, personal service, and reverence for life that were so eminently characteristic of the great man for whom it is named. Living and working together in an intimate community, young men and women study under the close personal and scholarly guidance of a faculty devoted to Dr. SCHWEITZER's ideal of service."

ATLANTIC COLLEGE IN THE UNITED KINGDOM, St. Donat's Castle, Glamorgan, South Wales. College in this case can be misleading, because of the interchangeability of this term when used by the English. This College aims to promote and provide international education at pre-university but post-high school level, i.e., at the British sixth form level. According to the *Half-Yearly Progress Report* (October, 1964), the aims of the College are:

> To promote international understanding through education; to break down national barriers in education particularly in the field of university admission, and to make education a force which unites, not divides. To achieve this, we intend to establish not just one College, but a number of Sixth Form colleges, each of which will offer to selected boys of different nationalities and high ability a two-year academic course immediately before entering universities in their own or other countries.
>
> To provide education specifically designed to meet future needs. To give first-hand knowledge of the outlook of other nations and to stress the teaching of foreign languages.
>
> To promote physical fitness and to satisfy the youthful instinct for adventure; to foster a spirit of compassion and a sense of obligation to the community.

In 1964, the College had 156 students from twenty-one countries (Argentina, Bermuda, Brazil, Burma, Canada, Denmark, France, Germany, Greece, Iran, Italy, Jordan, Lebanon, Malawi, Malta, Mexico, the Netherlands, Norway, Sweden, the United Kingdom, and the United States). The biggest proportion, sixty-eight students, were from the United Kingdom; part of the student body had financial assistance in the form of scholarships. Financial support took the form of grants from the British Government and business concerns.

CENTER FOR CULTURAL AND TECHNICAL INTERCHANGE BETWEEN EAST AND WEST (THE EAST-WEST CENTER) was established in October, 1960, by the United States Congress, by a rider to the Mutual Security Act of that year authorizing the State Department to provide a grant in aid to the University of Hawaii for the Center's establishment. It is administered by a Chancellor, responsible to the President of the University of Hawaii and the University's Board of Regents. Its budget is determined by the House Sub-committee on Appropriations for the State Department and administered by the Board of Regents of the University of Hawaii. Approximately $ 37,000,000 for buildings and operation of the program have so far been assigned.

The Center consists of three main divisions: 1) the Institute for Technical Interchange, which trains students principally for the U.S. Agency for International Development; 2) the Institute for Advanced Projects, the research arm of the Center; and 3) the Institute for Student Interchange. The purpose of the East West Center is stated as "the promotion of mutual understanding among the countries of Asia and the Pacific and the U.S." In pursuit of this aim, scholars and intellectuals from the U.S. and Asian countries come to the Center for a year's residence, and for attendance at four- to six-week seminars and week-long conferences. Research, articles and books on Asian development and Asian-American relations are developed. Students at the Center come from twenty-seven Asian-Pacific countries and from the United States, the ratio being approximately three Americans to one Asian.

The potential, in this instance, of developing a genuine world center for the study of cultural, social, political, and economic problems, awaits only a shift in thinking on the part of the State Department and the administrative officers of the University away from the bilateral cultural arrangements now made between Eastern countries and the United States, and a move toward a broader conception of the role of the U.S. in bringing about world understanding through education.

College of Europe, Dyver 11, Bruges, Belgium, was established at the European Cultural Conference in Lausanne in December, 1949, after a three-week preparatory session held in Bruges. The first academic year began in the fall of 1950. As part of the trend toward European integration, the College was to be a graduate research center to study the political, economic, social and cultural problems presented by the union of Europe.

The curriculum was not narrowly conceived to train civil servants for emerging European institutions but as a broadening of the mind and the development of a common point of view through an international and interdisciplinary approach. The course of study is eight months, and the College has sought to enable the students to become more completely aware of European realities through a general understanding of at least one other field of knowledge in addition to that in which he had previously studied. However, with the development of new European institutions, such as the Common Market, the European Coal and Steel Community, the instruction has assumed a more technical character to provide specialists to give leadership to these new institutions.

Six of the faculty are permanent staff, and visiting professors of different nationalities come at regular intervals. Eighty-five percent of the student body of approximately fifty are from Western Europe with some students from Eastern Europe – from twelve to eighteen nationalities are represented. All students and resident faculty live in a large hotel with community life considered an essential element of the College.

Half of the finances of the College of Europe are provided by the Belgian Government; the remainder by the Federal Republic of Germany, Great Britain, Luxembourg, the Netherlands, France, the European Coal and

Steel Community, and the town of Bruges. Other governments or institutions subsidize the College through scholarships. However, the College of Europe is independent of any government or intergovernmental organization.

Common Market European Schools, Conseil Supérieur de l'Ecole Européenne, Boulevarde de la Foire, Luxembourg. A system of secondary schools has been developed in the last ten years to serve primarily the needs of the children of the officials of the coal and steel organization of the European Common Market. The first school was organized at Luxembourg, in 1956, and other schools have been established in Brussels, Varese (near Milano), Karlsruhe, Mol (near Antwerp), and Putten (near Amsterdam). The schools are financed by the respective ministries of education of the six governments participating in the Common Market and by the coal and steel community organization.

The ministries of education of the six governments appoint an overall governing board which plans the curriculum; each of the schools is administered locally by a board chosen by the higher body and local parent and teacher organizations.

The faculties represent the six nationalities of the Common Market and are appointed by the respective ministries. The headmaster of each school is appointed for a five-year term only, after which he is to be replaced by some-one of another nationality.

The curriculum prepares students for a European baccalaureate which is designed to meet the university entrance requirements of all six Common Market nations, i.e., the French Baccalaureat, the German Arbitur, and university entrance requirements in the Netherlands, Belgium, Luxembourg, and Italy. The instruction is in Flemish, Italian, German, and French with English as a compulsory third language. All students are bilingual and many are trilingual.

European Institute for Advanced International Studies, Nice, France, was founded in 1965 by the International Center for European Training (C.I.F.E.) under the leadership of M. Alexandre Marc with the intention that it would be the beginning of an international university. This international university is to be composed of a consortium of graduate institutes, each dealing with some aspects of international and human relations and each founded and administered by one or more universities from countries in the Atlantic community, such as the United States, Great Britain, France, Germany, and Italy. The project received the support of the city of Nice which provided land, the beginning operating budget, and administrative buildings. Classrooms and other teaching facilities are provided by the University of Nice.

The first semester of the European Institute began in April, 1965, with thirty-one students from Europe, North and South America, and Africa and thirty professors from Europe and North America. The teaching and research at the Institute are centered around an interdisciplinary study of federalism, both in theory and as applied to European integration, Atlantic relations, and the developing countries. Additional institutes to be established at the Nice center will be Atlantic studies, East-West studies, study of the developing areas, study of American federalism, Latin American studies, and ethnopsychology. The international university is dedicated to the creation of new European and Atlantic scholars, capable of meeting the international issues of the modern world, while at the same time serving as a link among the countries of the Altantic community.

Friends World Institute, 5722 Northern Boulevard, East Norwich, New York. After five years of work by the Committee on a Friends World College, a New York State group of the Society of Friends (Quakers), the Friends World Institute opened in September, 1965, with thirty-eight students and nine faculty. The Institute will become Friends World College as soon as its assets and campus qualify it for a New York charter. The Institute is temporarily located at Mitchell Gardens, Westbury, New York, and is actively seeking a permanent campus in the area.

The Institute is an experiment in international and polycultural higher education based on a study of world problems. The four-year program involves six-month stays at each of seven centers around the world. For the first six-month period, the students attended seminars on various social problems and made an extended trip to Washington, through Appalachia and the deep South, observing and discussing poverty, regional development, the T.V.A., civil rights, cooperatives and Indian affairs. Then the class moved to Mexico for five months and will go to Scandinavia for study of Western Europe.

The Institute is initially organized into four programs: The Division for Resident Study maintains a campus in the United States with a resident four-year program leading to the B.A. degree. The Division of Study Centers Abroad will operate through seven strategically selected centers where a student will gain knowledge of the world through living, travelling, studying, and working for six months in each region. The Center for Peace Studies and Research will provide a graduate program leading to the M. A. degree, and The Summer Study-Travel program will operate a series of trips abroad for students in the Division of Resident Study.

Graduate Institute of International Studies, 132 rue de Lausanne, Geneva, Switzerland, was established in 1927 "to maintain ... a center for the study of contemporary international questions from the judicial, political, and economic points of view." Associated with the University of Geneva; approximately one hundred and fifty students, mostly doctoral candidates;

predominantly European faculty; mainly American and European student body; curriculum in social sciences taught by lectures, seminars, and student research from an international perspective.

MIDDLE EAST TECHNICAL UNIVERSITY (METU), 24 Mudafaa Caddesi, Yenisehir, Ankara, Turkey, provides an illuminating example of possibilities for future developments of the world university idea. The idea for METU originated in 1954, during a visit by Mr. CHARLES ABRAMS of the United States on behalf of the United Nations. Mr. ABRAMS originally suggested a School of Architecture and City Planning for Turkey; following the work of a UN Technical Assistance Mission in Turkey in 1955, the idea was expanded to include engineering and technological disciplines. With the help of UNESCO, a group of Turkish business, industrial, and educational leaders drew up a university charter which was approved by the Grand National Assembly of Turkey in 1959. In the beginning, only courses in architecture were available, but faculties in Engineering, the Arts and Sciences, and the Administrative Sciences were added, and the University expanded its concept in an international direction to serve the needs of the Middle East region rather than simply those of Turkey. "It is of incalculable value" says the METU catalog, "in building up understanding between nations for students of different origins and backgrounds to work and mingle together." There are faculty members from twenty countries, an international student body of three thousand with plans for an eventual enrollment of twelve thousand.

In the beginning, METU received financial help from the UN Expanded Program of Technical Assistance, and now receives funds from the United States AID program, the Ford Foundation, CENTO, and from "friendly foreign governments in the way of experts, equipment and books under bilateral agreements." The main source of funds is, however, the budget of the Turkish Ministry of Education. It is significant that the conception of a technical university should have expanded in the direction of including the arts and sciences, education and public administration, thus uniting technical and liberal studies through the demands of the region which METU serves. It is entirely possible that through expansion of the basic idea of a regional center for technical and social planning into that of a world center serving regional and world needs in the arts and sciences as well as in the technologies, the evolution of METU into a world university could take place.

NEW EXPERIMENTAL COLLEGE, Slotsherrensvej 21, Vanløse, Copenhagen, Denmark, was established in 1962 by AAGE R. NIELSEN as an "educational community designed to give students and professors from all countries an opportunity to study, do research, and work together to develop a world university." Students and faculty members pay their own expenses; there are no faculty salaries; the curriculum is determined by students and faculty on the basis of interests. Since 1962, approximately one hundred students, professors, and others have taken part in the experiment. There are occasional lectures; the main work is in seminars, discussion, and research.

PATRICE LUMUMBA UNIVERSITY OF FRIENDSHIP AMONG NATIONS (PATRICE LUMUMBA UNIVERSITY OR FRIENDSHIP UNIVERSITY), 5 Konskoy Proyesd, 7 Moscow, U.S.S.R., was founded in 1960, by the government of the U.S.S.R. and was named after the Congolese political leader. Admission is open mainly to students from Asian, African, and Latin-American countries. The University offers courses in engineering, agriculture, medicine, physico-mathematical sciences, natural sciences, history and philology, economics, national economic planning, and international law.

Most, if not all, of the students attending the university are holders of scholarships provided by the Soviet government. These scholarships cover tuition, free medical care, transportation to and from Moscow, a monthly allowance of ninety rubles for undergraduates and one hundred rubles for graduate students, and an allowance of three hundred rubles for the purchase of warm clothing. Each student pays his own board. In addition, students spending their summer and winter holidays in the Soviet Union are taken on "guided tours" at no cost.

Courses at the undergraduate level take five to six years; while graduate courses may extend from three to four years, including a one-year course in the Russian language. By 1964, there were 2,100 students enrolled at the University, with more than eighty countries represented. The University graduated its first class (228) on June 29, 1965. The entire cost of running the University is borne by the Soviet government. Administration rests with the Rector, the Pro-Rectors, and the Academic Council, which together constitute the University Senate.

VISVA BHARATI, Santineketan, District of Birbhum, West Bengal, India, was founded by RABINDRANATH TAGORE in 1921, ninety-three miles from Calcutta, as a world center for the study of international culture and the promotion of interracial amity and intercultural understanding.

Courses included studies in painting, music, oriental languages, philosophy, and literature. In 1951, by an Act of the Indian Parliament, Visva Bharati was incorporated as a residential university for study and teaching, as part of the system of Indian universities. The student body and faculty are international, the curriculum has an intercultural, international character, although the bulk of the students and teachers are Indian and Asian.

WORLD UNIVERSITY – INTERNATIONAL INSTITUTE OF THE AMERICAS, P.O.Box 22876, University Station, San Juan, Puerto Rico, opened in the fall of 1965, as the first unit of a world university. The founding of this Western Hemisphere institute is to be followed by the establishment of similar institutes in Africa, Asia, and other continents of the world. Each institute will feature the history, culture, and civilization of that continent in relation to the rest of the world. Dr. Ronald Bauer, Chancellor of the Institute, has stated that "education must be made available for all people on this earth, and it must be education with an international perspective. This world university system through its interrelated institutes on each continent will seek to break through the artificial barriers of history, custom and traditions, habits and politics, and antagonisms based on race, religion, nationalism, ignorance, poverty, greed or any other condition that tends to lower the dignity and well being of man anywhere." The International Institute of the Americas will stress the culture of Latin America and the United States, emphasizing the cultural contributions, common history, and problems of the Americas.

Another aim of the International Institute of the Americas is to offer a fully inter-related system of education that provides a formal educational program throughout life, beginning with the nursery school and continuing through elementary and secondary school, university, graduate, and adult studies with a special college for retired people who wish to continue their education. The Center for Undergraduate Studies, the Graduate Center for Inter-American Studies, the College for Adults, and the College of the Emeriti are the first to be organized with four hundred students attending the opening session of the Center for Undergraduate Studies and one hundred attending the centers for adult education. The faculty of fifteen are drawn from the Western Hemisphere and Europe, and an International Advisory Council includes Don Pablo Casals and Madame Pandit.

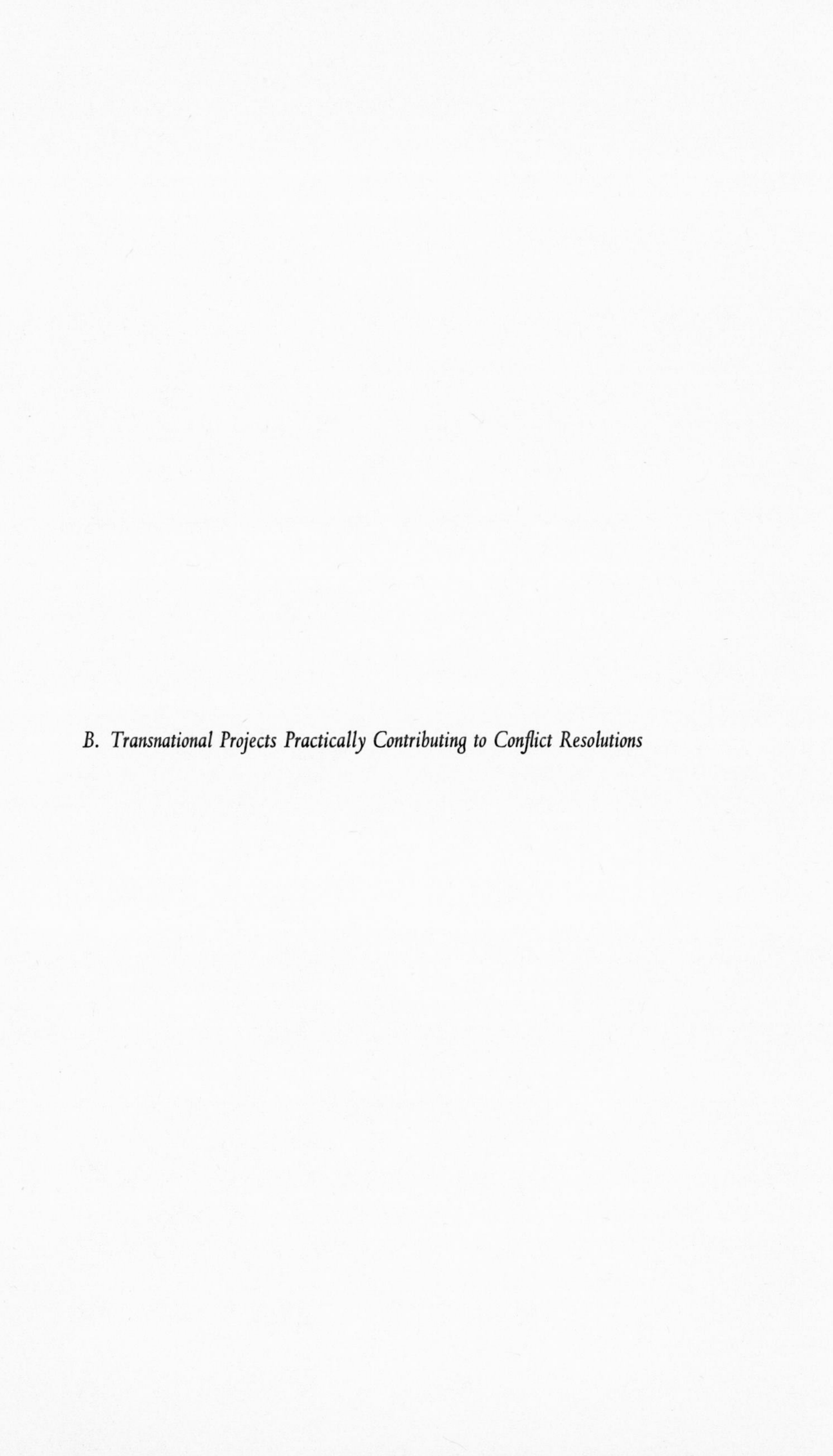

B. Transnational Projects Practically Contributing to Conflict Resolutions

The World Academy of Art and Science and the Creation of the World University

by

Hugo Boyko
President, World Academy of Art and Science

It was in Italy that after the Middle Ages some of the greatest men of all time brought Humanism and Renaissance to Europe and then to mankind as a whole. They paved the way for modern thinking and culture. The whole work of the World Academy of Art and Science is to a certain degree only a continuation of their thoughts and their work, and I am happy that our Third Plenary Meeting is taking place here, with the help of the Italian Authorities.

Two years ago, at the Opening Session of the Second Plenary Meeting of W.A.A.S. in the Parliament Building in Stockholm. I quoted the Founding Declaration of the World Academy, in which the two main purposes of our organization were set forth; I repeat them now: our aims are:

(1) to gradually build up a Transnational Forum in which the vital problems of mankind can be responsibly discussed and thoroughly studied by the best minds of our generation and of the generations to follow, from an objective, scientific and global point of view;

(2) to act as an objective advisory body for leading international organisations and for mankind as a whole, *outside of all group interests.*

I also explained the structural and organizational principles according to which the World Academy operates.

We are a numerically small but highly selective body, whose membership, during the first three years was, according to the statutes, restricted to 150 Fellow Members. Subsequently the statutes were amended and allow at present for a maximum membership of 300, distributed over all continents and adequately representing Sciences, Humanities and Arts, including the art of statesmanship. The enlargement of the membership was decided upon also in order to elect a considerable number from non-European or American races and creeds.

In order to make a personal contact with such personalities a round the world journey of the Honorary Secretary General was sponsored and a number of other journeys followed. During the two years since the Second

Plenary Meeting, group meetings were convened by the Secretary General in Iran, India, Thailand, Malaysia, Singapore, West and East Australia, Hawaii, California, Texas, New York, England, Scotland, France, Spain, Switzerland and Israel, in five separate journeys.

Such regional group meetings and an extensive correspondence enabled all Members and also invited experts in specific fields to discuss the various and very diversified problems as thoroughly as possible. Specific problems are dealt with by our Working Groups and Committees.

We live in a time where man has reached unprecedented mastery of the forces of nature. Concurrently, and perhaps causally connected with these very achievements, man has encountered problems, the solution of which is a conditio sine qua non for the further existence of the human race. Our progress in science and technology is not counterbalanced by that spiritual and emotional maturity which is indispensable for the harmonious application of our experience and knowledge to the benefit of the individual as well as to that of the various groups of mankind, and to mankind as a whole.

The upheavals to which the last few generations were subjected, have left in their wake a general deterioration of norms and values. The fear of catastrophy in which we live, makes the implanting of high ethical and moral values in the following generations more difficult than before, for what we are up against is man's loss of faith in his own capability to achieve peace and happiness.

The educational problem in this transition period of several generations has to be thoroughly dealt with by the most experienced educationalists, philosophers, sociologists and statesmen with the highest possible knowledge and wisdom, by cooperation on a global scale.

Our answer to these problems is twofold: we endeavour to show ways for the satisfaction of immediate needs by presenting new and original solutions for the population crisis and food production, and we are much concerned with the long-term educational effort required in order to achieve a satisfactory level of spiritual, emotional and ethical maturity.

The first two volumes of our publications are proof of it. The first dealing with these problems under the title "Science and the Future of Mankind", the second under the title "The Population Crisis and the Use of World Resources." The wide interest can be seen from the fact that the first volume has already a third edition, and the second volume even the fourth edition during the short time since their appearance.

Also our present Plenary Meeting symbolizes this dualistic approach: on the one hand, our Working Group on the productivization of deserts and wastelands has presented in its recent Symposium (Sept. 5–9 1965) new methods devised for plant growing with highly saline or sea-water as a further step in the peaceful conquest of deserts and wastelands for the production of food or of industrial plant raw material. On the other hand, the Council of the World University, meeting here for the first time,will consider ways and means for the consolidation of a transnational educational framework, where students and scholars from all continents will not only be concerned with research on problems of global importance, but will also imbibe and propagate the highest humanistic and academic values. The Council will further be concerned with the selection of the most suitable among those projects for Faculties, Schools, and actual research which have been proposed.

The establishment of the World University, which I had the privilege to propose a few years ago, is the direct result of group meetings held in Asia, Australia, America and Europe during which the basic idea was thoroughly discussed, until the present structure crystallized: A transnational network of old and venerable as well as newly established, most modern Institutions of Higher Learning and Research, each forming a Center for the study of a specific subject, but all cooperating and somehow coordinating with a view to strengthening a global outlook and deep concern with the principal problems of our world.

Our Council Member, SZENT-GYÖRGYI, Nobel Laureate in Human Physiology, expressed this in a few words in his letter of acceptance to me: "The World University presents the answer to an urgent need in our time." And in this time, in a world which has become so small that every spot in it can be reached in a matter of hours, where even the Antipodes are in calling distance, it is indispensable that problems should be considered for their potential global impact. It is the moral responsibility of Science to foresee the influence of its progress and achievements on humanity as a whole, and the World University will constitute a most adequate forum for this purpose. It will enable Science to plan research according to global needs and to concentrate the best minds on mankind's most urgent problems, but it will also have to ensure, in cooperation with enlightened statesmanship, the most suitable and adequate use of those forces of nature which we have learned to master during the last few decades.

Our efforts in this direction are generally acknowledged already. Thus during the past year the Secretary General and about twelve Fellow Members of W.A.A.S. were invited to the International Convocation on "Pacem in Terris," organized by the Center for the Study of Democratic Institutions. There, scientists and Statesmen of all continents, including U THANT, the Secretary General of UNO, met in order to discuss ways and means for the achievement of a lasting peace. This was another proof for the urgent need for Science to take its appropriate place in the management of human affairs. There I discussed, in a small group, with Stuart and Emily MUDD, Robert HUTCHINS, Lloyd and Mary MORAIN, Linus PAULING and others, the necessary practical steps for the foundation of the World University. The creation of this transnational University shall be the main contribution of W.A.A.S. to the "Year of Cooperation" of the United Nations Organisation, and it shall be a lasting one.

The same complex of problems, but considered from different aspects, was discussed during the Symposium of our Working Group on "Causes of Conflicts" under the chairmanship of Prof. George CATLIN, London. Here, the range of human conflicts was dealt with from the smallest unit, the individual, to group conflicts in society and up to conflicts between nations.

This Working Group will also discuss the enlargement and intensification of its work, as well as its potential ramifications in the framework of the World University.

I shall soon speak about the various Faculties apart from that on "Peace Research."

There is a certain common pattern in the development of man and of all his different races and cultures. Even in prehistoric times the transition from hunting and from nomadic life to agriculture and city dwelling made man look for peace, at least for his own group. Such a peace is theoretically possible to achieve by slaughtering or suppressing all potential enemies.

But it turned out that such a peace cannot be a lasting one. It is certainly not by mere chance that in the relatively short time of mankind's history of a few thousand years the great prophets of unity and of common ethical values appeared on earth with the vision of peace and happiness for all.

Everywhere where writing could communicate their thoughts to the following generations we can find the same visions at about the same period. The names may be different, the language stems from very different races and peoples, but their ideas and their ideals are surprisingly alike. They may be called LAO TSE or CONFUCIUS, BUDDHA or ZOROASTER, JESAYA or JESUS, we hear from them as the main goal "Peace on Earth and Happiness for all" for which they advise us to strive and to live in our spiritual and material struggle.

With the gradual growth of populations and colliding interests of peoples as one of the immediate consequences, peace was everywhere and always disturbed anew.

Now we have a completely new situation. It is certainly not by chance that in the new world which science and technology is creating and to a great part has already created, that in this new world similar thoughts are springing up in all corners of our globe, and that everywhere the élite among artists and scientists, an élite of statesmen and also the élite of the press is discussing the possibilities, and the ways and means for coming nearer to this goal.

In spite of the great population crisis, in spite of the threatening over-population and equally threatening nuclear war, or just because of it, the idea of a Unity of all men is becoming clearer and clearer. The great work of ECOSOC and the Specialized Agencies of the United Nations Organization, the various kinds of technical assistance, the efforts to help other peoples, frequently even to help the enemies of yesterday, are all proof of it.

In the multitude of ideas to overcome our perilous transition period one idea is of a particular significance. It is the idea of a World University. The transnational concept of Universities is in itself not as new as it seems to be. In fact the mediaeval Universities and also later ones had a transnational status; they had even extraterritorial rights. It was only in the nationalistic trend in the European countries of the time around 1800 that this transnational idea vanished.

What we are experiencing now is only a revival of this old idea. During the last few years, numerous projects for the establishment of such a World University have been worked out and presented to a broader forum by their authors. But all of them remain confined to the idea of an actual, physical center, a kind of international but locally determined campus, where people from many countries and races could meet and study.

We do not think that such an institute would apply under the present political conditions to our concept of a World University, or would apply to it in the foreseeable future. On the other hand, a close scientific cooperation, not bound by geographical limitations of any kind would factually lead to it. In this way, it will be possible to enlarge the traditional concepts of academic work and to combine efforts undertaken in different places of our globe into worldwide research on problems affecting humanity as a whole. In this way also the excellent work of scientific years and decades sponsored by the Specialized Agencies of UNO and the Scientific Unions would achieve a lasting value, far transcending their scientific one, and constitute a further step in the realization of the ethical aims of Science: Peace and Human Welfare.

The plan the World Academy is following provides as a first step the *Constitution of a Council*, a Council composed of personalities of worldwide renown, all acting and thinking along the lines I have described before.

After having constituted the Council, the Presidium of the World Academy of Art and Science and the Council of the World University will approach as a start a small number of Universities and similar Institutions of Higher Learning in various parts of the globe with the request that they should suggest a research subject for which in their opinion, they could serve as a world center for transnational research team-work. The research subject can be restricted or more encompassing, but it must have a potential of very strong or global impact on Human Welfare and must require by its very nature an international cooperation or coordination.

The respective University must be particularly suited for just this subject with regard to research personnel and/or equipment and geographical position, and the World Academy and the Council will have to give their approval, in order to avoid duplication.

Any Institution willing to act as a world center for one subject should be prepared to cooperate in one or more suitable projects for which other Institutions will act as centers.

After approval of its research subject, the Institution in question will have to indicate other Institutions which are apt to cooperate in this specific research scheme. It will then, supported by the World Academy, make contact with these other Institutions for further cooperation.

One of the great advantages of this plan is economic. Whereas all other plans are thinking of at least one great new campus, or of five or ten, our scheme is feasible or even better feasible without such a large expenditure. One single adequate campus would cost at least 20 million dollars. With this sum we shall have 20 cooperating Universities or, respectively, the Cooperating Chairs in them, and from a global point of view, with a many times higher efficiency.

Gradually this worldwide network of cooperating Universities will become increasingly close-knit, and the work on the various research projects will lead to the publication of annual or bi-annual reports, either by the World University alone or together with UNESCO or another adequate Special Agency of UNO.

During the last few months we have already carried out the first step, the constitution of the Council and also, in the second step, the approach to a number of particularly adequate Institutions of Higher Learning, we have successfully started.

The present status of the first Council of the World University is as follows: the 18 members in alphabetical order are:

The Nobel Laureate and Honorary President of the World Academy, Lord JOHN BOYD ORR of Scotland;

The Honorary Secretary General (now President of WAAS and for long years President of the International Commission on Desert Ecology and that of Applied Ecology) HUGO BOYKO of Israel; he is acting as the Dean of the Council;

The Nobel Laureate in Physiology, Sir JOHN ECCLES of Australia;

The Co-founder of plant sociology, Einar DU RIETZ of Sweden;

The President of the General Biology Division of the International Union of Biological Sciences, CARL GÖRAN HEDÉN of Sweden;

The President of the Centre for the Study of Democratic Institutions and former President of the University of Chicago, ROBERT M. HUTCHINS;

The Vice-Chancellor of the Chinese University of Hong-Kong, CHO-MING LI;

The leading Member of the Planning Commission of India, P. C. MAHALANOBIS, Calcutta;

The Vice-President of the Czechoslovak Academy of Sciences, IVAN MALEK;

The Member of the Presidium of the World Academy and Past President of the American Humanists Association, LLOYD L. MORAIN of California;

The Educationalist and Sociologist Prof. EMILY H. MUDD of Philadelphia, the first female Member of the Council;
The Vice-President of WAAS and Past President of the International Association of Microbiological Societies, STUART MUDD;
The Nobel Laureate and Vice-President of the WAAS, H. J. MULLER of California;
The Founder and first Vice-Chancellor of the University in Kuala Lumpur, Dato Sir ALEXANDER OPPENHEIM of Malaya;
The Vice-President of WAAS and former Senator of the Swedish Parliament HUGO OSVALD;
The Nobel Laureate in Chemistry and also Peace Nobel Laureate, LINUS PAULING;
The President of the American Division of WAAS, BORIS PREGEL;
The Nobel Laureate in Bio-Chemistry, ALBERT SZENT-GYÖRGYI.

This plan for a World University found an enthusiastic response not only with the Members of the Council but also as I have already mentioned, with a number of well known institutions of Higher Learning and many influential scientists; I mention for instance Brock CHISHOLM, the founder and first Director General of the World Health Organisation; Sir Julian HUXLEY, the founder and first Director General of UNESCO, and others.

The extensive correspondence up to now presents a number of very promising possibilities, which will have to be discussed and selected by the Council for their importance on the one hand and for their practical implementability on the other.

The stress in our activities will be laid on new original ideas and new lines of research but only on those which are of particular potential impact on Human Welfare. An important point of view will be the prevention of any competition with already existing international activities. If there is an overlapping then it should be in the form of complementation or even active support of such activities of others.

The following suggestions already received may serve as examples of the kind of program we have or we intend to build up.

The entire subdivision in Faculties, Schools, etc. will have to show this trend to independence from trodden paths, without, however, neglecting the advantages of traditional experience. Some of these suggestions are:

A *Faculty for Human Resources* with e.g.:

– a School for Brain Research (proposed by Nobel Laureate Sir John ECCLES)

– a Team for Education Problems of Prodigy and Particularly Gifted Children (proposed by the Vice-President of the Czechoslovak Academy of Sciences, Ivan MALEK)

– a School or Faculty for the Study of Symbols

– a Team for Research on Human Understanding (proposed by JOHN U. NEF, Chairman of the Center of Human Understanding of the University of Chicago) – all in close cooperation with UNESCO

– a School for Public Health Research (not application) in close cooperation with WHO (center propably in the Netherlands)

A *Faculty for New Approaches to Natural Resources* with e.g.:

– a Transnational School for the Ecology and Productivization of Deserts and Waste Lands (in close cooperation with FAO, UNESCO, WMO and ICSU), (proposed by Hugo BOYKO)

– a Transnational School for Wild Life Research (in close cooperation with UNESCO, FAO, IUCN, IUBS (proposed by Sir Julian HUXLEY)

A *Faculty of Education:* that means a Faculty for studying the problems of adequate education for the common interests of mankind as a whole. Thus for instance our education is apt to mislead the younger generation with respect to the history of other peoples, races, cultures, religions and their contribution to our common culture. A small substitute, also frequently misleading, is to be found in the cinema, in television, in books outside the school and textbooks.

We, the educationalists, have to learn how to overcome this gap and, I am sure, it will be one of our most difficult tasks; a task for which a teamwork of the very best will have to work in close cooperation with many others but particularly with and probably under the auspices of UNESCO.

This work is aimed at a long term goal and it will take many years before even the shape of the work to be done will be in sight, but it has to be started now and the transnational World University may potentially be the only framework, where all peoples can trust that the work will be done not only on a scientific basis but also to the utmost of human possibilities and objectivity actually outside of all group interests.

This Faculty will have to deal with common textbooks in many fields, primarily in history, but it will also have to deal with the great polycultural values.

A life-time may be spent in study of the cultural development of – let us say – Sweden or Czechoslovakia, Iran or India, Thailand or Bali or China or Japan, and so on, but what we have to learn is the common denominator, the sense of beauty expressed in various forms, the love of the neighbour inherent in the majority of all people in the same way as is the instinctive rejection of all that is strange to each individual. This *a priori* rejection is nothing else than the atavistic animal fear of all that is unknown or unaccustomed. It is this *a priori* and atavistic rejection of all strange individuals and peoples, with all its prejudices as consequence, which is one of the basic causes of quarrels and wars.

We shall have not only to find but to *stress* the common denominators of human development, the mutual interests, the mutual great powers of creativeness, in all their valuable differences and their potentially highly positive influence on mankind as a whole and for the *mutual* development. *We have to learn it in order to teach it.*

Today when our Antipodes are our close neighbours, – and they are in calling distance – we have to learn as much as possible about the values of all other peoples so that they will not be strangers any more to us, strangers subconsciously rejected without any reasonable cause; rejected *a priori* for another behaviour based on another education or another skin colour or another form of features and for nothing else. Reasons for rejection are more often than not constructed afterwards, not knowing that the real reason is only an animal fear. The Faculty of Education will have a wide field for research as well as for teaching.

Here, in the framework of this Faculty of Education the ideas of our distinguished Fellow and Council Member, Prof. MAHALANOBIS of India will probably find their place of implementation. Frequently studying in highly developed foreign countries by students from developing countries has as after-effect that the students cannot make the right use of their knowledge because of the completely different environment and background in their own country, and also for the lack of the rich equipment which they were accustomed to work with during their studies. Instead of enriching his people and his country by what he has learned, such a student takes, out of frustration, any political or administrative position, and the whole sacrifice of the country where he has been trained, as well as that of his own country, has been in vain.

If on the other hand visiting teachers of high level would go to the developing country for a while it would cost but a fraction of the very considerable expense to send a single student abroad, and the subjects could be taught in the developing country itself on the basis of the actual equipment available and with the necessary consideration of the natural background and the actual most pressing necessities. The stay in the country could easily be paid by any of the developing countries and only, practically, the travelling expenses of one man instead of a great number would have to be found.

Another Faculty will have to work in a similar direction but on other subjects.

A *Faculty of Peace Research*: This will have to work in close cooperation with existing or planned organizations and others, perhaps with the Hammerskjöld Institute and the International Institute on Peace Research, headed by our Fellow Member, the Swedish Ambassador to India, Alva MYRDAL.

Last but not least I should like to propose a *Faculty of Global Planning*.
To this I should like to add a few more words:

If we ask ourselves what are the main problems of mankind in the foreseeable future, then we are primarily confronted with the problems of overpopulation and those of education, further with the problems of Natural Resources, including energy, with Communication and Transport problems, and others in addition.

To deal with Human Resources means not only with individual and public health problems, but also with arts, religions and all other cultural and social components of human society. I shall not go into details here; other more authoritative thinkers will do this in one of our next volumes, which is in the editorial hands of Professor Ritchie Calder.

With regard to Natural Resources, Communication and Transport we are on the eve of many revolutionary discoveries and inventions. The energy problem is no more a fundamental scientific and technical problem. It has primarily already become an economic problem. Coal and oil will long before their exhaustion be substituted for by nuclear energy, hydro-electric power and solar energy. The speed of our scientific and technological progress is accelerating.

It was a symbolic act when – a few days ago – from the bottom of the ocean a call was sent to the two Astronauts travelling in space, and the latter communicated jokingly with their fellow pioneers many thousand meters below the surface of the ocean.

This was symbolic not so much of our achievements as for what man is striving for since the first man used the first tools and tamed fire. Before that the only way to survive was to adapt his body by genetic developments to new and unfavorable environmental conditions. From then on a gradual conquest of nature began by our own specific, mental power, and with steady acceleration. The fastest strides have been made during our own life time. They are so fast that our mental adaptability has not yet kept pace with them.

I remember with great enjoyment, I was then a boy of about 12 years, Bleriot's flight in Aspern near Vienna in Austria. An overwhelming enthusiasm spread through the thousands of spectators, when he succeeded to fly a very few minutes and several hundred meters about 15 meters above the earth. Next day came a cable from America that the brothers Wright remained a whole hour with their plane in the air and – this is the main point – nobody believed it.

Twelve years later we heard the aeroplanes with less enjoyment over our heads shooting with their machine guns into our front positions of World War I. Now we are on the eve of the conquest of space and on our way to the moon or still farther.

On our own planet we are on the eve of the conquest of deserts by using saline and sea-water with or without desalination, as we have heard during the last few days at our Salinity Symposium. This means that we may add in the near future areas in the total size of a great continent to the existing agricultural areas.

We are on the eve of utilizing the oceans for breeding instead of hunting, and to find new mineral resources beneath the surface much more effectively than heretofore by completely new methods. We can detect deep-lying ores even from airplanes by electromagnetic detectors, and soon we shall have the means to use the immeasurable mineral treasures beneath the bottom of the sea.

What we have not yet achieved, as I have mentioned before, is the mental preparedness for these victories of the creative power of our minds. To achieve this will need much research, including psychological, polycultural and brain research, and it will need much patience, education and careful planning.

Whether we are already ripe for global planning we do not know, but we must start and we must try. Of course, everywhere one of the greatest handicaps will be the inertia of the masses. May I bring as an example a comparison between agriculture in the United States and that of India: only 12% of the population in the United States are working in agriculture, but they produce considerably more than the whole population needs. In India this correlation is more than reversed. There almost three quarter of the population are working in agriculture and on no less fertile soils, but this great majority of the people is not able to produce the necessary minimum for the undernourished masses.

The problem is not as simple as the figures would show. The tremendous and locally most successful efforts of FAO to teach the use of new and modern methods instead of the primitive ones used for thousands of years will have the needed success and really effective impact on the standard of life of these 450 millions of people when also the mental and spiritual preparedness which is still lacking in the broad masses, will finally be achieved.

Here too psychological research has to be coordinated with agricultural plans and with many other branches in addition. How to coordinate them will be one of the most important tasks of the Faculty of Planning which will have to work in closest cooperation with the Specialized Agencies of UNO for any work, but particularly for any complementary work.

Some beginnings have already been made in this direction. There are regional projects of coordinated planning in various parts of the earth and here too the Special Agencies of UNO give a glowing example. We shall hear of such development projects in great river basins by one of our Members, Professor John Phillips, who is at present in Iraq and engaged in the great Euphrates project of UNO.

What we have achieved already and what we have to expect from science and technology gives us the conviction that we shall be able to overcome the great problems of our time: overpopulation, shortage of food and of other natural resources are certainly surmountable problems if we can shake off the mental chains of past millenia, the chains of egocentric group interests; or at least if we can come to some compromise for a period of transition. If we can achieve this, we shall obtain not only the survival to mere existence but to actual happiness and to real joy of life for all.

But in order to achieve this the necessary foundation is global planning. Only a transnational team of the best minds in science, in technology, in the arts and in statesmanship will be able to learn and to search how to plan and what to plan, and then only we shall be able to teach how global planning has to be done. This will be the manysided task of this faculty.

The idea of a lasting peace has been a latent idea in the élite of the human race for about 3.000 years or more, but it is only now that science has opened the ways to fullfil these dreams! We meet in a time of high tension and grave dangers to the human race. We are fully aware of this danger; in fact we founded the World Academy and we are founding now the World University as a defence against these dangers, as a defence not in an actual political sense but in a timeless sense.

It is my fervent hope and all our Fellow Members participate in this hope with me, that the World Academy and the World University will contribute a considerable share to this defence work, and that through our work we shall come nearer to the far goal, the final victory of peace and of human happiness.

Some Thoughts on Megabiological Research *

by

W. TAYLOR THOM, JR.
President, American Institute of Geonomy and Natural Resources, Princeton

INTRODUCTION

In order to aid in giving focus to the WAAS World Forum discussions now being held, the writer has felt constrained to ask three questions which follow:

(1) Do not world conditions demonstrate the imperative need for the prompt initiation of a coordinated, overall global program of Megabiological study and research?

(2) Would not the individual special-subject research programs, comprising the total program need to be carried out on a transnational basis and by volunteer "teams" of qualified cooperators to be recruited mainly from the staffs of university type-institutions the world over? and

(3) Should not the World Academy seek to trigger, stimulate and guide the activities of the suggested research-teams, thereby actually, though somewhat indirectly, moving the situation a long step forward toward the transformation of the world's many mushrooming "multiversities" into units being informally integrated *into* what could become an actual institutional *World*-University? A university in connection with which WAAS, as a non-institutional, informal and trans-national *Fellowship*, should perform functions such as are performed by the genetic pattern, enzymes and growth controlling hormones operative within the bodies of evolving

*. A definition of the term "Megabiology." The term "Megabiology," is coordinate with the terms "Microbiology" and "Macrobiology" and is a general one that embraces all structured, functioning and evolving mega-organisms such as

Legally-incorporated business organizations
Incorporated villages, towns and cities
National and regional governments
Universities and educational systems
Structured church organizations
Subsistence-village and tribal groups and "civilizations"
International bodies such as UN,–UNESCO and ICSU

"macro" individuals. As for example, within the bodies of human beings as these beings develop from embryo to infant; from infant to child; from child to adolescent; and, (ultimately) from adolescent to a poised, thoughtful and properly-motivated human personality.

THE IMPERATIVE NEED FOR A GLOBAL PROGRAM OF MEGABIOLOGICAL STUDY-AND-RESEARCH

There is obvious and imperative need for the formulation and activation of a series of parallel crash-programs within the field of megabiologic study and research.

For the crises developing in various parts of the world are tending to deepen and coalesce as mushrooming populations continue to grow at an accelerating rate. Individual human beings in fact possess certain critical characteristics, like those of uranium atoms. For if people become more and more compressed together, into supercritical masses, it has already been shown that they will begin to generate chain-reactions that can lead to lethal social explosions – not only on the urban or national or regional scale, but also on the total, global scale. Also the imperative need for coordinated programs of megabiological research is made evident by the mega-maladies which are responsible for the continuing spread of world-crises. Moreover these mega-maladies are clearly due to the operation of a few easily-identifiable root causes, causes such as are, themselves, really *dependent* functions of a single *independent* variable, namely, the *rate* of global population-increase. Therefore, if the causes of malady *are* thus known, should not recruited *teams* of megabiologists be able (speedily) to produce miracles like those which have been wrought recently by microbiological-and-medical research teams, teams that have gone so far toward conquering or controlling the major pestilences and nutritional-deficiency diseases that have recurrently or continuously so sorely afflicted human populations throughout history?

To be more specific the causes of current mega-biologic maladies are divisible into seven general groupings, as listed below.* For which reason should not the *total* megabiological research program also be composed of seven (coordinated) areas for study-and-research-with the work within each area to be planned and carried forward by trans-national volunteer *teams* of workers?

*. The Seven Groups of Root-Causes of Megabiological Malady;

(1) Inertia, Ignorance and Wrong "Imprintings" during Earliest Childhood; (2) Hunger and Want: (3) Fear and Hatred; (4) Lack of Morality plus Individual Irresponsibility; (5) Injustice, Oppression and Lack of Freedom; (6) Exploitation, Waste and destructive exhaustion of indispensable mineral-substance resources (vs the proper *cultivation* and *creative multiplication* of vitally necessary mineral-derived supplies); and (7) Egotism, Unfairness, Disloyalty, Treachery, and Arrogant Lust for Power.

SUGGESTIONS REGARDING THE RECRUITMENT AND OPERATION OF THE RESEARCH-TEAMS NEEDED

If a number of coordinated research projects are to be planned and staffed, the questions of "whether and how and where and by whom" should be given careful consideration by a small WAAS Ad Hoc committee after adequate discussions have taken place within the WAAS World Forum. Also, it may become clear that certain WAAS Fellows could provide excellent leadership for one or the other of the programs contemplated. This not only because of demonstrated interest and competence in the scientific and social areas involved, but also because of their proven capacities for inspiring and effective team-leadership.

It would be naturally expectable that particular men, in particular Departments (or Schools) in particular University-type organizations would stand out as logical recruits for the teams needed. And WAAS interest, diplomatically expressed, should help to gain the several consents needed for such recruitment while also helping to manage re-adjustments of the activities being currently carried by recruits, so that their recruitment would yield benefits in all quarters, rather than causing disruptions.

The grants-in-aid needed for the operation of the several programs should be sought directly by the committees concerned, with WAAS endorsement of applications (as to soundness and promise) if – and when – in order.

WAAS should hope to maintain liaison with the research programs initiated – in order to be available for consultation, when that would be helpful, and also in order to be able to render competent judgement upon the soundness of sub-projects for which further grants-in-aid would be needed.

THE STIMULATIVE-AND-CATALYTIC ROLE AND FUNCTION OF THE WORLD ACADEMY AS AN INFORMAL, TRANSNATIONAL AND NON-INSTITUTIONAL WORLD FELLOWSHIP

WAAS as a non-institutional, informal and transnational world Fellowship should seek fully to validate and continuously maintain

(1) An ability to maintain a World Forum "within which the vital problems of Mankind can be responsibiy discussed and thoroughly studied from an objective, scientific and global point of view." And

(2) A capacity to serve as a competent, informal and impartial advisor to the UN, UNESCO and ICSU; to their associated or constituent agencies or unions; and also to university-type organizations and regional or national political bodies.

Furthermore, in order that WAAS may be able to fulfill its objectives (1) and (2), just described – while also playing a proper role in connection with megabiological research programs of the sort here suggested, it would be necessary for the WAAS Secretary General to have an administrative assistant who could also be chairman of a small Ad Hoc, project-Planning Committee. And if such a committee were to become (at least for the time being) a part of the WAAS Secretariat, a moderate-size grant-in-aid should be sought (for support of the General Secretary's total office) – this grant-in-aid to be, perhaps, made so that the money thus earmarked could be expendable, at discretion, within a five year period.

CONCLUSION

In concluding our consideration of the world's need for megabiological research it may be a good time to review the matters of "objective, means and method" as these relate to overall WAAS policy and plan. And if we do, here and now, undertake such a review our conclusions would run about as follows:

(1) We should seek to join with the peoples of all the world in the building of Justice-under-Law, on a global scale – in order that the Hungry and the Needy may become able to earn – and – learn, thereby becoming able to earn their own self respect by being able to meet their individual and family needs *through their own efforts.*

(2) We should seek to encourage full use of the new means for effective administrative planning and control that have been made available by the development of team-planning, team policy-making (by consensus) and effective administration (by trained professionals). For the combined use of "team-approach plus electronic computers" has made it possible for human groups to solve those complex problems that are increasingly beyond both the comprehension and the control of *any* human individual, no matter how experienced or gifted.

(3) WAAS should scrupulously avoid all intrusions into the administrative activities of formal, *institutionalized organizations.*

(4) WAAS should avoid all competition with existent (or projected) Foundations which have responsibility for the custody of, and disbursement of, trust funds.

(5) WAAS should, by contrast, not seek permanent endowments, but, instead, seek grant-in-aid support for its work – hopefully on a 5, 10 or 20 year-period basis, such grants preferably to be expendable *at discretion within* the term of years specified.

(6) WAAS should give all possible support and encouragement to activities (such as those of the recent Pacem In Terris Convocation) whereby a proper psychological world climate can be induced, a climate within which the *inevitable competitions* between ideas and systems can proceed *constructively;* without bitterness; without the employment of unfair tactics; and without resort to that violence which destroys what it seeks to preserve. And lastly;

(7) WAAS should stimulate the peoples of all the world into assembling their existent unsatisfactory (fragmental) economics into a properly-functioning global economy. They should seek to gain Justice-under-Law and freedom for all by a proper employment of "Government of the People, by the People and for the People." All peoples should seek to so employ "the wisdom of the Human Heart" that it will be possible to give proper consideration to the rights and hopes of the children of the future, so they may not be condemned, even before birth, to lives of misery and hunger. And lastly, this same "wisdom of the Human Heart" should show us how that greatest of all evolving Mega-entities – a fully developed world society - may not only be animated by proper humane concerns, but also be guided toward intelligent and creative actions by a fully-developed, collective brain, a brain which actually already exists, in segments, within the "University world," merely awaiting a proper unification. Partly by a direct linking up of special brain-units (in tandem) and partly by an effective *cross*-linking (in parallel) of the world's two brain-halves. These two halves consist, respectively, of the Humanistic and the Scientific areas of emotional and intellectual responsibility. (For we must expect the world's characteristic schizoid behaviors to continue, so long as the two brain-halves are *not* effectively cross linked.)

Interindividual, International Conflicts and Cooperation

by

MIKAEL M. HOFFMAN

Director, Int. Center for Cultural, Educational and Relief Activities, Rönninge, Sweden

Since 1923 I have lived and worked among refugees, among students, teachers, youth-leaders, social workers etc. belonging to different nations and coming from various parts of the world. I have also had the opportunity to observe human relations between 1929–1933 when I was general secretary of the International Student Association with its headquarters in Berlin. At that time we were interested in actively involving foreign students in Europe in work for international understanding via study trips, conferences, meetings, work camps,discussion groups etc. Since 1936 I have been head of a unique institution called Agni, (in Swedish also Örjansgarden) which for 30 years has had participants and guests at its seminars and relief work amounting to over 40,000 from most countries in the world. 43 years of my life and work spent among individuals representing a great part of mankind constitute a vast field for observation and experiences.

INTRODUCTION

Human life is full of conflicts. On one side conflicts, on the other side cooperation. There are innumerable conflicts and components of the roots of conflicts. The new-born child is in conflict with his new environment: cold, hunger, air. His first cry is protest and fear as Dr. Karl MENNINGER writes in his book: Love against Hate. At the end of his life as an individual man is in conflict again with the cruel life, and he struggles with his death. During his life man may also be in conflict with his parents, other children, his wife and his children.

What is conflict? According to The Concise Oxford Dictionary, conflict is fight, struggle, collision, clashing of opposed principles etc.

There are many philosophical theories about conflicts and their cause. The German philosopher Oswald SPENGLER believed man to belong to the wild beast and to act accordingly. There has been much written about the struggle of life. NIETZSCHE has applied DARWIN's basic rule in the animal kingdom to human society. There is Christian belief in original sin and in Adam and Cain as bearers of the first conflict into divine and human order. The German philosopher and sociologist Professor Max HORKHEIMER said at the Evangelical Church Congress in Cologne this summer:

"Mankind is the most bloody, the most cruel species of the known world. Nothing was holy for him, neither truth nor religion, which he used as instruments of power"... But are conflicts really there because man is evil and are all conflicts of evil? Let us therefore ask, what are the highest aspirations of human beings. Recently one Bulgarian Communist monthly interviewed a few young people on this question – What is the sense of your life? Young people brought up in a Communist country answered:

"Fulfillment, to develope all my abilities, to be appreciated by people, to be loved, to meet one with whom to share in love all my life, to be happy, to be creative, to be always remembered by people."

I myself have asked this question about the goal, the aspirations a thousand times in our international centre and young people from Africa and America, Asia and Europe all gave the same anwser:

"To create, to be loved, to be."

The essence, or the conclusion, is that man's highest aspiration is to be, to exist as an individual, to remain either in eternal life or in deeds unforgetable, to fulfill or to realise within one's own unique life all potential abilities. This aspiration sometimes leads an individual into conflict with another individual's aspiration. But conflict is not in itself evil. On the contrary it can be a source of new energies, inspiring power to do better, to create. Without conflicts there is no life. Conflicts are of evil when one part (A) *prevents* the other part (B) in conflict from the fulfillment or realisation of B's life, that is prevents B from developing his potential gifts. This very often happens not due to man's inhumanity but due to man's immaturity, misunderstanding, and lack of empathy.

Can we study interindividual conflicts and cooperation scientifically? We know how difficult it is to make experiments in the field of human relations, because the object of experimentation is changing during the experiment, and does not give us reliable data, because he knows that he is being observed.

But, as we have been working for a long time, many years, on human relations there may occur configurations, situations which can be compared with other known situations and so serve us as a substitute for experiment. Other situations may occur which can serve as control for our research. In Agni we could use several groups for our experiments in human relations without group members knowing this.

We do not use statistical methods as sociology does. Their importance and scientific reliability are according to our knowledge sometimes overestimated. There is no time to give you relevant facts.

The scientific investigation of conflicts is rather new. An attempt is being made to apply in this research new terms with a background of mathematics. This, as is known, has been very successful in physics, astronomy, chemistry, partly in biology and linguistics. Our research methods include:

(1) Permanent attentative observation, collecting data.
(2) We draw comparisons, and
(3) Analyze
(4) We use given, not arranged, experimental situations
(5) Evaluation.

Our goal is integration of empiric and theoretical knowledge and research on interindividual relations and international education.

CONFLICTS

Let us now consider some of the most frequently-occurring conflicts. The two conflicting parts are called A and B.

(1) There are inside conflicts within oneself. A's aspirations are too large for him, he is unable to fullfil them. He lives in a state of permanent inner conflict. He is unhappy, irritated, he does not recognise the cause of his pain and is inclined to accuse irrelevant conditions and B as being responsible for them. A is unhappy because his program of tasks and duties forces him to do more than he is able to do. He is tired of being unable to manage his work. A's will is divided – the one part calls him to be responsible, to fullfil his duties; the other part is drawn to the contrary side, is tempted to appetite, is longing to satisfy some desire.

(2) Very often the origin of conflict is psycho-somatic, health-conditions. Many times I have observed how the digestive apparatus, constipation or diarrhoea, has caused bad temper, irritability, melancholy. When A is irritable he, as most human beings, seeks somebody to accuse as being responsible for his suffering. It may be B, and here is a conflict situation. Still more disastrous may be hidden disease. Symptoms of a disease may be then, unwillingness to fullfil obligations, aggressiveness either as automatic self defence or as explosive quarrelling. The person with hidden illness does not know the reason of his disorder. Perhaps he wishes to be left in peace, he accuses himself and others. Many conflicts originate from the soma, but the people around him, ignorant of the real cause accuse him morally as being lazy, irresponsible, a bad comrade, an evil man. That is our human cruelty. We need illumination as the majority of people still know very little of these facts.

(3) Another cause of human conflicts is the influence of the weather on human well-being. We have often observed how some sensitively-disposed people are dependent upon the weather. Often when we get up in the morning and observe the weather we can exactly foresee how some people will behave during that day. The director-general of the Meteorological Institute in Sweden, Mr. Alf NYBERG, pointed out in an interview with the

Swedish daily Svenska Dagbladet of 27th August 1965 the fact that low pressure, as can be proved, influences certain disposed individuals, but we still do not know why. We have now new branches of science: biometeorology and climate-medicine or climatological medicine, both of which can help us to understand better the more profound human motivations and behaviour. For instance, in a recently published report to the international climatological congress research group on this subject, doctors of medicine and climatologists draw attention to the fact that a stream of warm air in Scandinavia between November and January increases the frequency of apoplexy. Streams of cold air affect individuals with heart diseases. Gradual cooling over a long period of time increases blood pressure to an essential degree. Warm and humid weather increases the state of agitation in individuals disposed to schizophrenia. These examples are still only theories but they demonstrate very clearly the connection between the daily life of the individual and weather and climatic conditions. Educationalists must be more informed about these relations, so that they may, if necessary, teach how to counteract the negative influences of weather and climate. May I point out here some of the main causes of interindividual conflicts.

(1) Reality does not correspond to expectation. As a result, disappointment, pain and desire to act against the individual who has disappointed and caused pain.

(2) Weak ego:

(a) due to a long period of suppression (by parents, school, group),

(b) due to physical features different from the majority of people (too short, of small stature),

(c) due to persecution,

(d) due to social status etc.

The individual with a weak ego suffers from an inferiority complex. Often it is accompanied by the desire to strike somebody, to compete and to be victorious, even to the extent of crime. The individual with a weak ego is permanently hurt, he is pendulate between depression, general obedience and submissiveness on the one hand, and aggressiveness and the desire to be superior to his fellowman on the other. Alfred Adler – world-famous psychologist – physician and founder of the Individual psychology (1870–1937) considers conflict to be the clash of the two poles – inferiority complex and the desire to get power – to be the cause of most neuroses. When I met Adler in 1932 in Berlin at the International Congress for Individual Psychology, he told me that he considered this clash to be the most vital force in human life. My own observations indicate that this is often the case, but I prefer to put, instead of the idea of desire to get power, the desire to be, to exist, to be loved, to create.

(3) But of course there are individuals with the desire to get power or to obtain leadership in the group. There are many aspects of this cause of

conflict but I have to be brief – there is lack of time to satisfactorily illuminate these many important aspects in my address.

(4) Perhaps the most known conflicts are clashes of interest. Mr A is a shop owner in a little village. Mr B from another village arrives and opens a new shop. There is violent competition. Or, A and B apply for one scholarship, for only one professor's chair – it can be a noble competition but it can also be a struggle where all means are regarded by the two opponents as permissible. Then, we have not to forget the "Age of Rebellion"the adolescents. In the last days of August 100 adolescents were involved in a fight with police in Stockholm, Gothenberg, in England and elsewhere. Why? At the United Nations Congress on prevention of Crime (9–18 August) in Stockholm, I had the opportunity to interview many delegates. The American: adolescents want adventure, they want ideals – we have to provide these. The Russians: Youth is seeking heroism and ideals – we have to provide these. The Africans: Adolescents are vital, they want to be useful, they want adventure. We have to provide education and working projects, camps. Until now, I have been speaking about conflicts which are taking place in every group and society. But what about conflicts among individuals belonging to different nations, continents.

(1) It is normal to be attached to parents, family, tribe – to the group in which one is brought up. In ancient times it was also normal to meet a foreigner with distrustfulness. Deep in every one of us is still, maybe subconsciously, a tendency to apply our group's culture, behaviour, values to foreign groups.

Here I may only touch upon the causes of conflicts between individuals from different groups and nations.

(2) Primitive fear.

(3) Ignorance, lack of knowledge.

(4) Generalisations. (A Finnish man was drunk and hurt a Swedish man with his knife – all Finns when drunk are very dangerous).

(5) Conflict of interests.

(1) If Mr B, opening a new shop in a little village, belongs to a different group than Mr A the shopowner and the majority of his clients, then Mr A may use this as a focus to hit at, to arouse animosity towards Mr B and his group.

(2) Indoctrination of antipathy performed by different social forces such as state, political or religious parties and groups etc. Because we often

(a) do not have sufficient information,

(b) are lacking in knowledge of the basic facts,

(c) are unable to think independently,

(d) feel happier when we are in accordance with our group,

(e) are easily influenced by propaganda. Often in our human relations we fall victim to mass-suggestion and act accordingly as indoctrinated, as hypnotic subjects, identifying ourselves completely, and often unconciously, with the indoctrinaters, with aroused emotions, agressiveness and hatred,

(f) lack of empathy.

EDUCATION

Our research in interindividual relations teaches us that basic conflicts are common in all groups, in closed national as well as international groups. On the tree of human relations there are some branches with some particular features – we call them international relations, but international individual conflicts cannot be separated from the basic common human conflicts.

In order to overcome *negative* human conflicts in international relations, we have to tackle *also negative* basic human conflicts. To achieve interhuman international understanding and cooperation we have *also* to work on basic interhuman understanding and cooperation. The work on human, international understanding alone will, up to our knowledge, not lead to success. This conclusion was and is of great importance for Agni's work. We decided to work for education. A few weeks ago I had the opportunity to speak with several African leaders. Mr. K. from Guinea said: "In my country, Guinea, we began with economic and industrial development. But for that we need to work for social development – we are trying to do that now, but our people have to be educated first. When Mr. K. was speaking I drew a circle and wrote inside the circle: Education, industry, social welfare, where is the beginning of the circle: education or industry or social welfare? Nigerians answered: Our paramount need is education. Thailand: depends on the country. Senegal: all at once. But most of the Africans, South-Americans and Asians I met said: education.

AGNI

Agni was founded as an educational international institution in May 1936 in Sweden, near Stockholm. We have learned that many of the international congresses, journeys, sporting contests, etc. seldom affected and changed individual human relations. As general secretary of a large international movement of students from all over the world, I was seeking methods of work which could grasp the individual completely. I was tired of many shallow, beautiful words and strongly felt disaster drawing nearer and nearer. To grasp totally an individual to help him open his eyes, to help him to realize that he is a citizen of the world, that all humans are brothers, that his brothers are suffering from hunger, ignorance, persecution – to do that, I said to myself, we need a new form of school. I spoke with leading people from Europe and other continents and many of them encouraged me. Professor Albert EINSTEIN, Thomas MANN, RABINDRANATH TAGORE, Luigi PIRANDELLO, Werner HEISENBERG, Selma LÄGERLÖF, the

President of Czechozlovakia, Thomas MASARYK, Nobel Prize winners, scientists, writers understood signs of the time and somehow participated in the creation of Agni. During the time between the two world wars many people were blind, some believed I was mentally not normal. Well today more than 40,000 individuals live around the world, many of whom can witness what Agni meant for them. Many teachers, social workers, youth leaders, journalists etc. were former participants in Agni's seminars and are today working to realise what they have learned at our centre. Agni is a combination of an international university college, centre for international relief, a work camp, settlement, Indian ashram and Scandinavian residential folk high school. Young people from all corners of the world are coming to Agni to participate in international seminars in our work. Agni's seminars are residential, and participants are living and working with us. For 29½ years Agni has been experimenting in new methods, new education for interhuman global understanding and cooperation. Gradually we have discovered more efficient methods for this purpose. Here are some glimpses only:

(1) We have no employed people, no servants. Of the 25 or 40 participants only 8 or 4 share all the responsibility for the material well-being of the group (food preparation, everyday fresh flowers, lost property, first aid, garden, houses etc.)

(2) The way of living is simple. Simple food – no food or left over is thrown away, simple lodging – daily life is hard compared with the life in the west. Everything here reminds us of our suffering fellow-men in underdeveloped parts of the world – that is one reason for simplicity – the other reason is to create conditions which, in a self-evident way lead the participant to the mobilisation of all his positive emotions in order to be able to adapt himself to these conditions which may be for him quite new. There is a proverb: "Everybody likes us when we are white, who likes us when we are dark?" It is easy to advocate international brotherhood when we have comfort around us, it is difficult to do so when we are confronted with naked unpleasant realities. How often have I met people who were ready to donate large sums for refugees, but after meeting a few of them were disappointed and promised never to help one or another group of refugees. Human understanding means really understanding a man not only on Sunday but also a man in difficulties. Simple living means very close relations and an adventure.

(3) All participants spend every day a few hours on international relief work, sorting, packing, transporting relief materials. Agni helps suffering, poor, destitute people in various contries, among others in Greece, Italy, Poland, by sending to them gift parcels with clothes, food etc. Many participants share at Agni their first experience of relief work and we cannot underestimate the great, tremendous educational value of this work. A

participant who up to now had only talked about better human relations is now acting. He will never forget this first experience.

(4) Studies. In the afternoon, Agni is transformed from an international relief centre into an international university college. Participants change their clothes, everywhere are fresh flowers.

The study program can be divided into two parts. The first – we can call it theoretical – deals with (a) the present situation (cultural, economic) and its background reflected in the problems of different countries (b) guiding ideas in our time (science, literature, opinions etc) (c) international organisations and movements, relief work. Experts from different countries give lectures, sometimes also qualified participants.

The second part divides all participants into study groups according to their interests and activities. (Teaching profession, youth leadership, race relations, etc.) These study groups work with the view to presenting suggestions for remedies at the end of the seminar. The main question to be answered is not what U.N. or the president of U.S.A. can do, but what I as an individual can do to promote international understanding in my own field of work. International education cannot limit its work to providing knowledge and helping to develop intellectual abilities. It must also penetrate the participant's emotional life and awaken his hidden resources. In this connection I would like to remind you of the plenary meeting of W.A.A.S. in Stockholm in 1963, where Aldous HUXLEY appealed to W.A.A.S. to make thorough investigations simply as to how to awaken hidden human resources. I had at that time the opportunity of a long conversation with him and we exchanged our experiences, he with the psychopharmaticas as a means to improve human inter-relations and to open the door to the non-oral world. I on my part told him about Agni's new educational methods with the same goal.

(5) I will speak now about intensity. Intensity as an educational method has been applied at Agni for many years. To judge by the results this educational experiment was successful. What is intensity in education? To answer this question I would need more time than I have at my disposal here. In a few words it is rapid gradual intensification, heightening to the highest possible degree, to the maximum abilities of the whole scale of positive emotions, intellectual life and manual activity. Our experiment proved that we reached best results when this intensive life lasted 4–7 weeks. Using this method, Agni really grasps the whole personality, penetrates very deeply.

What a participant has experienced settles down in his subconciousness, remaining with him for his whole life. But this method must only be applied in connection with others, not in isolation. Here I mention the following four methods.

(6) *Empathy* seems to be one of the most powerful emotions to create better human relations. Empathy is the power of projecting one's personal-

ity into (and so fully comprehending) the object of contemplation. This is more than sympathy. Empathy is complete identification with another individual, it is the way to understand what is usually hidden behind the insurmountable walls of his personality. Empathy as a potential ability exists in every human, but often it is underdeveloped, not trained, partly due to the defence mechanism of one's own integrity or comfort, and partly because of lack of a teacher for the development of empathy. The foundation of empathy is knowledge, experiences, fantasy and to a great proportion self-knowledge. Self-knowledge requires courage, development of the ability to observe one's own motives, emotions, etc. It is empathy and its child compassion which can build bridges between conflicting parts, between enemies, and lead us into a higher, better human world.

(7) The word love is more than any other word used and misused and still this word is a symbol for a very great human force. We have made experiments in this field. Before starting a seminar we spent three days in making the decision to undergo an experiment in love.

We decided that for 6–7 weeks, during the period of our seminar, we would undergo an experiment with ourselves. We shall partly change our attitudes and behaviour. We shall not criticize but ask, not judge but learn, we shall observe ourself and fight our negations, we shall try to develop our sympathies, we shall influence our mood by our behaviour, our actions – we appear for instance in the morning with a smile, polite and friendly. The result of this experiment in love was astonishing. Participants wrote afterwards that this was a turning point in their lives.

(8) I spoke about emotional life. Humans have reason but in their lives they are to a great extent governed by emotions. International education has to deal with emotions, and has the noble task of directing them towards human brotherhood and the fulfilment of the individual's life. Music, song, social festivities, beauty through colours, flowers, clothes, intensive, abundant life between the two poles – simplicity on one side, high culture on the other, simple living and high thinking – manual work and intellectual activities on a high level – these are just some of the educational instruments we have used at Agni.

(9) The art of relaxation plays a very important part in the improvement of human relations and the richness of individual life. In small groups we train our ability to relax, using different ways and methods.

(10) Education for international cooperation is guided to a great degree by every seminar group itself. But every group must include a few former participants or individuals who are able to inspire the group. (I think if we were to collect sufficiently extensive data about the individuals we could then show a diagram of negative and positive influences). Enthusiasm is also an educational method.

(11) Young people are often inclined to accept theories and statements they have just acquired as evident, as absolute truth. They may discuss for

hours things of which they have no experience or knowledge. Unverified statements clash, mainly on social and political questions. Often they are indoctrinated by their governments, by political parties. Emotions are aroused. International education at Agni follows the old master SOCRATES. Go into the roots. Ask, learn to think independently! Govern your emotions! Ask! Understand, see deeper, see back-ground, see different sides of the problem, stay not on the surface of hatred and ignorance, but go deeper and seek truth.

For 30 years we in Agni have been surrounded by human conflicts and cooperation. During these 30 years we have been experimenting all the time. We have found that some methods were less and some more efficient. We are working for the establishment of institutions for Agni's international education in every country of the world. Agni's international education is not bound to one single institution in Sweden. It is, according to our experience, a proved, verified method which can be applied universally. For several years we have been working on research, collecting all the data of Agni's international education. For two years we have been preparing a global Correspondance Seminar on forms, methods and techniques in interhuman international cooperation.

We need a cross-science on the impact of international education on adult individuals. We need the cooperation of psychology, anthropology, sociology, medicine and criminology, among others.

I have the honour of extending greetings from Agni to the third plenary meeting of the World Academy of Art and Science. On behalf of Agni I wish also to congratulate WAAS on taking the initiative in the creation of a Transnational World University and wish you all success in the realisation of this urgent task. Here I would like also to assure you of Agni's readiness to cooperate fully with the proposed World University. Moreover, I have the honour to propose that WAAS and its World University constitute Agni as a world centre for research, either on broad lines as stated in our invitation to the Global Seminar on forms, methods and techniques in interhuman international cooperation, or on more restricted subjects:

(a) on the impact of international education on grown-up individuals,

(b) alternatively on the further restricted-subject – the impact of international education in residential colleges for adults,

(c) or alternatively on Agni's international education, whereby Agni's education is not considered as limited to only one institution, Agni, in Sweden. Actually this education is already partially applied and can be applied everywhere in the world.

The Significance of the Sociology of Cooperation for the Planning of a World University

by

HENRIK F. INFIELD

Our Council has done a great deal of preparatory work on the World University in some of which I had the privilege to participate. My field being that of the Sociology of Cooperation, I have tried to point out the significant contribution this discipline could make to the planning. As I see it, the very idea of a World University implies commitment to cooperation as a primary mode of operation. The discipline which deals with this topic is the Sociology of Cooperation. This discipline is relatively new. It has succeeded in establishing research centers in different countries and it has found its place in a few institutions of higher learning of the traditional kind. But it appears that in order to find its proper place it will need a frame work such as only a World University can offer. In this sense it might be said that the Sociology of Cooperation is a discipline in search of a World University.

At this point, it might be in order to indicate what we consider to be the nature and the scope of this discipline, and to describe briefly its development up to this date. As to the nature of the discipline I may be allowed to repeat, with slight changes, a specification I attempted in a recently published paper. To quote: "What distinguishes the Sociology of Cooperation from other social science schools and disciplines is not so much theory, method and techniques, as concentration on a specific topic, the topic of Cooperation. Viewed in the sociological perspective this topic shows three main characteristic aspects. These are:

(1) Cooperation as a general social process;

(2) as institutionalized in the Cooperative Movement;

(3) as a form of orientation which we believe to be particularly in accord with our present-day world and life view.

As a general social process Cooperation has been treated by several social science disciplines, such as Biological Sociology (BAGEHOT, KROPOTKIN and W. C. ALLEE); by Anthropology (MARGARET MEAD, GEORGE L. MURDOCK, RUTH BENEDICT, MARK A. MAY and LEONARD W. DOOB and

LAURA THOMPSON); Experimental Social Psychology (GARDNER MURPHY); and Industrial Sociology (ELTON MAYO and the Harvard School of Business Administration). While the treatment of these disciplines remains more or less "academic", the sociology of cooperation deals mainly with cooperation as practiced by the Cooperative Movement. It sees as one of the most important contributions made to social science by this movement the method it has evolved of social innovation. This method, applied most systematically, though not always with explicit awareness, by the so-called "modern cooperative community" is that of the sociological experiment as the prototype of which can be considered the development pattern of the Kibbutz.

It is therefore that the Sociology of Cooperation devotes its main attention to the modern cooperative communities, such as the Israeli Kibbutzim, the French Communities of Work, the Soviet Kolkhozi, the Mexican Ejidos, to mention only the topically most important ones.

In the sociological view these communities serve as testing grounds for the implementation of the more comprehensive possibilities of the cooperative orientation, the third main aspect of our topic. This orientation, to characterize it briefly, aims ultimatively at the fullest realization of man's constructive potentialities. The source from which it derives its notions are the particular cooperative values. These can be distinguished as being of a more generic and a more specific nature. Among the important generic cooperative values may be mentioned: human fellowship; the spirit of service in the interest of a world community based on order, kindness and harmony; respect for the opinion of others; and mutual sympathy. As to the more specific values, they can be described as partly economic and partly social. Main among the economic cooperative values are: production for use and service; common ownership of the means of production; and equitable share in its proceeds. Main among the social cooperative values are: the dignity of man ("masters of their own destiny"); his equality as a person; and his right to equitable participation in all decisions that concern himself." [1]

As to the development of the Sociology of Cooperation it is marked by progress from research to the use made of its findings in institutions of Higher Learning. In this sense the following account may at the same time serve as a brief survey of some of the existing agencies active in transnational education.

In its first phase, the phase of exploration, the field of the Sociology of Cooperation was cultivated mainly by several research centers. The first of these centers was the *Group Farming Research Institute*, New York City and Poughkeepsie, N.Y. Among the main studies carried out by this Institute were those of the Saskatchewan Cooperative Farms, Canada (1946); of the

1. See: H. F. INFIELD "The Therapeutic Use of the Clinically Applied Sociology of Cooperation". *Israel Ann. Psychiatry*. I. No. 1. 1963.

Israeli Kibbutzim (1949); of the French Communities of Work (1951); and of the Mexican Collective Ejidos (1952). The Institute published a Bulletin *Cooperative Living* (1949–1957), with subcribers in 31 countries, and a series of Group Farming Research Institute Monographs, in addition to several larger volumes.

The Group Farming Research Institute was instrumental in establishing several research centers in Europe, the *Bureau d'Etudes Coopirative et Communautaire*, in Paris; the *Centro di Sociologia della Cooperazione*, Ivrea-Milano, Italy; and the *Sektion für die Soziologie des Genossenschaftswesens* at the University of Cologne, Germany. Each of these centres carried out field studies of its own, recorded them in a series of monographs and in its periodicals, and each also published several more comprehensive volumes. The efforts of all these centers were coordinated in the *International Council for Research in the Sociology of Cooperation* (founded 1953). The I.C.R.S. established an *International Library of the Sociology of Cooperation* with publications in English, French, Italian, German and Spanish. Its periodical *The International Archives of the Sociology of Cooperation*, publishes bi-annually papers in three languages, English, French and Italian. Founded in 1957, it is now in its ninth year.

Having accumulated a sizeable body of knowledge in the new field, the Sociology of Cooperation was able to take its place at first in several smaller Institutions of higher learning. First among these was the Cooperative College at Loughborough, England, the educational institution of the British Co-operative Union. Its students come from all parts of the British Commonwealth of Nations as well as from Great Britain proper. In 1955 I was invited by the College to offer a Seminar on the Sociology of Cooperation to a group of selected students. The Seminar was repeated in the following year and the Sociology of Cooperation was subsequently included in the annual curriculum of the College. A similar Seminar was offered also at the *Albert Schweitzer College*, at Churwalden, Switzerland, an "International Education Center" as it calls itself, whose orientation derives from the philosophical writings of its namesake. The seminar was subsequently incorporated in the College's annual program. A significant place was assigned to the Sociology of Cooperation in the *Afro-Asian Seminar on Cooperation* held in Tel-Aviv, Israel, from Nov. 1958 to 1959. This bilingual (French and English) seminar, the first of its kind, organized by one Asian developing country for the other countries of Asia and Africa, was attended by over 60 participants, mostly government officials and leaders of farmers and cooperative organizations from seventeen countries. It marked a turning point in the relations of Israel with other Asian and African countries. Since then a permanent Institute for Trade Union and Cooperative Studies has been established in Tel-Aviv. It continues to attract leaders from Asia and Africa.

Regular courses and seminars in the Sociology of Cooperation have so far been offered in the main by three Universities: The Hebrew University,

Jerusalem, Israel, (1957–60); University of Argentina, Buenos Aires; and the *Ecole Pratique* of the *Sorbonne*, where the director of the B.E.C.C., Henri DESROCHE, has been appointed Professor of the Sociology of Cooperation and has estalished in recent years a Cooperative College which serves chiefly students from the French speaking countries of Africa.

It might be mentioned also, that provision has been made for the Sociology of Cooperation in two International Institutions which are still in the planning stage. One is the *International Institute of Ghandian Studies*, Benares, India. This Institute sponsored by the *Ghandi Peace Foundation*, was tentatively established in 1962 by Jayaprakash NARAYAN. Its curriculum assigned the Sociology of Cooperation an important place. Unfortunately the Institute failed to attract a sufficient number of students and had to be closed after a few months. NARAYAN, as he informed me, intends to try again as soon as circumstances allow. Still in the planning stage is also the Academy of R. W. CORTI, best known as the founder of the International Children Village Pestalozzi. CORTI has already acquired at Veticon, near Zürich, the land for his Academy, which he sees as a "supra-national center conceived in response to the ... urgent need for synthesis, integration and ever-increasing responsibility in the field of scientific research." He too plans to make the Sociology of Cooperation part of his program.

Finally it remains to be mentioned that a somewhat unusual application has been made of the Sociology of Cooperation at the Maon Yerushalayim, a psychotherapeutic institute of a Half-Way House type, established in 1960 in a suburb of Jerusalem, Talpiot. Here the Sociology of Cooperation in its clinical application helped develop the so-called "cooperative group psychotherapy." The Half-Way House began as a privately endowed institution. Its success prompted the Israel Ministry of Health to turn it into a governmental agency.

In the course of this, here briefly sketched, development, the Sociology of Cooperation arrived at certain conclusions which should be of interest to any planning of world education in general and perhaps also to our own planning of a World University. Two of these conclusions, it seems to me, deserve to be stressed in this context.

(1) Cooperation, in the sense of concern for the fellow man, is not something that follows automatically from any particular socio-economic group structure, not even from such a comprehensively cooperative one as that of the Kibbutz. It demands a special attention to the presence and the development of what I call the "cooperative potential," of the group and the individuals who form it. To this end I have developed certain techniques of assessment (the Cooperative Potential and Resoluteness Tests), as well as certain techniques designed for its development, as described in the above quoted paper.

(2) Whatever else the qualifications of those in charge of educating others for cooperation might be, they not only must have a thorough

acquaintance with the theory and practice of cooperation but must themselves possess a substantial cooperative potential.

The World University faces a situation in which some elemental forms of a world order aiming at intra-and intergroup or international cooperation have already begun to emerge. But the emergence is far from speedy. This poses, as far as world education is concerned, an interesting and challenging new problem. For education, in its commonly accepted sense, means the transmission of the *Kulturgut*, the inherited and acquired cultural values, from one generation to the next. The cooperative world order, however, far from being an established fact, is as yet merely more of a felt need. This suggests that world education must be creative education by the sheer necessity of having to create the very reality for which it intends to educate. With specific reference to our World University it appears that the Council favors what I would call a germinal procedure. It proposes to proceed by establishing chairs and research centers at institutions of higher learning in different countries. As the coordinating organ would serve the Presidium of the WAAS and the Council. They would constitute a world center for a transnational team of co-operating Institutions and/or single scientists. This method of organising a World University has been agreed upon, it is stated in the Circular Letter ci/65, in view of the practical difficulties which would face "under present political conditions" now and "in the foreseeable future" the establishment "of an actual ... international but locally determined campus, where people from many countries and races could meet and study."

This procedure, if I understand it correctly, contains an element essential to all planning for a true World University. This is the realization that such an University to be truly transnational cannot remain confined to one place but has to erect educational plants in different parts of the world. It is the manner of procedure that allows for differences of opinion. It can be done, at least to begin with, either in the manner agreed upon by the Council; or in the way the Friends Committee appears to plan its World College. One of the disadvantages which appears to me to be inherent in our Council's plan is that the procedure by chairs will have difficulty to establish the World University as a distinct institution. This danger, it seems to me, is avoided if, as the Friends apparently intend to do, the World University or college is organized along the lines of Oxford and Cambridge University, but extended to regional areas and to the world as a whole. (It might be noted that the State Universities in some of the American States such as for instance California, North Carolina or more recently New York, proceed by establishing Colleges in different parts of the state, all united in the given State University).

In both procedures the Sociology of Cooperation can find its place. Chairs of the Sociology of Cooperation, as I have shown, have been established at some well-known Universities; a chair of the same kind can easily be established within the framework of a World University as planned by the Council. This notwithstanding the fact that a full use of it can be made not in terms of individual chairs but in more comprehensive communities of scholars, which constitute the *Communitas communitatum* of a *World University*.

The first, and I believe important, contribution that the Sociology of Cooperation in this kind of planning would be able to make is to call attention on a point usually neglected in the plans for world education. This is the personal factor. If it is accepted that the intent of world education is intra- and intergroup cooperation, then the ability to cooperate of those who are in charge of such education must be of crucial importance. It is therefore my firm believe that such education must start with the education of the educators. It is obvious that a staff which is not definitively cooperative itself will hardly be capable of teaching others to cooperate. This is one point. Another is the fact that education for cooperation inplies orientation towards the future rather than towards the past. In its scientific program it will have to transcend the confines of conventional curricula and find, in addition to the established sciences, a place for the sciences which are just emerging, often from the combination and unification of two or more hitherto separate disciplines.

Just to outline such a program in its most general contours, it will have to be divided into three parts, as follows:

I. A preparatory term of a few weeks consisting of sessions devoted to the training in cooperation of the staff; and sessions devoted to the training in cooperation of the students by the staff.

As noted, some techniques for this kind of training are already available and additional ones can be developed.

II. A curriculum more or less as commonly offered by existing colleges leading to a Bachelor of Arts degree but modified so as to suit regional needs and requirements and containing a course on the Sociology of Cooperation as well as a seminar on Research Methods and Techniques in this field.

III. An advanced, or possibly postgraduate, curriculum. This would offer subject matter such as: Psychophysiology, Biochemistry, Geological Science, (Paleontology, Human Ecology, etc.) Cybernetics, Astronautics, Supersensorics, and something I like to call *Noosophy*, or the exploration of systems of Ultimate Orientation, or religion.

The Problem of the Health of the International Community in the Light of Research on the Causes of Conflicts

by

JULIAN ALEKSANDROWICZ

assisted by GEORG W. ALEKSANDROWICZ JR., MAŁGORZATA DOMINIK, and BARBARA MONNE (psychiatrists), PIOTR WESOŁUCHA (internist), JADWIGA FEDOROWICZ (sociologist), and ALINA SKOTNICKA (psychologist)

Director, 3rd Clinic of Internal Diseases, Cracow

Let me begin with a truism: The guiding line of the medical profession has been, since the beginning of time, the removal of human suffering, disease, and premature death, and their prevention.

The kinds of diseases and their frequency have, as we know, been different in different cultural epochs. New kinds of suffering and disease leading to premature death have originated and are originating from dependence on a changing biophysical and psychosocial environment.

Epidemics of infectious diseases were more frequent in the epoch preceding the discovery of bacteria. Many of those diseases have already been mastered because science discovered their causes and showed methods of fighting them. This has been done by representatives of the biological, chemical, and pharmaceutical sciences, as well as by representatives of the humanistic sciences and lawyers. International law, by rigorously enforcing the carrying out of vaccinations, quarantine, etc., today safeguards the community the world over against the spread of epidemics.

In our contemporary cultural epoch, disease of the cardio-vascular system precipitated by factors of a psychosomatic nature, malignant tumours including the leukaemias, and injury and deaths resulting from road accidents, have replaced infectious diseases as the most frequent causes of suffering, illness, and premature death. It is commonly known that the increase in the incidence of these diseases correlates with technological progress.

It may be supposed that in contemporary civilisation there must exist some insufficiently recognised factors which favour the increase of the above-mentioned diseases.

Experience gained in the prevention of infectious diseases permits us to anticipate that a decrease in morbidity will begin as soon as the pathological mechanisms of the most common contemporary diseases are recognised and knowledge of their prevention becomes universal.

We were guided by this thought when we considered the aetiopathogenesis of suffering, disease, and premature death of people treated in our clinic and when we considered the possibilities of preventing them. The subject of this report is the observation of the relation between the psycho-social environment and "organic neuroses."

Our observations were based on the examination of 2,520 patients admitted to the Third Clinic of Internal Diseases, Cracow Medical Academy, over a period of 28 months (1963 – 1965).

Before we discuss the Table, let us define the still controversial term "neurosis".

WALLEN believes that "neurosis is a way of life, bringing with it emotional sufferings." For our purposes, neurosis constitutes a reversible disturbance of intellectual and emotional phenomena comprised in the sphere of higher nervous functions – a disturbance which is due to the difficulties man experiences when adapting himself to his psycho-social environment. Those difficulties can be of an endogenous nature, resulting from personality difficulties, or of an exogenous nature – when the stimuli in the external environment are too powerful for man's adaptive capacities.

In the course of adaptation, certain stress factors are formed in the organism which, by neurohumoral means, can also produce organic changes and, in the course of the development of the disease, can lead to a large number of multiorganic symptoms of varying intensity.

Starting from the assumption that good health is the biological state in which man does not show any clinical symptoms of disease and fully enjoys physical and psycho-social well-being (by psycho-social well-being we mean a state of social usefulness in which the subject cooperates in improving the environment's existence), we believe that neurosis is a disturbance in that well-being, particularly in psycho-social well-being.

Our report is particularly concerned with the problem of neurosis.

TABLE I

Diseases of the blood	26%
Neuroses	31%
Mental illness	3%
Others	40%

Neurosis has become the plague of the contemporary world. BILIKIEWICZ states that the percentage of people suffering from neurosis and calling on general practitioners and specialists amounts to 30–50% of all patients. It would seem that we are witnessing today an explosive increase in the number of neurotic people and people ill with neuroses. This is confirmed by the report of MENNINGER of the USA among others (according to BILIKIEWICZ.[1] He says that during the First World War the percentage of men unfit, because of neurosis, for service in the US Army amounted to 2%, whereas in the Second World War the number rose to 12%. In 1917, 97, 577 US soldiers were hospitalised because of neurosis; in 1944 – 1 million.

As can be seen from Table I, the number of patients suffering from neuroses amounted, together with psychically ill patients, to over 1/3 of the

1. Tadeusz Bilikiewicz: Psychotherapy in general medical practice. PZWL, 1964.

total number of patients in our clinic at that period of time. The 3% of the patients mentioned in the Table, in whom psychotic syndromes were observed during their stay in the clinic, were firstly patients who had found themselves in the clinic because their dominating somatic ailments were more disturbing to the environment than their basic disease, and secondly patients with psychoses which originated in the course of diseases of the internal organs (e.g. cardiac psychoses). They were, of course, transferred to the psychiatric clinic for further treatment.

The neurotic syndromes which general practitioners most frequently encounter, are the so-called organic neuroses or, in other words, neurotic syndromes in which organic ailments come to the fore. Thus, there are for instance "functional" disturbances of the circulatory system or of the stomach, etc. which have no pathological basis when objectively examined. Quite frequently, only disturbances in the autonomic nervous balance can be found in these patients.

Another group of patients is those whose sufferings have a neurotic aetiology, but whose principal ailments have an organic character. Those organic impairments which are the result of neurotic disturbances are formed by so-called psychosomatic links, and they constitute a double problem. On the one hand, they require, of course, conventional treatment. On the other, they simultaneously require a psychotropic treatment, or, in other words, the same treatment as neuroses of other kinds. Whereas the first type of treatment is aimed at bringing the patients direct help, the second – psychotropic therapy – is designed to remove the sources of the illness and to prevent its recurrence. The majority of these patients present symptoms of high blood pressure, bronchial asthma, angina pectoris or myocardial infarction, stomach of duodenal ulcers, ulcerative colitis, etc.

In clinics for internal diseases one also finds patients in whom appear, in the course of hysteria, the so-called organic conversions, hypochondrico-hysterical syndromes, and patients whose sufferings express their neurotic experiences, e.g. fear.

These subjects who, as has already been mentioned, constitute more than 1/3 of the patients treated in our clinic, were examined and treated by psychiatrists, psychologists, and sociologists, in addition to receiving conventional therapy.

We should like to underline here that we are only in the course of working out the conditions and methods of our work and for this reason not all the patients in the above group were examined and treated in the same way.

The psychologists and psychiatrists made intensive inquiries with the majority of these patients. The psychiatrists instituted psychotherapeutic measures with the aid of different techniques, or indicated methods of psycho-pharmacological treatment. The psychologists tested the patients' personality. The sociologists examined the patient's environment, trying to find in it the elements of conflict. When they had found and defined them, they attempted, together with a sociological assistant, to eliminate from the environment the neurogenic element.

In the course of our observations we came to the conclusion that in the majority of patients suffering from neuroses the aetiopathogenetic elements had been an important cause of various conflicts which had their source in the imperfect and often even harmful organisation of social life, and not in the personal difficulties of a patient.

TABLE II

Supposed "principal neurosis-creative element"	No. of cases
Conflicts at work (disadvantageous interpersonal relations, fear of losing job or of retirement)	3
Lack of interest in work	3
Conflicts between parents and children	2
"Over-protective mother"	2
Conflicts in marriage resulting from character differences or from adultery	6
Housing problems	2
Personality difficulties (e.g. disproportion between intentions and capacities, hypochondriac personality features, etc.)	8
Total	26

As can be seen from the above table, in only 8 of the patients examined could the origin of neurosis be found in their personality features. In the remaining 18 cases the "external" elements arising from the social environment or suitable for correction by social intervention always played an essential part. Naturally, the character of "neurogenic elements" described here should be considered with utmost care for, so far, we have no sufficiently precise methods of describing objectively the degree of a patient's traumatisation by noxae existing in the social environment. Therefore, our results are only of an exploratory character.

We found that 160 of a group of 220 patients displayed external, environmental elements of conflict. The most common cause was living together in close contact with many others as sub-tenants; next came sexual conflicts and conflicts between employer and employee resulting from bad business management, etc.

This emphasis on the existence of external neurogenic factors supplies the Health Service with important arguments for demanding suitable changes in the psychosocial environment, thus helping to prevent such factors from arising. However, we realise the difficulties which will be encountered in changing the environment so as to ensure that disease-creative incentives of a psycho-emotional nature would be reduced to a minimum. Our intention was only to attempt to expose the most frequent noxae having their source in our psychosocial environment.

Hence, it also seems that the neurogenic conflict situations existing in the international community would also constitute an interesting subject and help to explain the source of neuroses and their organic consequences.

A trial analysis of these "external" neurogenic factors was carried out in 81 patients at our clinic, This group was divided according to diagnoses, the existence and role of neurogenic conflicts being defined at the same time, as shown in Table III.

TABLE III

Diagnosis	No of cases in the group	No of cases in which the neurogenic conflict situation was confirmed	Confirmed conflicts in groups:			
			Family groups	Professional groups	Neighbourly groups *	Wider social systems**
Ulcerous disease	46	36	15	11	7	3
Other neuroses	25	15	9	3	0	3
Suicides	11	11	2	1	0	8
Total	82	62	26	15	7	14

* By neighbourly conflicts is meant interpersonal relationships, the basis of which is contact in a confined space (mostly common accommodation).

** By wider social systems is meant those interpersonal relationships which form a man's psychosocial environment.

The conflicts listed in Table IV were those most frequentley observed in the group discussed above.

TABLE IV

Type of conflict	Number of cases in which they were confirmed*
1. Disintegration of traditional groups, threatening the natural tendency towards stabilisation	10
2. Rush for social success, in cases where the psychic possibilities of the individual were limited	17
3. Inequality of social development between different co-existing individuals	5
4. Disturbance of accepted values	9
5. Faith shaken in traditional moral standards and upbringing	19
6. The appearance of aggression, based on past experiences (war reminiscences)	9
7. Increasingly complicated problems of the organisation of work and of adaption to technological progress	11

* Since the conflict situations in different cases consisted of various factors, the numbers given, referring to the number of cases in which the individual factors were confirmed, are higher than the figures for the number of cases in which the conflict situations were confirmed.

This Table shows only certain characteristic proportions in the emerging social phenomena.

A similar situation has been affirmed by Dr. Ewa Broszkiewicz, a psychiatrist, based on an examination of our patients suffering from diseases of the cardiovascular system. These investigations, carried out in the course of psychological rehabilitation, will be described in a separate report.

The result of our work takes the form of a preliminary report and may raise some doubts. We ourselves are also not free from certain doubts regarding the methods; nevertheless, our observations permit us to draw the following general conclusions:

(1) The conflicts originating in the external environment of patients have a decisive pathogenetic significance for the origin of neurosis. These facts have been confirmed more frequently than was previously accepted on the basis of traditional methods for the diagnosis and therapy of internal diseases.

(2) Patients with neuroses who are admitted to internal diseases clinics can be more successfully treated with the help of psycho- and sociotherapeutic techniques than with classic internal treatment only.

(3) We cannot help feeling that analysis of the social environment of patients with neuroses, their reeducation and their immunisation by psychotherapy will give better and more lasting effects than the pharmacological treatment used in traditional clinics for internal diseases.

(4) The list of conflict factors observed in our patients shows that the disease-creative stimuli are most often conditioned by factors resulting from the current situation of the contemporary world. The environment of contemporary man's existence was formed not only by natural forces but particularly by the people themselves. They organised their psychosocial environment which stipulates the forms of interhuman relations. It is therefore in their power to organise their environment and their interpersonal relations in such a way as to eliminate disease-creative incentives.

AFTER-THOUGHTS AND PROPOSALS

The microclimate of a clinic reflects in a way the surrounding macroworld – the biophysical and psychosocial environment of both the national and the international community. Hence, it permits a socio-medical plumbing of the "causes and effects" existing in a given environment, which result in psychosomatic health or illness.

Man reacts with a limited number of symptoms of the psychosomatic organism, sometimes felt as a disease, to the innumerable and constantly changing number of environmental stimulants. Today, all over the world we are passing through a stage of explosive increase in suffering, disease, and premature death.

The results we present of our investigations on the influence the environmental situation has on the origin of neuroses, reflect to a certain degree this situation. Although they refer to a small group of patients coming from the neighbourhood of our town, we have reason to believe that the neurogenic factors existing in other parts of our country and indeed in the world, although different in their essence, are identical in their ultimate effect.

The psychotraumatic stresses originate in the family environment, in the school environment, in the environment at work, etc. Psychotraumatising noxae are in character as well as in number the result of contemporary culture. This culture is made up of both the forms of human behaviour which can favour health or cause illness, and of knowledge about the world placed in the framework of technical and physical humanistic and biological sciences. "Culture" also expresses itself by assimilating existing intellectual values and by forming new ones. The most essential criterion of culture is perhaps the development in man of all that which is really human (Cardinal KOENIG).

Both the biophysical and psychosocial environments are in a dialectical relationship. They are formed not only by natural forces but particularly by the actions of the people themselves. Therefore, only people can organise these environments so that they will favour health, and not illness.

Many of the factors which disorganise the environment have their source in the technocratic structure of contemporary civilisation. They ought to be recognised both by the community generally and by the small groups of administrators, particularly by those who cure and those who are cured, by subordinates and by those in power.

In the contemporary period of mankind's history, in the period when the fate of the world is at stake, it is necessary to enlarge our knowledge about man and about the factors which are the causes of interhuman conflicts, as well as our knowledge about their consequences in the form of psychic and somatic health and disease.

A special part could be played here by investigations into the mechanism of one of the most dangerous pathogenic stresses, i.e. hate in its various forms, beginning with envy and finishing with homicide and genocide.

It is self-evident that only a healthy man can organise a healthy biophysical and psychosocial environment. On the other hand a sick man i.e. a man who has no feeling of full physical and psychosocial well-being in the sense of his usefulness in cooperating in the improvement of the environment) cannot, because he does not know how to organise the environment so as to save himself and others from suffering.

Our goal – as can be seen from the findings which we have presented here – was to make a contribution to the gathering of facts which could facilitate the elimination from the environment of causes of human suffering. These facts ought to be widely advertised.

Previous trials of advertising them, conducted in the Cracow community, were based on transferring to the community the results of clinical observations. With this aim we organised "The Year of Kindness," "The Little Parliament of the Cracow Region" – dedicated to the culture of life and work. So successful were the results of that educational action that the authorities recommended its further dissemination, which constitutes the first stage of freeing the psychosocial environment from pathogenic stimuli. A further stage is the propagation of the necessity of passing a law safeguarding the individual against psychical traumas in the same way as he is safeguarded against physical injuries, and an attempt to reform medical studies (law on psychical health) which, in their syllabus, ought to consider the fact that contemporary physicians cannot exercise their function of counteracting suffering independently from those specialists, technological, biological, and humanistic who – often unconsciously – create suffering by transforming the natural environment.

It seems that contemporary technological progress in the sphere of mass-dissemination of information offers, as never before in the world's history, great possibilities of propagating ideas. We ought therefore to place on the educational syllabus those ideas which naturally emphasise that which unites people, and not that which divides them. This way seems closer to achieving our aim, namely to educate and pacify contemporary man's greatest foe – that is, other men.

The after-thoughts presented here should not be taken as recipes. They are rather a register of problems to be solved. Undoubtedly, one can maintain that the sources of sufferings are indissolubly connected with the essence of human existence and will never be avoided. Hence, all attempts at organising and forming the psychosocial environment in such a way as to decrease suffering are bound to be unsuccessful. The problem is whether one should cease to resist and let things slide, or whether one ought to strive to reach aims which are apparently unattainable.

For in the same way as the once Utopian dreams of space travel have now become true, so the dream of science serving the welfare of all people of the world, those living now and those to be born, can become a fact. This will undoubtedly be decided by science.

For just as a world of machines and technological civilisation could not be organised by man without knowledge of physical laws, so the formation of an environment favouring the welfare and health of humanity will not be achieved by him without a knowledge of the laws of psychology, sociology, cultural anthropology, and other branches of humanistic sciences integrated with medical science.

Our experiences of the microworld of the clinic permit us to elaborate a principle that consciousness and cognition and investigation make it possible for man to control and master his biophysical and psychosocial environment.

For todays' period of explosive development of communications means that humanity, as never before, has the possibility of realising the Utopian vision in which mankind constitutes one community united by the ideas of brotherhood.

In the realisation of that vision an individual will be judged by criteria of honesty and dishonesty, by intellectual and ethical criteria, rather than by social, genetic, or financial criteria.

We all realise that tomorrow's world will depend on the amount and quality of knowledge which we pass to the younger generation and especially to the youth which we entrust with administrative and governmental functions over social groups. Therefore the organisers of pedagogical institutions training the world's leaders should strive to eliminate from such studies people with unsuitable moral standards and intellects.

The role of inspirer and coordinator of the multidirectional international therapy of the world community devolves upon the World University, which will be the highest in hierarchy – the Alma Mater Universitatis.

All that we can add to what we have already said, is to wish the World Academy of Art and Science, the initiator of the World University, every success in its attempts to fulfil the hopes we have placed in it.

REFERENCES

1. Aleksandrowicz, J.: A trial to adapt the traditional clinic of internal diseases for the contemporary treatment of neurosis. *Mental Hygiene*, 1963, 47, 3: *483*.
2. Aleksandrowicz, J.: Technic, Humanism and Medicine. La Scuola in Azione, Milano, 1963, 15.
3. Aleksandrowicz, J., Bożek, A., Gizowa, A., Kaczanowski, K., Kępiński, A., Orłowska, A., Skotnicka, A., Zurowska, A.: Psychosoziologische und anthropologische Untersuchungen an Leukaemiekranken. *Zeitschr. f. psycho-somatische Medizin*, Göttingen, 1963, Nr 1.
4. Aleksandrowicz, J., Brożek, A., Kaczanowski, K., Piaskowski, B.: Anthropologische Untersuchungen an Leukaemiekranken. *Haemat. Hungarica* 1964, 4, 2: *381*.

The Fundamental Importance of Brain Research

by

Sir John Eccles
Professor of Physiology, Australian National University, Canberra

I have only recently been honoured by election to this distinguished Academy, but since then I have given much thought to the high ideals of our Academy and to the manner in which I might be able to help in the realization of these ideals. Central to these ideals is the concept that we must strive to foster and develop the fullest possible life for mankind, not just here and now, but indefinitely into the future. It is my belief that we will be successful just in so far as we appreciate the nature of man and plan accordingly.

As I come to consider the nature of man, I discover that I have direct access to privileged information about one – namely myself with my self consciousness. Please do not fear that I am going to use this assertion in order to develop a solipsistic thesis. I shall be at pains to show that I have to recognize an equivalent self consciousness in all other human beings. My philosophical position is diametrically opposite to those who would relegate conscious experience to the meaningless role of an epiphenomenon.

Is it not true that those experiences most commonly with us are accepted without any appreciation of their tremendous mystery? Are we not still like children in our outlook on our experiences of conscious life, accepting them and only rarely pausing to contemplate and appreciate the wonder of conscious experiences? For example, vision gives us from instant to instant a three dimensional picture of an external world and builds into that picture such qualities as brightness and colour, which exist only in perceptions developed as a consequence of brain action. Of course we now recognize physical counterparts of these perceptual experiences, such as the intensity of a light source and the wave lengths of its emitted radiation; nevertheless the perceptions themselves arise in some quite unknown manner out of the coded information conveyed from the retina to the brain. I hope you feel the wonder of this gift of vision which adds such riches to our experiences. Perhaps it is easier still to appreciate the miraculous transformation that occurs in hearing from mere congeries of pressure waves in the atmosphere to sound with tone and harmony and melody, all of which are *created* as a consequence of the complexities of the neuronal patterns developed from the inflow of acoustic information.

I hope these simple examples convey to you some impression of what I mean when I refer to the wonder of the conscious life that each of us experiences. Yet it seems to me that this post-Darwinian man has in this age lost the sense of his true greatness and of his immeasurable superiority to animals. At this present primitive level of understanding of man's brain and of its role in ordering behaviour, it is often maintained that man is merely a special type of computer. I will readily agree that this can occur for special regions of the brain. For example in recent years my research has been concentrated on the cerebellum which is a highly differentiated organ of the brain specially concerned with the control and the finesse of movement. As one tries to understand how the cerebellum performs this task, one is virtually constrained to think of it acting essentially as a computer, but with principles of operation radically different from present-day computers. However, the cerebral cortex contrasts with the cerebellum by its much more complex and diversified structure and functional performance. Moreover, we have to recognize that certain highly complex and diversified actions of the cerebral cortex and the associated subcortical ganglia give rise to conscious experiences.

There is no evidence, whatsoever, for the statements often made that, at an adequate level of complexity, computers also would achieve self-consciousness. With that extravagant claim there may be added the further assertion that computers may achieve a higher status of evolutionary development than man, so that we would be relegated to some servile role, just as animals are to us. If there were even a remote risk of such an eventuality, I would recommend Samuel BUTLER's "Erewon" as prescribed reading for all students, and I would found a society advocating the dismantling of computers before we had to murder them! Those who assert that, as soon as some computer achieves the requisite degree of complexity, it will have a self consciousness, have completely failed to recognize that the most complex cerebral activities usually do not result in a conscious experience. As yet we are quite ignorant of the special circumstances which attend cerebral activities that are giving rise to conscious experiences.

Again we have the extraordinary doctrine that all behaviour is determined solely by inheritance and conditioning. It is unfortunate that the advocates of this doctrine have been blind to the fact that its logical consequences make its assertion meaningless; for this action of assertion by them must be recognized by them as merely the result of a prior conditioning, and of value merely as a tribute to the effectiveness of this conditioning. The denial of free-will and the advocacy of a universal determinism is justified within the scientific frameworks of the now-discredited 19th century deterministic physics and of a primitive type of reflexology as an epitome of brain performance. My position is that I have the indubitable experience that I can by thinking and willing control my actions if I so wish, though in normal waking life this prerogative is exercised but seldom. I am not able to give a scientific account of how thought can lead to action, but this failure serves to emphasize that our present physics and physiology are too primitive for this most challenging task of resolving the antinomy between our experience and our present primitive level of understanding brain function.

After these general considerations, I would like to enlarge upon the theme of conscious experiences and the brain. Some of the leading neurological investigators in the world devoted a study week to this subject here in Rome almost a year ago, and some remarkable conceptual advances were there reported. It was agreed by all participants that every conscious experience – every perception, thought and memory – has as its material counterpart some specific spatio-temporal activity in the vast neuronal network of the cerebral cortex and subcortical nuclei, being woven of neuronal activities in space and time in the "enchanted-loom" so poetically described by SHERRINGTON. I would further go on to say that, no matter what one's philosophical or political position, there must be general assent to the proposition that the study of the brain is central to the scientific investigation of the nature of man. The functioning of the brain gives us all that matters in life, not only our immediate perceptions, as I have illustrated by vision and hearing, but also all memory, emotions, thoughts, ideals, imagination, technical skills, and above all the creative achievements in art, philosophy and science. It is a common but erroneous belief that the marvellous technical skills of a musician are due to the refinements of performance of his muscles in arms and fingers and of his touch sensibility; but in reality all this refinement of learned skill is in the memory patterns in the brain of the musician, which is acting from moment to moment on some synthesis of memory patterns with the information fed in from the sense organs of muscle, skin and of joint.

In the last 10 to 20 years there has been enormous progress in the understanding of the simpler aspects of brain structure and function. This basic work has been on the properties of the unit structures of the nervous system, the nerve cells, on the modes of communication over nerve cells by propagated impulses and between them at the functional contacts or synapses and on the simplest functional patterns of nerve cell organization. It provides a sound foundation for further progress; and, thanks to the great power of the new micro-techniques, its success has been beyond the most sanguine hopes of a few years ago. Yet all this progress serves but to give an immensely wider and deeper vision of the fantastic problems that lie ahead. We can now be confident that the almost infinite complexity and variety of the neuronal network that could be formed by the ten thousand million nerve cells of the cerebral cortex endows it with potentialities adequate for any achievement, even for that displayed in the performance of the highest intelligence. I have hopes, too, that we are on the threshold of understanding the basic principles responsible for the laying down of memory traces, which we may envisage as being due to an enduring enhancement of synaptic efficacy with usage. In this way a neuronal pathway that is activated by a particular sensory input will, as a consequence of repeated activation, achieve a kind of stabilization by means of the enhanced synaptic functions of its neuronal linkages, and so be available for recall in memory when there is an appropriate input into its circuitry.

Yet all this progress serves but to give an immensely wider and deeper vision of the fantastic problems that lie ahead. If we are to regard the brain as a machine, it enormously transcends in its variety and flexibility any man-made machine, such as a computer. If it is to be regarded as a communication system, such as an automatic telephone exchange, it is of a quite different order from anything that we can devise, comprising, as it does, more than ten thousand million neurones linked up in the most unimaginably complex and subtle manner. And, as I have already emphasized, it has in addition the extraordinary emergent property of providing self-consciousness, at least when in certain states of activity.

The most remarkable examples of experiments on brain function and consciousness have been reported by SPERRY in which surgical separation of the commissures linking the two cerebral hemispheres was made in order to control intractable epilepsy; and mercifully it was successful therapeutically. These subjects display no gross signs of incoordination of response, nor do they display or report any signs of splitting of their mental unity, such as might be called a mental diplopia. But truly remarkable findings have been revealed by appropriate testing. The dominant hemisphere is that containing language representation, and to all inputs into that hemisphere, the subject responds normally and reports normal conscious experience. However, all inputs selectively made into the other or minor hemisphere fail to give the subject any conscious experience, nor can the subject voluntarily initiate any motor actions stemming from that hemisphere, which contrasts with the normal voluntary evocation of movement from the dominant hemisphere. Yet the minor hemisphere is capable of quite complex and skilled tasks in response to information reaching it from sense organs selectively feeding into it, as may be arranged by inputs from the appropriate visual field or cutaneous receptor field. We can summarize the situation of these patients by stating that the goings-on in the minor hemisphere never come to their conscious experience, nor can they voluntarily affect these goings-on. Essentially, the splitting of the brain has left the conscious subject in normal relationship to the dominant hemisphere with the normal "two-way traffic" between brain action and conscious experience, whereas with the minor hemisphere there is no such "traffic", but instead this hemisphere functions as an unconscious computer that is capable of complex actions in response to input and is also capable of learning. I allude briefly to these extraordinary findings in order to illustrate the way in which neurological research is giving rise to the most extraordinary discoveries that have great significance both to philosophy and psychology.

If the value of research is to be measured in relation to its intrinsic importance to man, then brain research must rank as incomparably more important than space research, which commands a very much greater financial support. No doubt much of this inflated support is forthcoming because of its real or imagined value for military strategy and political status. I don't care much about the lavish expenditure of money on space research. What I do care about is that it is attracting such a large proportion of the highly intelligent young scientists. This is a real tragedy, and I hope it will be possible to limit its impact. For example, I think it is urgently necessary to oppose the emotional attraction of space research by the development of a counterattraction in the greatest of all intellectual adventures, the attempt by man to understand the working of his own brain.

There need be no fear that this attempt to understand the brain scientifically will lead to the removal of the "final illusions of man about his own spiritual existence," which would be the claim of some positivist scientists as well as philosophers. On the contrary the framework of a quite inadequate and primitive concept of the brain provides the medium in which flourish the materialistic, mechanistic, behaviouristic and cybernetic concepts of man, which are at present so dominant. Of course I fully support scientific investigations on behaviour and conditioned reflexes, and in fact all the present scientific programs of behaviouristic psychology. All of this work is a type of physiological psychology. Furthermore, I agree that much of human behaviour can be satisfactory explained on the basis of concepts developed in relation to these experiments. However, I differ radically from the behaviourists in that they would claim to give a complete account of the behaviour of a man, whereas I *know* that it is not adequate to provide me with an answer to the question: What am I? It does not explain me to myself, for it ignores or relegates to a meaningless role my conscious experiences, and to me these constitute the primary reality – as to each one of you – each for himself.

I have an equivalent objection to the assertions of evolutionists that my brain, and therefore my consciously experiencing self is fully explained by the magnificent creative process of thousands of millions of years of evolution. I readily accept all that they postulate in respect of my brain, yet I find my own consciously experiencing self not satisfactorily accounted for. The creative evolutionary process is to me an incomplete explanation of the origin of myself. I believe that we have to recognize that there are great unknowns in the attempts that have so far been made to understand the nature of man. And the further we progress in research the more we will realize the tremendous mystery of our personal existence as a consciously experiencing being.

Yet, as I have mentioned above, great progress has been made in our attempts to understand the mode of operation of the simplest levels of brain action with the secure foundation provided by the study of the properties of the units of the nervous system, the nerve cells, and of the functional linkages between them, the synapses. Moreover, we now have considerable insight into the organization of the simplest patterns of neuronal linkages. What is now needed is the concentrated efforts of the highest intellects in such diverse fields as mathematics, physics, communication theory, chemistry and molecular biology, in order to transform the present level of investigation into fields as yet unknown, One can envisage that it will be necessary to have revolutionary developments in both the experimental and theoretical methods of probing into this vast field.

But, you may well ask, what mode of action would help in bringing about these most desirable recruitments into the field of brain research? Several of us neurophysiologists and neuroanatomists have discussed possible procedures. There has been general agreement that it is urgently necessary to establish in Europe a Brain Research Institute that would have a permanent research staff at the highest possible level and with research fellowships and scholarships for temporary staff that come for one or more years of research training. In addition the Institute would function as a centre for specialist symposia and for what may be called study courses of several weeks duration. These study courses would provide opportunity for scientists from other fields to discover the nature of the problems arising in brain research and to explore the possibility that they may be able to utilize their own technical and theoretical abilities in the furtherance of brain research. As yet this project of a Brain Research Institute remains as a germinal idea. But I feel most strongly that brain research is the greatest challenge confronting man, and that supreme intellectual efforts are urgently needed in attempting to meet this challenge and so to embark on the greatest adventure that man can ever undertake.

In conclusion I would suggest that this project of a Brain Research Institute has affinities with the concept of a World University that is being considered at this present meeting of the World Academy of Art and Science. It was with this in mind that I asked Dr. BOYKO if I might present to you a brief account of the present status of brain research and of its transcedent importance for the future of mankind.

Certain Criteria for Application to Large-Scale Irrigation Projects in the Developing Countries

by

JOHN F. V. PHILLIPS
Professor, University of Natal, Pietermaritzburg

BACKGROUND

It might be asked what prompts me to discuss so significant and also so debateable a topic as criteria considered to be useful in assessing the prospects for the developing of large-scale projects depending upon the control of rivers and aimed, in part, at the provision of water for irrigation, power and other needs.

My reply is that for long I have been interested in and, during the past two decades have been able to study several kinds of large-scale projects in the still less developed parts of the world. Although some of these projects have not been based upon the control of rivers, they, nonetheless, have presented opportunities for evolving criteria, some of which are applicable, *mutatis mutandis*, to propositions involving the control of rivers and utilization of the waters for various purposes. (In some respects my concept of pre-decision criteria is comparable with SINGER'S (1964) point about pre-investment activities.)

It has become fashionable to decry the East African Groundnut Scheme (H.M.S.O.: 1947; 1951), but may I humbly say that, in addition to its producing services advantageous to Tanganyika in particular and East Africa in general, that vast undertaking kindled in me thoughts leading to the evolution of criteria of the kind included here.

After my preparing reports upon that scheme (PHILLIPS: 1950A; 1950B) and – during the ensuing eight years – seeing something of the prospective Volta River Project in Ghana and also of various undertakings, either actual or projected, in parts of Trans-Saharan Africa, Latin America and South-east Asia, I drew together my thoughts regarding the kinds of criteria found helpful in assessing the potential utility of great projects (PHILLIPS: 1959; 1961). Subsequent experience in the one-time Federation of Rhodesia and Nyasaland (PHILLIPS et al., 1962) and in South Africa (PHILLIPS: 1964; 1965) has refined these criteria further. Recently, I have considered these in relation to the remarkable Euphrates Project in Syria (Agricultural Panel of International Experts: 1965).

Emergent from these and other opportunities of examining criteria at first hand has been the privilege of exchanging ideas with authorities upon the development of great projects in various parts of the world. While I am indebted to those who have discussed with me the points made here, I accept sole responsibility for any that appear either self-evident or farfetched.

SELECTED CRITERIA: AN OUTLINE

The study and the interpretation of the reciprocal influence of all forms of life, lower, higher and human, and the stage upon which they have their being, the environment, constitute *ecology*. I have learned to base my studies of the development of any enterprise upon the *ecological approach* – that which attempts to examine and interpret the implications of the meshwork of physical and biological factors and of the social, the political and economic conditions and potentialities involved. In essence the objectives of the *ecological*, the *synoptic* and the *holistic* (SMUTS: 1926) approaches are synonymous: to endeavour to see any particular subject under investigation *as a whole*, and to evaluate simultaneously its relation with any other relevant subject within either a similar or a related environment.

I derive *the criteria* outlined below from the font of ecology and, for the purpose of illustrating my theme, I select criteria believed to be significant in the assessing of the potential utility of projects dependent – wholly or in part – upon the harnessing of rivers. While some of the criteria are inherently more significant than others - numbers (1), (2), (4), (8), (9) and (10) – there is an interplay among them all. The intensity of the implications of this obviously varies according to the kind of project and, indeed, with the particular undertaking. Some criteria naturally do not apply to certain kinds of projects.

(1) *The proposition should be conceived and examined as a whole.*

All factors of the physical environment, all biological phenomena and all matters relating to man – social, economic and, where necessary, political – relevant to the assessing of the significance of a project should be examined, correlated and interpreted as far as information permits.

Inevitably this implies weighing all the criteria that follow and, according to the nature of the project, its prospective bearing both upon the region in which it might be set and upon any related project. Moreover its effect upon the general economy of other regions within the same socio-economic setting should be examined.

Examples could be cited of the failure resulting from not appraising projects *holistically*, but suffice it to mention the East African Groundnut

Scheme and a high proportion of the irrigation projects of earlier and more recent vintage in Asia, Latin America, North America and Africa. Examples illustrating the advantages of *holistic* study are the Tennessee Valley, the later phases of the Gezira in the Sudan and the four undertakings outlined later.

(2) *The objectives must be precise initially and throughout.*

This axiomatic statement is unfortunately necessary as some projects have foundered because either of vague objectives or imprecise defining of changes later found to be essential. But this is not to advocate illogical inflexibility in objectives. On the contrary, it might well be imperative to modify and even alter either one or more of the objectives in the light of experience, but this must be done methodically and with the informed knowledge of all concerned, in all appropriate quarters and levels, within and beyond the developing authority.

Some multi-purpose projects have suffered because of the ill defined priorities in objective and a tendency for the directing authorities to "ring the changes" without giving clear thought to the repercussions.

(3) *Where feasible, projects should be set within either sites or regions simultaneously both naturally and potentially economic.*

It often happens that a natural setting is *ipso facto* one potentially *economic* and thus particularly suitable for the development of a project. We see this in a river system so situated as to provide water for a terrain bearing potentially irrigable soils of promise for specific crops of higher economic value. Conversely, a river system, while ideal in itself, might not command a sufficient extent of irrigable land to render development economic but might be none the less valuable for socio-political reasons.

Examples of projects both naturally and economically well situated are the Tennessee Valley, the Gezira, some irrigation schemes on the Egyptian Nile, in India and South-east Asia, and the Snowy River Project in Australia.

(4) *The scope and intensity of the preparatory and continuing examination of the following features must be adequate:*

(A) PHYSICAL FACTORS

(Such as *meteorological* data for the general guidance of the water regime and also for the forecasting of floods; the *hydrological* regime of the catchment; and the nature and distribution of the principal soil associations, series and phases and their potential productivity for economic crops.)

(B) BIOLOGICAL PHENOMENA

(Basic *bio-ecological* information; the responses of the most suitable economic crops, their management and rotation; the role of livestock and their economic significance; the production of forestry plantations for timber and pulp or of woodlots for shelter and fuel; and the nature and significance of the more important diseases of man and beast to be overcome.)

(C) HUMAN RELATIONS

(Particularly the detailed logistics of population before, during and after the development of the project; the operative sociology of the people, both indigenous and naturalized, within the region and, also, the advantages and the problems likely to emerge from the bringing in of either related kinship groups or other communities.)

(D) ECONOMIC FEATURES

(Notably, wherever applicable, the nature of subsistence cropping and of livestock husbandry, their promise and difficulties: the actual and the potential economy of progressive pastoral production; cash crops of appropriate levels of yield, price, marketability and financial return over a reasonable period; primary industries possible because of either local or otherwise suitably distributed raw materials, such as minerals; the prospective "backward and forward linkages" of secondary industries in relation to agriculture, forestry and any other primary industry (HIRSCHMAN: 1958); and the nature, scope and potentiality for commercial services of all kinds inherent in a thriving business community.)

(E) PROSPECTIVE REGIONAL IMPACT UPON THE ECONOMY

(Both within the region in which the project is to be established and in contiguous and other regions producing commodities either similar or related to those scheduled for the new project.)

Clearly this gamut of interrelated criteria presents a challenge of more than ordinary complexity. It is rare that the constituent factors are adequately examined prior to a decision being taken about the development of a project. Among those enterprises characterized by their being based upon a more than ordinary intensive and extensive pre-investment study of the above and other factors and features are the Tennessee Valley, the Snowy River, the Volta and the Euphrates, while, to a lesser degree and in a different sense, the Tugela Basin is also worthy of mention.

(5) *Where larger or great rivers are involved, a significant measure of control of flood waters is imperative.*

The wastage and havoc resulting from the unbridled flooding so often involved in the life of the larger and the great rivers need no description. In the interest of the saving of life of man and beast, the protection of property, the better usage of land and of water commonly so precious during the drier seasons, there is every argument in favour of the wise conservation of this indispensable asset.

While the control of maximum peak floods occurring at indefinite but often very long intervals (once per century or even once per millenium) is, of course, either so difficult or indeed impossible, suitably designed schemes dependent upon a dam or series of dams do indeed control the second tier of great floods. The plans for the Volta, the Orange and the Euphrates Projects do provide for the satisfactory regulation of the run-off at realistic values.

The conservation of the catchments in many projects is still, however, far less effective than desirable and indeed possible. The modern designs of reservoir spillways do achieve a certain amount but much more would be gained were mechanical and biological control of the catchments to be many fold more effective than hitherto. Administrators and conservationists have still much to cover in policy and to achieve in practice before this approach to control is markedly more efficient than it is today. Indeed, the technical and the financial implications of catchment rehabilitation are among the most complex challenges cast to ecologists, pastoralists, engineers and economists.

(6) *Where the nature of the project permits, pilot trials should be instituted as early as possible and, preferably, before a decision to procede is made.*

Emerging from some of the resounding failures of great enterprises since the last War is an interest in establishing *pilot* schemes for the trial of the principles and details of practice, procedure and production.

Irrigation projects lend themselves particularly well to a preliminary testing, provided they are reasonably free from the political and related complications still all too common in so many countries.

The socio-economic and the socio-political aspects of a project do not usually permit of adequate trial *before* a decision is taken to implement the main project, but it is sometimes possible to arrange trials in the transfer, settlement and technical education of farmers upon specially prepared pilot areas, in advance of a main development programme. An instructive example of this is seen in the decision of the Euphrates Project Authority, Syria, to develop some 70,000 acres for the 50-60,000 people to be transferred from the bed of the prospective reservoir. The Volta River Preparatory Commission, because of the complex project, could not arrange a general pilot scheme, but it stimulated interest in trials covering the irrigation of selected soils for the production of much needed commodities. It inaugurated also the collection of much information upon the sociological and the economic implications of a transfer of a larger number of human communities.

(7) *It is desirable, if not essential, to decide as early as possible whether a project has socio-political significance either distinct from or inherent in an economic potential.*

Had it been understood from the outset that the East African Groundnut Scheme had clear and high-priority socio-political objectives, as well as food producing and economic ones, it possibly might have been judged less severely when its impending failure became apparent. Some of the criticism, levelled at the Orange River Project by those who doubt the economy of so grand an enterprise orientated more to agriculture than to industry, might also be modified were there to be a statement regarding any socio-political objectives there might be in addition to those of economic kind. Beyond the obvious economic objectives of the Volta Project there is also a grand venture in the resettlement of many communities upon a sound socio-economic basis – a circumstance which has made additional friends for the undertaking. The Euphrates Project is unquestionably the more acceptable to many because, in addition to its prospective economic contribution, it purports to accelerate the implementation of Syria's agrarian reform, so dear to the rural communities and the government alike.

A reticence on the part of an administration in defining the proportionate role of socio-politics in a project is, of course, understandable, because of the manifest difficulty of timing such an enunciation with an upward surge in its own popularity.

(8) *The nature of the prospective impact of a project upon labour should be assessed, as realistically as possible, prior to its inception.*

It is comparatively simple to estimate the number and the distribution of the various categories of labour required for the constructional stages, but more difficult to do so for the subsequent productive ones. Failure to ensure a suitable flow of labour of the desired cadre during this continuing phase could prove a serious obstacle to a satisfactory tempo and level of achievement.

(9) *An assessment must be attempted of the physical and the human infrastructure both actually existing and clearly required within a reasonable period.*

These criteria are important even in comparatively well developed countries, but are imperative in those at a lower level of economy.

The existence of even modest *physical* infrastructural needs, such as roads, railways, fuel and water supply, is significant in accelerating the tempo of the creation and the productivity of a project. The absence of or poverty in these presents great obstacles to the rate of progress and adds enormously to the costs of initial development. This was one of the several potent causes of the failure of the Groundnut Scheme, set as this was in the backblocks of an under-developed country in a very largely under-developed continent.

While a poor *physical* infrastructure effectively impedes progress, the lack of a fairly advanced indigenous *human* infrastructure acts even more severely. The poverty in education, even at the lowest levels, in semi-skilled and skilled labour and in technicians cannot be overcome quickly. Likewise serious gaps in the social services, such as public health, education, a sense of civic responsibility to contribute to the general welfare of either a community or the State itself, are not closed in a few years. Here again the Groundnut Scheme was at an appalling disadvantage, whereas the Volta Project was more fortunate because of the much longer opportunity for the local people to benefit from primary, sub-technical and higher education.

(10) *The principal kinds of problems likely to result from or, at least, to be accentuated by the development of a project, must be envisaged.*

An irrigation project could, for example, cause an intensification and an extension of malaria and schistosomiasis in man and beast, while in parts of tropical Africa river blindness (*Onchocerciasis*) is spread through the intimate association of man with water. Salinization ("brak") is due *inter alia*, to the unskilled, careless application of water to soils with impeded drainage. Constant vigilance, therefore, must be exercised by all concerned!

(11) *Tourism and recreation must be considered as prospectively important economic and social features of a project.*

A high proportion of the irrigation projects in the tropics of Asia, Africa and Latin America are far from centres experiencing even the simplest elements of public health services and the barest necessities of urban life now common to the more developed countries. It might well never be possible to provide anything much for the tourists at such projects except where climatic conditions and exceptional scenery or other pre-eminent attractions could justify this.

Where development is within fair striking distance of either progressive foreign lands or the more developed sectors of a particular country, it is feasible that tourism could play an economic role. Each project suitably set in attractive surrounds warrants consideration as to the suitability of its climate, distance from large centres of population and any other advantages.

Recreation for local communities is more widely feasible and should be encouraged by medium of self-help – aided where necessary by trained state personnel and funds.

(12) *Special features of aesthetic and scientific interest should be studied well in advance of the inundation or any other serious disturbance of the site of a project.*

A classic and encouraging example is, of course, the interest and the challenge presented by the archaeological treasures in parts of the area to be inundated by the great Aswan Dam. Many another project is likely to present features of outstanding interest, demanding either study or removal in specimen form. In the interests of the world of learning and of the nationals of the country concerned, it is desirable that local and overseas authorities combine to decide what is worthy of study and salvage and for organizing such financial and other aid as may be justifiable.

Although not classifiable as a criterion, the possibility of an irrigation project becoming either *economically or technically obsolete* should not be forgotten. Setting, design, construction and economical potential are among the criteria which could render a project far less effective than is acceptable by modern standards: when, indeed, a new project might be a better investment than a tinkering with the existing one.

THE CRITERIA AS APPLIED TO FOUR GREAT RIVER PROJECTS

(A) Space dictates that I merely note some of the outstanding features of these enterprises.

(I) *The Volta River project, Ghana*

At the control point, Akosombo, the Volta drains a catchment of 40–50,000 square miles, maintains a flow of 125–350,000 cubic feet per seconds (cusecs) at peak but only about 1,000 during the driest period. This great fluctuation is to be regulated to 38,000 cusecs.

This remarkable multi-purpose enterprise embraces the construction of a lake of over 3,500 square miles and the establishment of an aluminium processing plant. The project is to be capable of: – generating hydro-electro power (about 1,023 megawatts) for the smelter and for general use in related and other industries and services; the irrigation of 300–500,000 acres of *humid* to *subhumid* terrain; and supplying water, for primary and other purposes, over a wide area; furnishing facilities for extensive water transportation, for tourism and for the establishment of fresh-water fisheries. A distinct impetus to the general economy at present mainly dependent upon Cocoa and wide diversification therof are envisaged. (JACKSON: 1956; 1964).

(II) *The Orange River project, South Africa*

The Orange, at the main point of control, has a run-off of about 60% of its total volume at the mouth; this derives from no more than 6% of the total catchment of 328,000 square miles and amounts to about 6 million acre-feet. The maximum peak flood is some 500,000 cusecs at the mouth, but there is great seasonal variation in flow. It is planned to control floods up to about 150,000 cusecs. Some 300 million tons of silt are estimated to reach the Atlantic annually.

This multi-purpose scheme aims at the irrigation of about 700,000 acres in *arid* to *subarid* terrain, in the catchment of the Orange and, by diversion, in the catchments of the Sundays and the Fish rivers; to furnish water for primary, industrial and other uses in various urban centres and for rural communities; to provide facilities for fisheries, tourism and recreation; and to generate power for pumping, for industries and for other purposes.

Long tunnels, linking the great river with the two rivers mentioned, are dramatic features. (Secretary for Water Affairs: 1962; GREEN & FAIR: 1962; S.A. Ass. Adv. of Sci.: 1963; 1965.)

(III) *The Tugela River Basin, Natal, South Africa*

The catchment is 11,300 square miles, the flow is 4,000–8,000 cusecs at the mouth, with wide seasonable variation and the silt deposit is 9–12 million tons to the Indian Ocean. It is feasible that some 520 MW could be generated, were there suitable provision.

This enterprise is based largely upon the gradual and further development of the catchment of the Tugela and its influent surrounds (THORRINGTON-SMITH 1960; PHILLIPS: 1964). This development will depend to appreciable extent upon the harnessing of the river, so as to provide water for primary and other industries, primary purposes and probably about 150–200,000 acres of irrigation. The presently more economically vigorous European agriculture sector and the much less vigorous Bantu one (but now in the process of able rehabilitation by the Government) are likely to benefit. It is feasible that primary industries – for example, iron and steel and oil from coal – will be established; these would act as stimuli to "backward and forward" linkage, that is, "satellite" industries. (THORRINGTON-SMITH: 1960; Town and Regional Planning Commission: 1964).

(IV) *The Euphrates River project, Syria*

At its control point at Tabqa, in Syria, the Euphrates has an annual estimated run-off of about 20 million acre-feet. At present the flow fluctuates between 170.000 to 7,000 cusecs, but this will be regulated. The silt load at the point of control is estimated at about 100 million tons per annum.

This great multi-purpose project aims at furnishing water for some 1.5 million acres of irrigation and also for primary and industrial purposes. Its socio-political and economic objectives of establishing large numbers of farmers upon relatively small farms (12 to 25 acres) is in keeping with the State's policy of land reform. Cotton is to be the major source of foreign exchange, but further contribution is expected to be the stimulation of other general cash and subsistence farming. About 1,000 MW will be generated for pumping, industrial and other purposes. (Press (German): 1962; Technopromexport (Russian): 1963; NEDECO (Dutch): 1963; 1964; Kahale: 1965; Advisory Panel of International Experts: 1965).

(B) Rough tentative assessment of the four projects in terms of the criteria outlined

I illustrate, in the table below, my tentative application of the criteria under discussion: –

A BROAD AND TENTATIVE ASSESSMENT OP THE CRITERIA APPLIED TO THE VOLTA RIVER PROJECT

THE ORANGE RIVER PROJECT, THE TUGELA BASIN AND THE EUPHRATES PROJECT

(According to a scale of 10, where possible)

CRITERION	VOLTA RIVER PROJECT	ORANGE RIVER SCHEME	TUGELA BASIN AND INFLUENT SURROUNDS	EUPHRATES PROJECT
(1) Conceived and examined holistically	10 (Outstanding in its holistic concept)	6 (This might be higher when fuller information is available.)	7	8
(2) Precision of objectives	10	8 (This might be higher when fuller information is available.)	7 (The nature of the concept renders precision difficult.)	10
(3A) The setting is a natural one	10	10	10	10
(3B) and has economic potential	8 (Difficult to assess, but aluminium, power, water-supply, agriculture, fisheries and tourism could render the project economic.)	6 (This is difficult to assess at present. Agricultural and industrial development could be economic, agriculture of itself less likely to be so; tourism and fishing could be important.)	8 (Agriculture could play a much more important role but other vigorous industries are essential to a satisfactory economy. Tourism could be very important.)	8 (Some uncertainty is due to the economy of cotton decades ahead, but doubtless *intensive* farming will give good returns. Industrial development could be significant.)
(4) Adequacy of the scope and intensity of the preparatory and continuing examination of: –				

CRITERION	VOLTA RIVER PROJECT	ORANGE RIVER SCHEME	TUGELA BASIN AND INPLUENT SURROUNDS	EUPHRATES PROJECT
A *Physical Features*				
(i) Meteorological data and forecasting of floods	6	4	6	5
(ii) Hydrology	6	6	6	6
(iii) Pedological and other soil data	8	4	7	6
(iv) Irrigation potential	8	6	4	8
	28	20	23	25
B *Biological Features*				
(i) Bio-ecology	8	6	8	6
(ii) Crops: (Irrigated)	6	6	6	7
(iii) Livestock	4 (Cattle; possibly some sheep)	6 (Sheep)	6 (Cattle, sheep)	4 (Sheep)
(iv) Forestry/Woodlots	8 (Silviculture of *humid forest* and establishment of woodlots in *subhumid* areas)	? (Not applicable at present; possibly woodlots under irrigation)	8 (Timber pulp: exotic)	5 (Woodlots occasionally irrigated)
(v) Study of public health problems	8 (Malaria, Bilharzia, Onchocerciasis and other diseases)	7	7	7
	34	25+	35	29

CRITERION	VOLTA RIVER PROJECT	ORANGE RIVER SCHEME	TUGELA BASIN AND INFLUENT SURROUNDS	EUPHRATES PROJECT
C *Human Features*				
(i) Population logistics	8 (Intensive studies have been made)	4	4 (Bantu; much still remains to be done)	7 (Good progress has been made.)
(ii) Sociology	8	5	7	7
	16	9	11	14
D *Economics*				
(i) Subsistence cropping	6	? (Not applicable except locally)	6 (Mainly Bantu; some Indian)	8
(ii) Progressive pastoral industry	4 (Mainly cattle)	5 (Sheep)	6 (Mixed)	5 (Sheep; later cattle)
(iii) Cash cropping	7 (Cocoa and other forest crops; cotton, sugar, rice)	6	7	8 (Cotton mainly)
(iv) Primary industry other than Agriculture	8 (Aluminium, other minerals)	? (Possibly minerals)	7 (Possibly iron/steel and oil from coal)	8 (Cotton mainly)
(v) Appropriate secondary industry	7 (Forward and backward linkages with aluminium	6	7	6
(vi) Commercial services	8	7	7	7
	40	24	40	42
E *Prospective regional impact*				
(i) Upon region in which it is to be set	10	10	8	10
(ii) Upon other relevant regions	9	8	8	9
	19	18	16	19

CRITERION	VOLTA RIVER PROJECT	ORANGE RIVER SCHEME	TUGELA BASIN AND INFLUENT SURROUNDS	EUPHRATES PROJECT
(5) *Control of flood waters.*	8 (The regulation of the annual flow at 38,000 cusecs is planned.)	8 (To control about 150,000 cusecs)	? (This could be considerable, but an estimate is impossible because no specific dams in prospect.)	8 (A marked effect would be experienced in lower Syria and in Iraq)
(6) Are pilot trials necessary and, if so, are they envisaged?	(Not applicable – except in irrigation trials, already embarked upon)	(Not applicable – except in irrigation trials)	(Not applicable – except in irrigaticn trials)	(An agro-socio-economic project: 65–70,000 acres concurrent with construction of dam and the related irrigation works.)
(7) Has the project socio-political significance?	(Yes, in keeping with socialist policy; could be highly significant.)	(The socio-economic implications are clear; it is not evident that there are any socio-political implications.)	(This is mainly socio-economic in respect of the Bantu sectors, in keeping with policy; there might be socio-political implications in the Bantu homelands.)	(In keeping with the State's agrarian reform; highly important in this respect)
(8) Impact on labour, actual and prospective	8 (Important in construction and later stages: production of aluminium and many other activities)	5 (Important in the constructive stages and, probably also, in the continuing phases: agricultural and industrial labour alike)	8 (Probably considerable as development progresses – particularly through the industries established on the Bantu homeland borders)	8 (Important in the construction stages and also in agriculture and industry as the project developes.)
(9A) *Physical infrastructure* (*a*) *Existing* (road, rail, water, communications, fuel, power etc.)	8 (Port of Tema, rail, main and feeder roads, townships: remarkable achievements)	4	7	5

CRITERION	VOLTA RIVER PROJECT	ORANGE RIVER SCHEME	TUGELA BASIN AND INFLUENT SURROUNDS	EUPHRATES PROJECT
(*b*) Further infrastructure envisaged	8 (Power, lake transport)	6	4	6
(9B) Human infrastructure (Prospective: e.g. social services, such as schooling, health, arrangement for employment)	9 (Remarkable provisions	6	7 (Not applicable at present, but would require attention already fair to good)	7
(10) (Possible problems traceable to the development of the project (e.g. "brak" in soils, livestock and human health hazards – such as Malaria, Bilharzia)	10 (Despite excellent studies and planned precautions re Malaria, Bilharzia and other diseases, serious health problems might arise: special problems in irrigation of certain "difficult" montmorillonitic soils are likely.)	6 (A relatively low rating of problems, such as "brak"; "fluke" in beast, Bilharzia in man)	6 (Local "brak"; "fluke" in beast. Bilharzia in man probably important)	6 (Gypsum near the surface could present problems on areas being irrigated. Bilharzia could spread.)
(11) (Tourism and recreation	8 (Foreign visitors would be attracted.)	8	8	9
(12) (Attention to aesthetic and scientific features)	10 (Remarkable efforts have been exerted to obtain information.)	8 (Being borne in mind)	? (Not applicable at present, but doubtless would be high.)	8 (Archaeological)

RESPONSIBILITY FOR THE CO-ORDINATION, PRESENTATION AND ADMINISTRATION OF GREAT PROJECTS

Although the form of administration of a great irrigation project is not always linked with criteria of the kind summarized it is so vital to the success of an enterprise that I comment upon it.

An examination of the Tennessee Valley, the Gezira, the Volta and the Euphrates Projects reveals that all fall under specially constituted bodies. A wide range of similar enterprises has definitely demonstrated the desirability of administering both the preparatory and the post-constructional phases by a body not within the orthodox public service: a *quasi-government* entity – a board, commission, authority – established by statute and directly responsible to either the Head of State or his deputy.

Such a body should be empowered to deal with all the multifarious aspects of the administration of the project, thus avoiding time-consuming bureaucratic procedure. Decision and action within specific but wide limits are the essence of the powers of such a body. To place a project under the control of a State department, even a scientific-technical one such as either a Department of Irrigation or of Agriculture, often entails bureaucratic procedure and timetaking splitting of hairs about a multiplicity of petty detail! On the other hand, the progress made by the Tennessee Valley Authority, the Snowy River Board, the Volta River Authority and the Euphrates Project Authority testifies to the greater efficiency achievable by either an independent or a *quasi-government* authority.

Indeed, in some countries, an additional extraordinary criterion of the prospective success of a project could well be whether this is to be directed by a State department or a special authority – with the odds strongly in favour of success being won more rapidly and effectively by the latter!

As the precise constitution of an authority must depend upon local circumstances, I do not attempt to outline, even in its principal essentials, the terms of references of such a body. I do stress, however, the absolute necessity for the body not only being protected from political pressure but also knowing itself to be free!

It is to be hoped that in due course the Orange River Project and the Tugela Basin enterprise will enjoy the privilege of serving this kind of authority. This is not to criticize either the technically most able State department at present responsible for the first named, but rather to plead for an administration inherently stronger than any State department ever could be. The Tugela Basin enterprise awaits, in turn, some such special directing organization.

REFERENCES

Agricultural Panel of International Experts (1965): Report on the Agricultural Aspects of the Euphrates Project. Mimeo., Euphrates Project Authority, Damascus.

GAITSKELL, A. (1959): Gezira. Faber, London

GREEN, B. P. & FAIR, T. J. (1962): Development in Africa. Witwatersrand Univ. Press. Johannesburg.

HIRSCHMAN, A. O. (1958): Strategy of Economic Development. Yale, New Haven, Conn.

H.M.S.O. (1947): A plan for the Mechanized Production of Groundnuts in East and Central Africa. Cmd. 7030, London.

H.M.S.O. (1951): The Future of the Overseas Food Corporation. Cmd. 8125, London.

HORWOOD, O. P. F. & THORRINGTON-SMITH, E. (1963) Metropolis. *Optima*, Dec., Johannesburg.

HORWOOD, O. P. F. (1964): The Economics of Development in the Tugela Basin. in: Symposium on the Development of the Tugela Basin, Town and Reg. Planning Commission. Pietermaritzburg, Natal.

JACKSON, R. (1956): Report of the Preparatory Commission Volta River Project. Vols. I–III, H.M.S.O., London.

JACKSON, R. (1964): The Volta River Project. *Progress*, 50 (2802), Unilever, London.

KAHALE, NOUREDDEEN (1965): The Multi-purpose Euphrates Project Mimeo., restricted; Euphrates Project Authority, Damascus.

NEDECO (1963): Investigations into the Euphrates Project Area on Irrigation and Drainage Requirements. 2 vols., Mimeo., restricted.

NEDECO (1964): An Agro-Economic and a Socio-Economic Evaluation of the Euphrates Project. 3 vols., Mimeo., restricted.

PHILLIPS, JOHN (1950A): Kongwa Working Party Report. Overseas Food Corporation, Mimeo., Filed in records Tanganyika Agricultural Corporation, Dar-es-Salaam.

— (1950B): Southern Province Working Party. Overseas Food Corporation, filed in records Tanganyika Agricultural Corporation, Dar-es-Salaam.

— (1959): Agriculture and Ecology in Africa. Faber, London.

— (1961): The Development of Agriculture and Forestry in the Tropics: Patterns, Problems and Promise. Faber, London.

PHILLIPS, JOHN et al. (1962): The Development of the Economic Resources of Southern Rhodesia, with Particular Reference to the Role of African Agriculture. Govt. Pr., Salisbury.

PHILLIPS, JOHN (1964): Some Tentative Thoughts about the Agricultural, Forestry and Related Development of the Tugela Basin and its Influent Surrounds. for Town and Reg. Planning Commission, Pietermaritzburg, Natal, Mimeo.

— (1965): Aspects of an Ecological Approach in the Development of Great Projects such as those for the Orange River. *S. Afr. J. Sci.* 61 (3), 69–75.

PRESS, DR. (1963): Report on the Euphrates Dam in Syria for the Purpose of Flood Control, Low Water, Increase of Power Generation and Irrigation. MS., restricted.

SECRETARY FOR WATER AFFAIRS (1962): Report on the Proposed Orange River Development Project. W.P. x-62, Govt. Pr., Pretoria.

SINGER, H. W. (1964): International Development: Growth and Change. McGraw-Hill, N. York

SMUTS, J. C. (1926): Holism and Evolution. London

SOUTH AFRICAN ASSOCIATION FOR THE ADVANCEMENT OF SCIENCE (1963): Orange River Development Conference. *S. Afr. J. Sci.* 59 (10).

— (1965): Symposium on Science and the Orange River Development Project. *S. Afr. J. Sci.* 61 (3).

TECHNOPROMEXPORT (1963): Project Report for Gravity Irrigation of One Hundred Thousand Hectares in the Basin of the Euphrates River. Mimeo., restricted.

THORRINGTON-SMITH, E. (1960): Toward a Plan for the Tugela Basin. Town and Reg. Planning Commission, Pietermaritzburg, Natal.

— (1964) The Physical Planning of Development in the Tugela Basin. in: Symposium on the Development Potentialities of the Tugela Basin, Town and Reg. Planning Commission. Pietermaritzburg, Natal.

APPENDICES

APPENDIX I

Summary of Report of the Committee on Peaceful Settlement of Disputes, of the National Citizens' Commission, to the White House Conference on International Cooperation, Washington, D.C., November 28 – December 1, 1965.

The peaceful settlement of international disputes has proved a perpetual challenge, because of the inability of international organization to regulate some of the most vital questions of peace and war. The two main approaches to this problem here suggested call for the combined efforts and insights of the government official with his responsibility for deciding on policy alternatives; the scholar and expert outside government whose approach may be that of historical research or the conceptual framework into which the policy decision fits; and both groups as they consider the obligations of states as members of the United Nations and its procedures as methods for carrying out policy decisions. It is fully recognized that some states do not consider the peaceful solution of a dispute is in their national interest.

The first approach is the development and maintenance of United Nations procedures, and continuing study under the auspices of the General Assembly of the process of peaceful settlement as a Charter obligation. Such study would draw together the views of the many states who have become United Nations members since the last such studies in 1950. Especially useful are third-party institutions for objective development of facts, and the mediator to suggest paths of settlement. In negotiations looking toward a permanent settlement, a panel of mediators appointed by the Secretary-General is recommended, reconstituting and emphasizing the rarely used Panel for Inquiry and Conciliation created by the General Assembly fifteen years ago. The importance of flexibility in the instructions of mediators and the timing of their activities and reports is also developed. One indication of a well-ordered community is the use of judicial methods for settling disputes. Wider use of the International Court of Justice is to be encouraged. One move toward such wider use would be withdrawal by the United States of its own self-judging reservation to the Court's compulsory jurisdiction. While these procedural alternatives are not new, they are available, should be practical for use, and well understood by states.

United Nations members have a Charter obligation first of all to seek a solution by one or more of the peaceful alternatives.

But there remains the hard question of settlement of a dispute when the policy of one party involved is to keep the dispute unresolved, to apply the direct or covert use of force or subversion, or to dictate a unilateral solution. The procedures outlined do not of themselves provide response to such a policy. In some cases such a policy may be drawn in part from a disputant's very different conceptual approach to international organization from that here developed. Long-term attention should be given to the conceptual framework for policy decisions. The General Assembly as part of its studies might consider the art of mediation and the extent to which the experience in handling labor disputes within a state can be transferred to the handling of international disputes.

The second approach, a continuing conceptual study involving a dialogue of the government decision-maker and the scholar is an investment likely to produce insights about the nature of existing international systems. It suggests a learning process about the need for peaceful change and could demonstrate the common interest of states, even those with differing values, in this process over the long term. This is an approach and not an answer. It suggests looking beyond the familiar to some of the new ideas of the social sciences, thus drawing on a wider area of scholars. Such a study would develop possible classifications of types of disputes, relating them to overall relations between the states involved. It would examine psychological factors, such as how each party sees a dispute and its own role in it. This has been called "the reality image." Suggested investigation should range from historical research so organized as to provide data for new measurement techniques, to the more experimental techniques of the social sciences, including simulation techniques and construction of models. The study would necessarily involve a critical examination of assumptions about the United Nations, such as the effect, if any, of its economic and social activities on its political activities, and the nature of the concept of self-determination in relation to lasting political settlements. Research would include the broad concept of stable peace as a problem of social systems.

Here then is a task for the present – the strengthening of procedures for peaceful settlement and for the next two decades, if so much time is given – the conceptual study of organized society. This task deserves all the wisdom and vision which can be brought to bear on it.

APPENDIX II

A Selection of Organizations and Associations Interested in Concepts of World Education

by

HAROLD TAYLOR

Education and World Affairs
522 Fifth Avenue, New York City, N.Y., U.S.A.

Friends World Committee for Consultation
Woodbrooke, Selly Oak, Birmingham 29, U.K.
Secretary, American Section: HERBERT M. HADLEY, 152-A, North 15th Street, Philadelphia 2, Pennsylvania, U.S.A.

Hague Academy of International Law,
Peace Palace, The Hague.
Secretary-General: Major-General J. B. DE JONGH

Institute for International Order
11 West 42nd Street, New York City, N.Y., U.S.A.
President: EARL OSBORN

International Association for the Advancement of Educational Research
Schlosstrasse 29, Frankfurt/M.W., Germany
Director: Dr. W. SCHULTZE

International Association for the Exchange of Students for Technical Experience
c/o Dr. KLAUS WYNEKEN
Kennedy Allee 50, 532 Bad Godesberg, Germany

International Association of Universities
c/o International Universities Bureau,
6 Rue Franklin, Paris 16
Secretary General and Director: H. M. R. KEYES

International Association of University Professors & Lecturers
Rozier 6, Ghent, Belgium
Director: Professor A. HACQUAERT

International Council of Scientific Unions
2 Via Sebenico, Rome, Italy
Secretary General: Professor D. BLASKOVIC

International Institute for Educational Planning
7 rue Eugene Delacroix, Paris 16, France
Director: Dr. PHILIP COOMBE

International Institute for Labor Studies
Geneva, Switzerland
U.S.A. Office: 917 Fifteenth St., N.W., Washington, D.C., U.S.A.
Director General: DAVID A. MORSE

International Peace Research Association
Polemological Institute, Ubbo Emminsingel 19, Groningen, Netherlands

International Peoples College
Elsinore, Denmark
Principal: VAGN H. FENGER

International Theatre Institute
Annexe de L'UNESCO, 6 rue Franklin, Paris 16, France
Secretary General: JEAN DARCANTE

International University of Comparative Sciences
13 rue du Post, Luxembourg, Belgium

New Education Fellowship
c/o Miss Y. MORSE
55 Upper Stone Street., Tunbridge Wells, Kent, U.K.

Rotary International
1600 Ridge Avenue, Evanston, Illinois, U.S.A.
General Secretary: GEORGE R. MEANS

Society for the Psychological Study of Social Issues
c/o CAROLINE WEICHLEIN, Executive Secretary,
P.O. Box 1248, Ann Arbor, Michigan, U.S.A.

UNESCO Institute for Education
Feldbrunnenstrasse 70, Hamburg 13, West Germany

UN Research Institute for Social Development
Geneva, Switzerland

Vittakivi International College
Havho, Finland

World Association of World Federalists
Burgemeester Patijnlaan 49, The Hague
Executive Director: J. W. BEUMER

World Confederation of Organizations of the Teaching Profession,
1227 Sixteenth St., N.W., Washington 6, D.C., U.S.A.
Secretary General: WILLIAM G. CARR

World Federation of United Nations Associations
1 Ave. de la Paix, Geneva, Switzerland
UN Representative: HILARY BARATT-BROWN, Rm. 1055, UN, N.Y.C.

World Organization for Early Childhood Education
134 bd. Berthier, Paris 17, France.
UNESCO Representative: Mme. S. HERBINIERE-LEBERT

World University Service
20 West 40th Street, New York City, N.Y., U.S.A.
Director: JOHN SIMONS

World Veterans Federation
16 Rue Hamelin, Paris 16, France
Secretary General: NORMAN ACTON

APPENDIX III

Bibliography

Books and Articles on World Education

by

HAROLD TAYLOR

BARTLETT, STEPHEN W. "A Dialogue Between Cultures." *Saturday Review*, XLVII (July 18, 1964), *44–47*.

CHATURVEDI, H. Tagore at Shantiniketan; A Survey of Dr. Rabindranath Tagore's Educational Experiment at Shantiniketan. Mathais' Publication, 1934.

COMMAGER, HENRY STEELE, The Year Book of Education 1964 Education and International Life. New York, Harcourt, Brace and World.

ELVIN, H. L. Nationalism and Internationalism in Education. (Foundation Oration). Goldsmith's College, London, 1959.

Federation of American Scientists Committee for a United Nations University. "The Need for a U.N. University." *Bulletin of Atomic Scientists*, XVII (March 1961), *111–13*.

FIELDS, ROBERT. "World University in the Making." *The Student*, VIII, 5 (May 1964), *26–27*. (Published by COSEC – the Coordinating Secretariat of National Unions of Students.)

KILPATRICK, WILLIAM HEARD. "Creation of World University Advocated as Peace Center." *New York Times*, August 28, 1962, *30*.

LAUGIER, HENRI. "Pour une Université Internationale des Pays Sous-Développés." *Bulletin of the International Association of Universities*, VIII, 3 (1960).

MARC, ALEXANDER. "Mission of an International University." *International Social Science Bulletin of UNESCO*, IV, 1 (Spring, 1952), *225–29*.

MCNEIL, ELTON B. "An International University." *Bulletin of Atomic Scientists*, XVIII, 8 (October 1962), *23–24*.

"Netherlands International School." *The Times, London, Educational Supplement*, 2561 (June 19, 1964), *1689*.

OTLET, PAUL, Address to World Federation of Education Associations. Proceedings of the First Biennial Conference of the World Federation of Education Associations .Edinburgh 1925.

— Sur la Creation d'une Université Internationale. Brussels, (1920).

PERLMUTTER, OSCAR WILLIAM. "Foreign, International and Supranational Education." *The American Review; A Quarterly of American Affairs*, III (Autumn, 1963) *69–91*. (Bologna, Italy.)

RABINOWITCH, EUGENE. "Pugwash-Coswa: International Conversations" *Bulletin of the Atomic Scientists*, XIX, 6, (June, 1963), 7–12.

RUSSELL, BERTRAND. "Proposals for an International University." *The Fortnightly*, CLII (July, 1942), *8–16*.

SALAM, ABDUS. "A New Center for Physics." *Bulletin of the Atomic Scientists* XXI, 10 (December, 1965), 43–45.

SIMEY, T. S. AND FLETCHER, F. T. H. "Report on an International Institute of the Social Sciences." *International Social Science Bulletin of UNESCO*, III, 3 (Autumn, 1951), *634–41*.

STALEY, EUGENE. "A Proposal for a United Nations University." *VOC... Journal of Education* (Tuticorn, India), II, 2 (August, 1962), *12–18*.

STOKER, SPENCER. The Schools and International Understanding. Chapel Hill, N.C., University of North Carolina Press, 1933.

STRØMNES, MARTIN. World Education for Peace; A proposal for Special Leading Centers in World Education. Regionally Distributed under the U.N. by UNESCO. Oslo, Oslo University Press, 1959.

TAYLOR, HAROLD. "The Idea of a World College." *Phi Delta Kappan*, XLIV (June, 1963), *399*–402.

— "The Idea of a World College: Experiment in Global Education." *Saturday Review*, XLVII (November 14, 1964), *29–32*.

UNESCO, Department of Social Scien ce. "The Proposed Establishment of an International Social Science Center." *International Social Science Bulletin of UNESCO*, III (Autumn 1951), *644–55*.

Subject Index

Name Index